Violent No More

In this third edition of *Violent No More*, Michael Paymar has updated the entire book with new stories, interviews, and several significant chapters. If you are a man reading this book, it is likely that you have already been abusive to your wife or girlfriend. ... yourself in the stories throughout ... will realize that change is not only ... fulfilling life. You will see that you ... can help you change. If you are a co ... ...or you are probably working with clients w ... ...ve been court ordered or have volunteered for your domestic abuse groups. This book will be a helpful resource for you and an important guide to working with the men in your groups.

This edition includes a Foreword by Anne Ganley, PhD, and interviews with Edward Gondolf, PhD; Jacquelyn Campbell, PhD; David Adams, EdD; Barbara Hart, JD; and Glenna Tinney, MSW.

About the Author

Michael Paymar, MPA, has worked in the domestic abuse prevention field for over thirty years. He and his colleague, the late Ellen Pence, authored the ground-breaking curriculum *Creating a Process for Change for Men Who Batter*, the most widely used model in the world. They worked together at the pioneering Domestic Abuse Intervention Project in Duluth, Minnesota, creating the Duluth Model. He wrote the award-winning documentary *With Impunity: Men and Gender Violence*. As a member of the Minnesota House of Representatives for almost two decades, Michael Paymar authored legislation to combat domestic and sexual abuse and sex trafficking. In this third edition, Michael Paymar provides insight into gender violence and offers hope for men who want to change their behavior and live violence-free lives.

Praise for *Violent No More*

"Violent No More fills a void by speaking with authority and authenticity directly to men who batter to challenge their historical and current attitudes, beliefs, and behaviors. It also speaks to women who have lived and are living with men who batter. This book should be on the bench of every judge in the country and on the recommended reading list for probation and parole officers, law enforcement, prosecutors, defense attorneys, magistrates, clergy, social service providers, and members of the health care system."

— David J. H. Garvin, MSW, LMSW
Founder of Alternatives to Domestic Aggression and
Batterer Intervention Services Coalition of Michigan (BISC-MI)

"Violent No More is a man-to-man conversation that should be taking place between every father and son, and among men who are true friends with each other. Regardless of whether you are a man looking into his own violence, a woman interested in the problem of domestic abuse, or a professional with years of experience, read this book from start to finish. It offers men who batter the wise voice of guide, thoughtful critic, cheerleader, compassionate coach, and fellow traveler. Michael Paymar courageously invites each man to find his own voice while carefully listening to the voices of women. The stories in this book point us to a hopeful light—men can find the source of real power: respect, equality, trust, love, and nonviolence. Paymar has found the perfect balance between compassion and accountability that we who work with men who batter so fervently seek."

— John Beams, JD, LSW
Cofounder of the Center for Nonviolence, Fort Wayne, Indiana

"Finally, someone has written a book for men in offenders groups. *Violent No More* is written to men, using the voices of men. It poses the most central questions to men who batter: How did I get here, and what does it take for me to change?"

— Ellen Pence, PhD
Cofounder of Duluth Domestic Abuse Intervention
Project and Founder of Praxis International

"This important book speaks frankly to men about domestic abuse. Michael Paymar challenges men to change the beliefs they have about women, power, and relationships. His suggestions give direction and hope. I highly recommend this book to all men who want to stop hurting women."

— Susan Schechter, MSW
Author of *Women and Male Violence*
and *When Love Goes Wrong* (with Ann Jones)

"In this updated edition, Michael Paymar moves our thinking forward by exploring relationships in which men who have battered not only have changed but also have stayed with their partners. His exercises for men who have stopped their violence and are working to transform their relationships are highly recommended. They are also very useful for the general male reader and for counseling programs. This is a valuable and courageous work!"

— Fernando Mederos, EdD
Director of Fatherhood Engagement,
Massachusetts Department of Children and Families
Author of *Programs for Men Who Batter:
Intervention and Prevention* (with Etiony Aldarondo)

"*Violent No More* challenges men who batter to face and change their behavior. This book is also important for women as it helps them better understand their abusive partners. Counselors and domestic violence workers would be wise to make *Violent No More* a must-read for the men in their groups."

— Catherine Waltz, PhD
Barry University School of Social Work

"A highlight of the book is the many inspiring stories by individual men of their violence and their process of change. This book should convince any man that we can and must stop violence against women."

— Paul Kivel, violence-prevention educator
Author of *Men's Work: How to Stop the Violence
That Tears Our Lives Apart*

"As a street cop I investigated more domestic abuse cases than I want to remember. I saw the terror in the eyes of the victims. I confronted the offenders who tried to convince me that their behavior was a justified response to provocation. When I became the chief of police in Seattle, I wanted my officers to understand the dynamics of battering. I also wanted to address the fact that, to my dismay, too many of my officers were also perpetrators.

"I read Michael Paymar's groundbreaking book *Violent No More*, which he has now thoroughly updated. It's as important today as when I first read it. Police administrators should read it. Line officers should read it. Men should read it."

— Norm Stamper, former Seattle Chief of Police
Author of *Breaking Rank: A Top Cop's Exposé
of the Dark Side of American Policing*

"*Violent No More* presents compelling accounts of men who struggled to end their violence against their partners and describes the changes they made in their thinking and behavior to make that happen. The updated version includes timely information on the co-occurrence of intimate partner violence and combat-related PTSD, important in aiding service members who are returning from Iraq and Afghanistan. Abusive men will find compassion and hope in these pages, while professionals in the field will find useful strategies to assist men in building loving, nonviolent relationships with their partners and children."

— Denise Gamache
Director, Battered Women's Justice Project

"*Violent No More* joins the small shelf of books that are essential for every therapist and counselor. We therapists *will* encounter abusive men and women who are being abused. We need to understand how to detect the phenomenon of domestic violence and how to intervene, for as Paymar acknowledges, counselors have often been part of the problem rather than the solution. This highly readable, even gripping book is written for men and the counselors who work with them. It is full of stories and exercises (there is now an accompanying workbook). Along with books on battered women's experiences, like *When Love Goes Wrong*, this book is a must-read for us. Why? Because having this knowledge can save lives!"

— Gus Kaufman Jr., PhD
Licensed Psychologist, Cofounder of Men
Stopping Violence, Atlanta, Georgia

"Violent No More is an effective tool for educating our colleagues about the dynamics of domestic violence and the work of batterer intervention programs. By hearing directly from both the men and women who've experienced domestic violence and from Michael Paymar, one of the most respected practitioners in the batterer intervention field, readers get a firsthand picture of what domestic violence looks and sounds like in all its forms. They are able to clearly identify the cognitive and behavioral changes required of men who want to change. They also become aware of the safety concerns for survivors.

"As we move into earlier interventions, other professionals—teachers and professors, nurses and doctors, human resources personnel, social workers, psychologists, and faith leaders—will all benefit from this book. It is unfortunate that courses in domestic violence are not part of the core curriculum for graduates in the social work or counseling/psychology fields. *Violent No More* should be required reading for practitioners in these disciplines."

— Carol Arthur
Executive Director, Domestic Abuse Project,
Minneapolis, Minnesota

Project Credits

Cover Design: Brian Dittmar Design, Inc.
Book Production: John McKercher
Copy Editor: Kelley Blewster
Proofreader: Alexandra Mummery
Indexer: Jean Mooney
Managing Editor: Alexandra Mummery
Rights Coordinator: Stephanie Beard
Publisher: Todd Bottorff

REVISED THIRD EDITION

VIOLENT
no more.

►► Helping Men End Domestic Abuse ◄◄

Michael Paymar, MPA

Foreword by Anne Ganley, PhD

An imprint of
Turner Publishing Company

Turner Publishing Company
424 Church Street • Suite 2240 • Nashville, Tennessee 37219
445 Park Avenue • 9th Floor • New York, New York 10022
www.turnerpublishing.com
Copyright © 2015, 2000, 1993 by Michael Paymar

Library of Congress Control Number: 2015934013

Manufactured in the United States of America

9 8 7 6 5 4 3 2 1   Third Edition   15 16 17 18 19

Contents

Important Note

The material in *Violent No More* is intended to provide a guide for men dealing with the issues of domestic abuse. Every effort has been made to provide accurate and dependable information, and the contents of this book have been compiled in consultation with other professionals. However, the reader should be aware that professionals in the field may have differing opinions, and legal policies may differ from state to state and are changing constantly. The publisher, author, and editors cannot be held responsible for any error, omission, professional disagreement, or outdated material.

The ideas, procedures, and suggestions contained in this book are designed to encourage men to work with their personal violence and abusive behavior, but are not intended to replace a professional program. If you have any questions or concerns about applying this information, please consult a domestic abuse intervention program or a licensed therapist. The author and publisher assume no responsibility for any outcome of the use of these materials individually or in consultation with a professional or group.

Foreword

by Anne Ganley, PhD

You may be picking up this book for the first time in a bookstore, at someone's home, or in the public library. Maybe you went online because you know you have a problem. Perhaps someone (your friend, your child welfare worker, or your lawyer) gave it to you, or it was assigned reading in a domestic abuse program. Or you may be reading it for the second, third, or fourth time. Whatever brings you to this book, welcome to the pages that follow and the journey you are about to begin.

This is a special book. It exists in part because men like you asked for it. When I opened a domestic violence intervention program, the first at a Veterans Affairs medical center, no such book was available. It was not until Michael Paymar wrote the first edition of *Violent No More* that men had a book of their own to support them on their diverse journeys to becoming abuse free.

In the early years of our batterers' intervention program, men would ask me if there was someone they could talk with outside of their group, someone who knew and understood what they were going through. While they appreciated the program staff and their peers in the group, they just wanted to talk with a guy who had been there and had been successful in stopping his abuse. Or maybe, a few asked, was there something they could read? One by one I attempted to connect them with another man with whom they could identify, but it was a hard match at times, for each man's experience of being abusive was unique. Some were poor, others wealthy; some highly educated, others had barely completed grade school; some were religious, others not; some were men of color and some not; some were in the military, some not. Their relationships were different as well: some long term, some new; some with children, some without; some had compliant partners, others had challenging partners. Some men had issues other than their abusiveness, such as addictions, health problems, or mental health concerns; others did not. The only thing they had in common was that they all were or had been abusive to someone they loved.

When the first edition of *Violent No More* appeared, I greeted it with relief. Here, finally, was a book that told many men's stories, not just one or two. The stories were not only of the abuse but also about the change process. The book was readable, it was practical, and it offered hope. I told everyone who entered the program to buy it. I wanted each man to have his own copy to use throughout the year-long intervention program. And use it they did.

As I listened to the men talk about their experiences of searching for a copy of the book, of having to ask for and then purchase it, I became aware that buying it, with its challenging title, was sometimes their first experience of confronting their denial of their abusiveness. Then, as they went through the orientation phase, they were assigned the first four chapters, one at a time. They could read ahead if they wanted, and many did, but they had to be prepared to talk about the assigned chapter in the first group meetings. Sometimes there was a nonreader in the program who had another group member as a reading buddy, and as I entered the room early to prepare for the session I might hear one man reading the assigned section softly to the guy sitting next to him.

As the men went through the more intensive phase of the program, we focused on the remaining chapters. Then the book would reappear during the maintenance phase, in which men who had successfully completed the first two stages met once a month to give each other support in staying abuse free. Once again the men would bring in their copies, sometimes using them to look at the positives or to look at the more subtle ways they were being controlling in their families. They would talk about how the goals of equality, respect, and teamwork in relationships outlined in the book were attainable or were hard to reach at times.

Over the years I saw the tattered books again and again. I would look over shoulders and see sections highlighted or marked with "me, me, me" in the margins, as a man identified with a particular passage. Sometimes when a group member would bring up an issue or question, he would use a section of the book to make his point, saying, "Remember in the book, where the guy says...?" Group members would argue with each other, jabbing with their fingers at certain paragraphs to emphasize their position. And some would even laugh, saying, "See, I'm doing just what the guy says in the book. I'm just trying to get my way in this discussion."

Yes, the book got used and many of the men genuinely liked it. They said they felt challenged both to act differently and to think differently. They said they never felt talked down to or preached at. And, of course, they said they liked hearing from a man...and from all the men in the book. They liked that the book was direct and to the point. And, yes, the book made my job a little easier. I had a tool that the men liked and that complemented the work they were doing in their programs.

So here you are, reading the Foreword to the new, improved edition of *Violent No More*. This edition has follow-up interviews with some of the men and women whose stories appeared in the first edition. The men talk about what has happened in the years since they made changes and about their need for an ongoing, daily commitment to be abuse free. The men say this is true even if they're part of a couple who chooses to stay together following the completion of the intervention programs.

In addition to reading this book yourself, I encourage you to give it to others. You need to develop a team of people who support your new behavior. Many of you have created a circle of folks who are silent when they know you're hurting your partner. You have become skilled at explaining away your behavior. You minimize it, deny it, and sometimes lie about it. Or you blame your partner, your children, your family—anyone and anything outside of yourself. You seek out those who won't challenge you. Oftentimes you convince family, friends, neighbors, your minister, your family law lawyer, the child welfare worker, your AA sponsor, your kids, the courts, your probation officer, and even your counselor that "there is no problem...and anyway, it's really my partner's fault." If others don't collude with you, you just avoid them. By doing this, though, you have made the task of changing that much more difficult. We cannot change things we don't see we are doing. We cannot see what we are doing and change if others do not hold us responsible for what we have done and for making the necessary change.

There are people in your life right now who want to help. They cannot be supportive, however, if they do not understand your responsibilities and their role in your change. Give this book to the person you abused so that she knows she has no responsibility for changing your behavior. It is not her job to take all—or even part—of the responsibility for your abusiveness. It is not her job to support you or even encourage you as you try to change. It is her job to take care of herself, to help herself and the children heal from your abusive control, and to reclaim her life—with or without you. Whether she loves you or not, she cannot help you with this particular change.

Give this book to your teenage or adult children, not as a plea for support or forgiveness, but so they, too, can look more honestly at what your abuse has done. As with your partner, their job is not to help you with your job. The book may help free them of the burden of trying to change you.

Give this book to family and friends so they can understand that what will help you most is for you to take full responsibility for all that you have done. The book will guide them away from blaming your partner, from making excuses for you, and from ignoring the seriousness of what happened. It will guide them in how to remain supportive of you while challenging you to live abuse free. It will guide them in how to hold you accountable for the changes you must make. To paraphrase a well-known saying, "Good friends don't let good friends abuse others." But oftentimes friends do not know what to do, and this book can help.

Give this book to your counselor, your doctor, your minister, rabbi, imam, your AA sponsor, your commanding officer, your supervisor... anyone who knows you and knows about the abuse. The book will help them understand you and understand that they can best help you by holding you accountable. Just because they are professionals doesn't mean they know much more than you do about domestic violence. They want to help but do not always know how.

Sharing the book is part of your being more honest with yourself and others. Honesty will make your work easier. There will come a time when you will add your own story to all the stories in this book. And there will come a time when you may give this book to another man to encourage him to start the journey to self-change. When you find it hard to read the book or you feel stalled in your efforts to move forward, remember the men in the book and also the many men who have read the book before you. Each of them struggled to look squarely at what he had done, to take full responsibility for his behavior in order to be free to change and to become who he wanted to be in intimate relationships.

In the third edition of *Violent No More* there are three new chapters. One addresses prevention of gender violence. The author asks you to be courageous by helping to challenge our culture, which bombards men and boys with negative messages about women and what it means to be a man. You can stop being silent. You've experienced firsthand the destructiveness of domestic abuse. Now you have an opportunity to help other men and boys stop the violence before it starts. You can give back by working with other changing men and women in your community.

There is also a chapter on assessing risk and danger. Most of the men in our groups are amenable to change if they make that choice, but there are some participants who continue to pose safety risks to their partners, children, and communities. Due to these risks, we are required to monitor them more intensely and work more closely with victims and advocacy programs.

For the tens of thousands of American men and women who have fought in Iraq and Afghanistan, the author has added a chapter on military personnel and veterans returning from war who commit intimate partner violence at home. For some, their abusive conduct preceded their serving in combat, while for others it may have become apparent only afterward. The author acknowledges co-occurring conditions, without excusing domestic offenders from taking responsibility for their abuse or blaming their combat experiences for their behavior.

To the counselors, group facilitators, probation officers, and child welfare workers who are working with men who batter, I strongly recommend *Violent No More* and the new accompanying *Violent No More Workbook*. The easy-to-use workbook has thirty-six exercises that parallel the chapters in the book. It is an effective supplement to counseling programs that work with court-ordered offenders or for men volunteering in your program. Participants can either complete the exercises at home or work on them together in a group.

Violent No More contains helpful ideas for effectively facilitating groups, stories from men and women, examples from the groups that enhance our understanding of the change process, and reminders of the importance of remaining resolute that victim safety must be central in our work. In a revised chapter for practitioners, the author addresses the discord and controversies in our field and challenges us to not lose sight of the long history of men's violence against women when suggesting new directions that may be injurious to battered women.

Violent No More is primarily a book for men who want to stop hurting their intimate partners, but it is also a useful guide for counselors who are on this journey with them.

— Anne Ganley
July 2014

Anne L. Ganley, PhD, is a psychologist in private practice and Clinical Associate Professor in the Department of Psychology at the University of Washington in Seattle. For twenty years she was the coordinator of domestic violence programs at two Veterans Administration medical centers. Dr. Ganley has developed model protocols for identifying, assessing, and responding to either domestic violence victims and/or domestic abusers in a variety of health, mental health, family law, and child welfare settings. She is a nationally known writer, consultant, and trainer in the field of domestic violence.

Preface

To the Men Courageous Enough
to Read This Book

I wrote *Violent No More: Helping Men End Domestic Abuse* for men who want to stop hurting the ones they love. It holds out a hand to men who have been and are violent in relationships with women, helps them understand what is behind their abuse, and offers guidance on how to change. It is a practical guide, based on years of working with men who have been violent, and written with the knowledge that most men who have battered are willing and ready to change—once they know how.

In the years since *Violent No More* was first published, I have appreciated the letters and phone calls I've received from men who have been helped by this book. Many of them have told me they no longer feel so alone after reading the stories of other men. They liked the book's emphasis on personal responsibility. They told me it gave them hope and the belief that they have the tools to change. And many of them have also sought help from domestic abuse programs and counseling in their communities.

To the Committed Counselors and
Group Facilitators Who Do This Work

I'm honored that so many practitioners have used *Violent No More* in their counseling groups and as a resource for men and women seeking help to end the violence. The exercises for men to practice what they are learning now appear in a separate workbook. Many counseling centers and domestic abuse programs purchase *Violent No More* and the workbook for their participants. Others require the men to pay for the book and workbook.

To the Partners of Men
Who Are in Domestic Abuse Programs

My intent was to write a book that would speak directly to men who batter. I didn't anticipate that *Violent No More* would also be helpful to women who have been abused by their husbands and boyfriends. Many battered women have contacted me to discuss their own situations. Some wondered whether their partners would, or could, change. Others realized that the stories of men and women in this book were very similar to their own life experiences and found solace in the fact that change can happen. Still others had their gut feelings confirmed—for now, they needed to leave the relationship.

Domestic abuse is defined as the use of physical violence in an intimate relationship. The term also includes intimidation, threats, emotional, psychological, and sexual abuse, as well as any other behavior one person in a relationship uses to control the other. Thousands of women are killed or seriously injured by their partners every year. Violence in the home is lethal—and it is illegal. But even though society is finally saying that domestic abuse is unacceptable, it still occurs in about 25 percent of American homes and is even more prevalent in other countries.

This book is not only for men who have been violent in the past but also for men who are concerned that their current behavior is hurting the ones they love. If you are violent, you know on some basic level that your behavior is wrong. If you are reaching out for help, this is the first and most important step. The next steps will not be easy, because ending violence, abuse, and controlling behavior requires struggling with long-held beliefs that will be difficult to give up.

Somehow and somewhere, men learn destructive attitudes and behaviors. The relationships of men who abuse their partners are like minefields: Nobody knows when things might explode and all hell break loose. Living in the minefield is terrifying. Inside, most men who batter know it doesn't have to be like this. All of us have the ability to experience fulfilling relationships that provide meaning and love in our lives.

In this book you will meet many men who have made major changes in their lives. You will read their stories and probably relate to some of them; others may shock you. Yet most of these men did change, and they are living proof that men who have been violent in relationships *can* change.

You will also read the stories of women who have been battered. Their experiences will help you understand the perspectives and feelings of women who have been beaten by their male partners. If you are not currently in a relationship, think about past relationships as you read these stories, and apply what you learn to future partnerships.

I encourage you, in addition to reading this book, to seek help from programs in your community that work to end domestic violence. You will need this support, because it is important to talk to people who have dealt with these issues firsthand. Overcoming violence and abuse in a relationship is hard work and can be lonely and frustrating. Like the men you will meet in this book, you will probably go through certain stages in your journey back from violence, a process that may take weeks, months, or years. First, you will begin to understand the big picture: "Where did I learn this behavior?" Second, you will apply the big picture to your own experiences. This stage may be difficult; facing up to personal faults usually produces internal resistance, yet it is a necessary step. Third, you will put into practice what you have learned. Whether or not you are currently in a relationship, you will begin to see things differently as you apply some of the suggestions in this book to your life.

At the end of the book are three new chapters for practitioners working with men who batter. It is important for those of us in the trenches to continue to have meaningful discussions about our techniques and principles. We do honorable work. This field is constantly evolving, and there are many promising practices that can enhance our efforts.

For men, if you agree with the direction in which this book takes you, I hope you will continue the process of change so your life becomes healthier and more satisfying. Remember, change takes time, but it is worth every bit of effort that you make. I wish you luck and success in your journey.

Acknowledgments

I want to acknowledge and thank the women and men in my life who have helped shape my thinking about relationships, sexism, and men's violence. First, I owe a debt to the battered women who have struggled to change our collective consciousness about the roots of domestic abuse. It is through their continuing struggle and commitment to end violence that someday we may see a more egalitarian and peaceful world.

I also want to acknowledge my colleagues, past and present, at the Duluth Domestic Abuse Intervention Project and the Battered Women's Justice Project, where I worked for nearly three decades. Their courage and unceasing dedication have permanently improved the lives of many women and men, and their efforts have provided a guiding light to many communities around the world.

I owe a special debt of gratitude to the men and women who volunteered to share their life experiences for this book.

I want to thank my friend, colleague, and mentor, the late Ellen Pence, for reviewing the original drafts of *Violent No More* and for being supportive of me all these years. Ellen was a true pioneer in this field and one of the great leaders of the battered women's movement.

I also want to acknowledge the late Allan Creighton for his insight and help with the first edition of this book, which came out in 1993. Allan was the founder of Men Overcoming Violence and the Oakland Men's Project. I'm in debt to Anne Ganley for writing the Foreword to this third edition. Anne is a nationally known writer, psychologist, and trainer on domestic abuse; her work with veterans is especially noteworthy.

I want to acknowledge Edward Gondolf, PhD; Glenna Tinney, MSW; Jacquelyn Campbell, PhD, RN; Barbara Hart, JD; David Adams, EdD; John Beams, JD, LSW; David Garvin, MSW; Denise Gamache, MSW; Chuck Derry; Graham Barnes; Gus Kaufman Jr., PhD; and Scott Miller for their contributions, insight, and ideas. I want to thank Kiran Rana, former publisher of Hunter House Publishers, for encouraging me to write this third edition.

For years Kate Regan has edited the work that Ellen Pence and I collaborated on. I was thrilled when she agreed to work on yet another project with me. Ellen was smiling from the heavens as we wrote and rewrote the manuscript. Thanks to Alexandra Mummery and Kelley Blewster for their thoughtful rework of the manuscript.

And, finally, a heartfelt and loving thanks to my partner and wife, Laura Goodman, who not only has stood by me for years but also encouraged me to write this updated version. She provided incredible feedback, advice, support, and love throughout the process.

Introduction

Every fifteen seconds in the United States,
a woman is beaten by her husband or boyfriend.

Thirty percent of all female homicide victims
are killed by a partner or former partner.

One out of every four men will use violence
against a partner at some time in their relationship.

Children are present during 80 percent
of the assaults against their mothers.

One in six women
have been stalked in their lifetime.

No community is immune to domestic abuse. Emergency rooms sew up cuts, fix broken bones, and treat bruises. Overcrowded shelters provide temporary safety and emotional support to victims. Offenders get arrested and protection orders are issued, but the courts are already overwhelmed and the jails overcrowded. And the violence continues.

When does it stop? How will it stop? And, finally, who is responsible for ending it?

Laws alone will not end domestic abuse. Men must stop the excuses and end the silence. Ultimately, men who batter must make personal decisions about how they want to conduct their lives. Over the years I have talked to hundreds of men who have battered their intimate partners. Most men who hit once usually hit again. And most of them said that their abusive behavior escalated until they finally got arrested or decided to seek help.

Men who are violent or abusive often project an attitude of not needing or wanting to change. Deep down, most of them know that something is not right. They start new relationships with high expectations, only to see their abusive behavior tear them apart. They medicate themselves with drugs, alcohol, and cynicism about life and relationships. Their friendships with other men are frequently superficial. They see their children acting out in inappropriate ways because of what is happening at home, and they don't know what to do. They see their partners, who once loved them, turn away in anger and in fear. All too often they end up alone, out of touch with their own feelings and cut off from the company and affection of others, pretty much trapped....

If this description sounds familiar, I hope you will continue reading.

There is no single profile of a man who is violent. Abusers are rich, middle class, and poor, blue collar and white collar, old and young. Some grew up with violence in the home, and others did not. Some have college degrees, and others dropped out of school. Some batter when they are drunk, and some when they are sober. They come from all races, religions, and cultures.

Men are not naturally violent, but we learn that violence is a powerful and effective response to settling disagreements. All men grow up with a feeling of entitlement based on their gender, but not all men choose to use violence. We can reject the cultural conditioning that spawns violence. We can discard the sexist belief that women are less significant than men. We can teach our sons and daughters that men and women are equal, that intimate relationships should be respectful, and that violence is not an acceptable way to resolve conflicts.

Why Write a Book for Men Who Batter?

A book like this can be a catalyst for personal change. By understanding how and why you got where you are, and by recognizing your own potential to change, you can begin a healthier life.

Back in the early 1970s I was very active in political and social causes. The women's movement was just beginning to blossom, but like many other men at the time I failed to understand the rage and frustration women felt at men's sexist beliefs and the institutional roadblocks they experienced in our society. My attitudes about women were not very different from those of the men I have worked with who have battered an intimate partner. Even though I had never battered, my sexism was real. I thought on some level that men were better or more competent than women. It was not until female friends confronted me that I began questioning my beliefs and attitudes. At first I became defensive. But then I decided to accept the confrontation not as criticism but as a challenge to look deeper. I eventually realized not only that my sexism was wrong but that it got in the way of my friendships and my ability to be intimate in relationships with women.

I decided to get involved with a small group of men who were meeting to discuss issues related to sexism and violence against women. I had recently been elected to the Duluth City Council and chaired a public hearing on sexual violence. Many people testified, and many good ideas were presented. Still, I felt frustrated at our inability to do more about ending gender violence in our community.

At about the same time, several women in Duluth began organizing the Domestic Abuse Intervention Project (DAIP). Organizers were insistent that society has an obligation to ensure that its citizens aren't victimized, whether in their neighborhoods or in their homes. The year the organizers began their work, a particularly gruesome homicide occurred—after enduring years of brutal beatings, a young woman shot her husband in the stomach with a shotgun. When the paramedics arrived, the man was literally in two parts. This incident and a growing concern about domestic abuse paved the way for a public response to what had been considered private violence.

The DAIP changed the way the criminal justice system, law enforcement, and human-service providers—social workers and counselors—responded to domestic abuse cases. The DAIP was instrumental in persuading the Duluth Police Department to re-examine and ultimately change its arrest policies. When the DAIP was organizing what became known as the Duluth Model, police officers were attempting mediation in domestic abuse cases or separating the couple by asking the offender to leave for the night and "cool off." Too often he came back and continued or escalated his violence. Under the new policy, police began arresting offenders if they suspected a crime had been committed. The DAIP also secured agreements from city and county attorneys to prosecute offenders and from judges to sentence them if convicted. In lieu of jail, most offenders were placed on probation and given an opportunity to change their behavior by attending domestic abuse classes. This is where I came in.

The organizers of the DAIP invited me and nine other men to a meeting. They explained the goals of the program and asked if we would be willing to meet with men who had been arrested under the new policy. The hope was that if we engaged other men who were harming their intimate partners, perhaps they would listen. Perhaps they would realize that they needed help. I volunteered.

After an arrest was made, the battered women's shelter would call me and give me information about the case. The next morning I would go down to the jail and meet with the man who was detained so I could hear his explanation of what had happened. Many of the men I met with seemed pleased to have someone to talk to. One of my objectives was to get them to see the impact their violence was having on their families—and its destructiveness. I talked about our counseling program and the help we offered.

Most of the offenders were stunned to be in jail. For many a secret was finally being exposed. Some were honest with me and said they wanted help. Of course, sitting in the bowels of the old Duluth jail may have influenced their receptiveness to my offer of assistance. Still, I believed that many of these men truly felt remorse and were apprehensive about what was going to happen next.

Other men were angry and defiant, blaming their partners or the police. They would deal with their problems themselves, they said. They made it clear they did not want or need any help from me or my program.

Each of these men had fallen in love with a woman and made a commitment to some kind of relationship. So what had happened? How did the loving, smiling husbands I saw in the wedding pages of our local newspaper become the angry, hurt men I was now seeing in jail cells?

The time I spent talking with these men affected me profoundly, and I started asking questions. Were they so terribly different from me? I reached back into my childhood and began remembering the messages I had received about men and women: "Men should be in charge." "Men are smarter and more logical than women." "Men settle disagreements in a *manly* way—through fighting." "A man is king in his home, his castle." Was there a connection between these childhood messages that most boys get and the prevalence of domestic abuse in our society?

The relationship between men's violence and what society tells us is the right way to be "male" became much clearer when I began conducting groups outside the jail for men who battered, and later when I became the Men's Program Coordinator for the DAIP. In the beginning the majority of the men in the groups were there because they were ordered by the court to attend. I remember feeling nervous as I walked into my first group. Would the men be angry at me because the court had forced them to be there? Would they talk honestly about their abusive behavior? Would they want to change? Would they even listen to me?

My first group was held at an old community center in Duluth. At the start of the meeting I asked the men to form a circle. They reluctantly carried or dragged their chairs to the middle of the room. Some looked angry, others bored—and we had not even begun. A few looked resigned to the situation and even seemed open to whatever was going to happen.

Most of the men were dressed casually, except for Don and Bradley, who wore suits. Howard, at fifty-five, was the oldest man there. The rest were between twenty and forty. Some of the men had been in trouble with the law before, but for most this was a new and embarrassing experience. One man, Paul, had volunteered to attend. He said he did not want to be abusive anymore and felt he was losing his family.

I introduced myself and told the group I realized many of them did not want to be there, but I hoped they would be open to what the program had to offer. I said that sometimes something bad or uncomfortable has to happen before we're ready to make changes in our lives. I said I wanted them to know I believed each of them *could* change—if he wanted.

Then I asked each man to introduce himself and explain why he was there. At first they were quiet, but gradually they started to talk.

As I thought about it afterward, I saw that the men had talked about their violence and relationships with women in three ways:

One group believed that men and women have separate and distinct roles: The man should be the head of the house. It didn't matter if the woman was contributing financially to the household; they believed that "someone has to be in charge." To them, this belief meant that if their partners challenged their authority, then admonishment—even if it became abusive—could be seen as a justifiable response.

Another group stated that their problems with their partners were mutual, and the violence was a result of conflict in the relationship. They admitted that the violence was wrong but believed their partners had pushed or provoked them.

A third group—a couple of men, including Paul—said emphatically that their behavior was wrong. These men seemed truly disturbed by their actions. They were seeing the effects of their violence on their partners, their children, and themselves. They seemed to have hit bottom. Their moral compass not only was indicating that their behavior was wrong, but now it was guiding their desire to change.

The initial group sessions were challenging because the men had such varied beliefs about their behavior, coupled with a high degree of discomfort about having to attend. By the eighth session, however, most of them were talking freely, with much disagreement and debate. One night I wrote the word "sexism" on the board and asked what it meant to them and whether it had anything to do with domestic abuse. The following discussion took place ("Michael" refers to me):

> **Don:** Sexism is when men treat women as unequal. You know, if women are paid less for the same job than men, that's sexism.
> **Paul:** I think it's a belief that men are better than women. Most boys get taught that early on. I did. I guess if we believe that men are superior, then women are obviously somehow inferior.

I asked how sexism might contribute to hitting a partner.

> **Paul:** Well, for some men, they think of their wives as property, and you can do what you want with your own property.
> **Michael:** It's interesting that you talk about wives as property. Until the end of the nineteenth century, there were actually laws listing the reasons a husband could beat his wife. He was expected to discipline her and keep the family in line.
> **Howard:** Yeah, but don't you think things are changing with all this feminist crap? My wife works and she's free to do what she wants.
> **Michael:** Why do you say "feminist crap"?
> **Howard:** I just think some of it has gone too far.

Needless to say we had a lively discussion that night. At the next session several men told me they had not really thought about the connections between men's violence, women, and sexism.

In later groups we talked about entitlement (believing you have privilege or power over another) and why a woman would resist an unequal relationship with a man. Gradually some men in the group began to recognize that they resorted to abuse and violence when their partners resisted being controlled. This was an important insight. Other men struggled with the ideas being discussed, while still others participated but remained unconvinced.

After six months the first group of men had completed the program. Each said he had learned something from it. All vowed they would not be violent again. Paul talked about how much his relationship with his wife had improved. I told him I thought he had worked hard and I appreciated his honesty. Bradley and his partner had split up, but he was sure that in his next relationship he would not make the same mistakes. We all said our good-byes, and I felt good about the experience.

Three months later I got a call from the women's shelter telling me that two men had been arrested for domestic assault the night before. I got to the jail at 7:00 AM and was led down a line of cells to the meeting room. The first man brought in for me to talk to was Paul. He had smashed the headlights of his wife's car with a baseball bat and threatened to kill her.

I was stunned and disappointed. I was so convinced that Paul had turned the corner. Of all the men in my first group, Paul seemed to have truly grasped the issues. He had talked eloquently about men and women needing to respect each other, stating that violence in a relationship was wrong. He had made a commitment to handle conflicts with his wife differently—and now here he was, in jail. I asked him to explain what had happened.

Paul said he hadn't wanted to go to a party the night before and didn't want his wife, Robin, to go either. This is what Paul told me:

I told Robin I was too tired to go to the party and said it would be really nice if we just stayed home together. She said she'd been counting on going for several weeks and wanted to go. So I said go ahead, even though I didn't want her to go. I was stewing all night long thinking if she really loved me she wouldn't have gone. And then I started wondering why she wanted to go to the party so badly. It was two in the morning before I heard the car drive up. I was so mad. I went outside with a baseball bat and she ran back into the car. I started screaming for her to get out, and when she didn't, I started smashing the car with the bat and threatened to kill her. The neighbor called the police.

This early experience with Paul taught me that understanding the problem of violent and abusive behavior intellectually (as he did) does not necessarily translate into changed behavior. There's a saying frequently used in chemical dependency treatment: "You've got to walk the walk, not just talk the talk." Knowing what you need to do to change and saying that you ought to change are not enough; you have to put the new behaviors into practice as well. I had to keep reminding myself that many of the men in our groups would return to old, familiar territory and, unfortunately, would batter again.

I choose to put my energies into this work because I think we as men have a responsibility to end men's violence. I believe it is simply inexcusable that women today still feel unsafe among their friends, partners, colleagues, and lovers. Male violence has been our historical legacy. Our prisons, battlefields, streets, and homes have been marked by our violence. It needs to stop. I believe, to put it a little simplistically, that it is much more "manly" to deal with our own violence: to accept the challenge of struggling with it without violating ourselves or others and of releasing it so that we are, truly, violent no more.

A Note to the Reader

This book is written for men who are abusive and violent toward their female partners. In no way am I claiming that men have not also been victimized by women in intimate relationships. Women do assault men: They use violence in self-defense, they use violence in retaliation, and some women initiate violence. In Duluth about 10 percent of the offenders arrested for domestic assault are female; most, but not all, were using violence in self-defense or in retaliation. A small percentage could be classified as women who batter. In these incidents men who are being battered should surely have the same protection and access to resources that battered women have.

I do not condone women's violence, but it is clear from my experiences in this field that men and women use violence in very different ways. Most men who have had violence used against them by their female partners are not also experiencing the kind of fear, intimidation, and coercion usually associated with being battered. Most men who have been assaulted by their female partners are not also experiencing sexual violence or the threat of being raped. Most men who have had violence used against them by a female partner will freely admit that they could escape from the immediate abusive situation or end a violent relationship without fear of retribution. We cannot ignore the power differential between women and men.

This book doesn't address same-sex battering, which is far more prevalent than originally thought. Men who are victimized by an intimate male partner should seek help from domestic abuse or counseling programs or from LGBTQ organizations in their community.

The people interviewed in this book are real, but some of their names have been changed to protect their privacy and that of their families. Some men have gone public with their stories and have given me permission to use their real names. The persons and events described in the group sessions are often composites based on real people and events, but the names have also been changed.

Finally, a few words about the language used in this book. Over the years, we have defined domestic abuse in many ways. When we're referring to it in a legal sense, we typically use the term "domestic assault" or "domestic violence." Some advocates and practitioners in the field use the word "battering" to describe not just physical violence but intimidation, coercion, threats, and other abusive tactics when the intention is to dominate an intimate partner. Not all men who are abusive to their intimate partners fall into this category.

Recently researchers and practitioners in the mental health field have been using the term "intimate partner violence," or IPV, rather than "domestic abuse" or "battering." The thinking behind this new definition is that "domestic abuse" can be applied to all kinds of violence in the home, including the abuse of a child by a parent. I will continue to use "domestic abuse" because it is how most men in our groups define their behavior.

I also tend to use the term "men who batter" when I'm talking about a man who uses violence (even sporadically) and also uses other abusive behaviors to control his intimate partner.

Although counselors and people in the criminal justice system may be reading this book (three new chapters at the end of the book are addressed specifically to them), the primary audience is men—men who have battered or who recognize that their abuse is becoming a problem in their lives.

Domestic abuse, while certainly not a new phenomenon, wasn't talked about a generation ago. Now a whole field has emerged, with researchers and practitioners making claims and counterclaims about how people change. We all have a piece of the truth. Men who want to stop hurting their intimate partners and the counselors working with them are on a journey together.

A Challenge for Men

Two roads diverged in a wood, and I—
I took the one less traveled by,
And that has made all the difference.

▸▸ ROBERT FROST ◂◂

Andy's Story

Andy was born in Duluth, Minnesota. Like some of the other men in this book, he grew up with domestic abuse in his family. He was arrested for domestic assault and was ordered to attend our program. Andy has struggled to understand the roots of his violence. He has been violence free for more than fifteen years and now works with other men who have been abusive to women.

> I remember coming home from school, and my father had my mother by the hair. It was obvious that she'd been crying because her mascara was smeared and her face was all puffy. He had a knife in his hand and he said to me, "Do you want me to kill this bitch? Because I will!" I was crying and begging him not to hurt her.
>
> He battered her all the time, and I never saw her fight back. She was always trying to accommodate him. Sometimes it would work and sometimes it would piss him off more.
>
> My brothers and I were always getting into fights, and my dad thought that was perfectly normal. If we complained or came to him, he would say we had to settle it like men.

I got a lot of my attitudes about girls and women from my father, but mostly I think society provided very negative messages about families in general. For me to get beat by a girl in a sports event was the ultimate in humiliation, and my father always told me you shouldn't hit girls, yet he battered my mother. He died when I was eleven.

I met Debra, and we started to live together. The worst violence I remember was when Debra said something about me at a party and I got embarrassed. When we got outside I grabbed her and threw her to the ground and started pounding her head on the sidewalk. She was screaming and terrified. My brother ran over and tried to get me off of her. He said, "Andy, you're going to kill her!" I'm not sure if I would have, but I stopped.

I thought Debra provoked my abuse. She would call me names or criticize my parenting abilities or say something she knew would piss me off, and I felt totally justified in letting her have it.

I usually blamed Debra for the violence. When she would come home late, I felt justified in hitting her. On some level I knew it was wrong, but I believed she brought it on herself. I always thought if she would just stop resisting me and do as I said, she wouldn't get hit.

After being violent I would try to get her to see that what I did wasn't that bad. I'd say, "You don't have any marks on you," or "Other men would have done worse." If I'd slapped her, I'd say later, "Well, I didn't use a closed fist."

One time we got into a fight in the bedroom and I pushed her and she fell over the nightstand by the bed. She ended up with a broken arm and had to have a cast. A couple of weeks later we were over at our friends' house, sitting around the table, and they asked what had happened to Debra's arm. She made up some story about tripping and falling. I was really uncomfortable and I got angry at her because I was embarrassed in front of our friends.

At the time I never felt that Debra was afraid of me. If you had come into our house back then and asked me about her being afraid, I would have said, "Hell, no!" I mean, why would she sleep with me if she was afraid, or why would she call me a fuckin' asshole if she was afraid? If she was afraid of me why would she say, "You're a sissy; go lay down by your fuckin' bowl by the dog. What are you going to do, hit a woman again?"

Debra was also violent with me. She was tough, and at the time both of us were into the bar scene. Sometimes she would throw things at me, slap me, or try to kick me. Actually I was glad when she did that, because then I would feel totally justified in beating her up. There were times I would goad her by getting in her face, calling her particular names so she would strike first. When she did it would give me the green light to knock the hell out of her. After all she hit me first. I was never afraid of her. Sometimes I would laugh at her after she hit me.

I rarely apologized unless the violence was really bad. When I apologized there was still this hint that it was her fault. I expected her to forgive me, and I would get really angry when she wouldn't. When she didn't accept my apology, I would say, "You fuckin' bitch, you started this stuff, and now look at you!"

I never thought she would leave me, but she did. The police came to our house three times but never arrested me. When they came I would be real calm and wouldn't show them my anger, and Debra would be real agitated. I would tell the police it was her fault and that she started the fight. They would go over to her and tell her not to provoke me.

Finally they did arrest me, because they had told me to leave the house after an incident and I had come back. I was charged with assault. I was really mad at the police, the justice system, and Debra. I felt no one was listening to my side of the story and everyone was blaming me when I thought Debra was just as much to blame. I threatened Debra, telling her if she didn't get the charges dropped I would really hurt her. She went to the city attorney, but they wouldn't drop the charges.

I was ordered into the counseling program and was really resistant at first. I didn't think I belonged there. I would say in group, "What about her violence? What am I supposed to do when she slaps me?" The counselors would challenge me to look at my violence and not to focus on her. It finally started to sink in, and I realized that Debra didn't have to change for me to change.

After four or five group sessions something happened for me. It was actually freeing to take responsibility for my own behavior. It was challenging to examine my beliefs. I began to enjoy going to groups and talking about this stuff with other men. Even though I started making changes, it wasn't enough to save my relationship with Debra. I guess too much had happened between us—too much pain and too much of my violence—for us to heal as a couple.

I waited a long time before I decided to get involved in a new relationship. I wanted to be sure I had worked through my issues around wanting to control women. I also wanted to be absolutely sure I would be nonviolent in any future relationship.

I told Beth, my current partner, about my past. It was a risk, but I felt she should know that I had battered Debra. I think it's important to be honest and accountable. Today I'm constantly challenging my beliefs about men and women. In my current relationship I try to be aware of my body language, because I'm a big guy and I have a loud voice. I need to be careful about how I respond to Beth when I'm angry. I'll always need to monitor myself.

In the past I was frightened by the prospect of women rejecting me, so I tended not to give too much, not to be too vulnerable, for fear I'd get hurt. I think part of it was my upbringing as a male. Men don't share feelings, men don't cry, men are supposed to be strong. It's an unfortunate attribute I see in the men I work with, and it's something I need to work on.

When I was battering, it never occurred to me that I didn't need the tough-guy image or that relationships with women could be different. Since I've made these changes in my life my relationships with women and men have changed. When I'm with men I'm really aware of sexist comments and attitudes. I don't want superficial relationships with people.

I'm optimistic that men who batter can change. Some of the changes are small and the process is slow, but I believe it can happen. It's been more than ten years since I battered, and

I've been completely violence free. Yet I still take an inventory of what I'm doing in my life.

When I started running groups in Duluth it was a real eye-opener. The men who were coming into our groups were so angry, just like I was. They were angry at the police, the courts, and their partners. I know this will sound strange, but the best thing that ever happened to me was getting arrested. I finally had to look at my behavior. I had to stop conning everyone, including myself.

Andy's Story Years Later

I sat down with Andy five years after our initial interview. I wanted to find out what had changed in his life, how he has remained nonviolent, and what advice he had for men in similar situations. Andy has been married for many years to Beth. He has gone back to college and earned a degree in psychology.

On His Past

An important element in my change process was the way people held me accountable when I got arrested. And that people believed I could change. When I was ordered into the Domestic Abuse Intervention Project, the group leaders and my probation officer all believed in me—that was important to a twenty-one-year-old who was going down the wrong track. When I began the group I was kind of scared. I mean I'd never talked to people about my feelings before, and I'd never been asked the kinds of questions they wanted me to answer. Group process? Bar stools were the closest I ever got to a group. But the process turned out to be comfortable—I wasn't told I was bad, but I did get challenged in a very respectful and helpful way.

On His Current Marriage

When I told Beth about my past use of violence, I think she was a little nervous about getting into a relationship with me, and for a while I think she was rightly checking me out. We were in love, but our first two years of marriage were definitely rocky.

Our initial problems occurred when I moved into her house. Beth and her kids all had a certain way of doing things, and I was thrust into their environment with their rules. Beth thought that I was avoiding conflict and that I wasn't committed to the relationship, because I was working long hours, so in her mind we couldn't work through our problems. We had some very big compatibility issues.

On Dealing with Conflict

During those first two years of marriage, when Beth and I would argue, I would sometimes get sarcastic and raise my voice, and at other times I would just shut down and withdraw. I would usually apologize when I was acting in an inappropriate manner. This was a painful time for both of us.

It was at about this time that Beth told me there were times she was scared of me. I couldn't believe it. She would say, "You know, you're a big guy, and when we get into an argument, if you raise your voice, it makes me afraid sometimes." She would then qualify these statements by saying, "I don't believe you'll physically hurt me, but I still feel afraid." I never sensed she felt this way, because she wouldn't shut down or retreat from any conflicts we were having. When she confronted me about this, it really floored me. I didn't want to own it, I didn't want to entertain it, I didn't want to feel it, and I didn't want to hear it. I so desperately didn't want her to be afraid of me, but she was.

Here I was, working with men who batter, and I'm very visible in the community because of my work, and here Beth is telling me that sometimes she's fearful. It was really depressing. All I had ever wanted was to be a loving husband to Beth and a loving stepparent to the kids. I wanted her to love me, approve of me, and think I'm somebody special. So when she told me about being scared, I felt like a monster. I hated it.

She would say things like, "You know you have this history," and I would really resent it, because I was not the same person I was back when I was arrested. I would get angry when she would put me in that framework. I felt she was playing the trump card and that was that—everything's over now, I can't do anything and I can't say anything.

On Working Through Problems in His Marriage

We were both determined to work things through. We went to marriage counseling and I went to individual counseling. We separated twice because we recognized we both needed to make some changes, or else we would wind up in divorce. The separation was helpful. We took the time to sort things out and find some better ways of communicating. We're a lot more honest with each other now. I don't walk away from conflicts anymore, and we work through our problems. We've actually set up times for dealing with issues.

On His Childhood, Anger, and Healing

I was pretty severely damaged as a child. I experienced and witnessed a lot of abuse and pain, even though my memories of that time are a little hazy. I don't have as much anger inside me today about my family, because I've done a lot of healing over the years. At the time Beth and I were having problems, I decided I wanted to do some "family of origin" counseling and try to get in touch with what my childhood was all about. I interviewed several counselors until I found one I thought would be helpful. I think my separation from Beth was in part a motivation for me to go back into therapy. It was also at this time that I started thinking about my dad. I finally got to a place where I could forgive him, and I miss him today. I asked my mother about my childhood, but she didn't want to talk about my dad's abusive behavior, so I let it go.

Working on improving yourself is so critical to personal growth. I have a men's group that meets every other week, which is really important to me. We talk about personal growth, relationships, and gender issues, and I get strength from them. I've had a lot of healing experiences over the years, and consequently a lot of my anger has diminished.

On Spirituality

I really think my faith in God has been important to my change process. I draw strength from God when I pray, and there's a lot of wisdom in the scriptures about love, trust, and respect. In my work with men who batter, I really stress the importance of being "plugged in" in some way. Religion, spirituality, whatever—just do something for self-improvement.

On Talking to His Stepchildren about His Past

My three stepchildren know I went to jail and they know I'm an alcoholic. Telling them was a decision that Beth and I made together, and it was relatively easy. They know that, in part, the reason I do this work is because of my past violence. They are very accepting. My relationship with these kids has been just super.

On His Life Today

Beth and I have a great relationship today. She's my best friend. We have a level of intimacy that's very special. As I said the first two years were a struggle, but we worked things through. I believe if those kinds of problems surfaced again, we would recognize the signs and deal with the issues in a heartbeat. This comes from a deeper level of commitment to our relationship that simply wasn't there those first two years of our marriage. We often talk about our relationship and how far we've come. There have been times that we just hold each other, and we're brought to tears because of how deep our love and intimacy are today. We have created a process for checking things out with each other. The love and respect that we have for each other are very powerful.

While I didn't interview Andy for this latest edition, I have continued to have contact with him over the years. He's currently conducting workshops on domestic abuse with Beth, and he's also working for a victim–witness program on the West Coast.

I often share Andy's story when I conduct workshops. I tell his story because (Andy would confirm this) without intervention by law enforcement officers, the criminal justice system, and a dedicated domestic abuse program, Andy's life may have turned out very differently. At the time that he was battering his wife, he felt totally justified doing what he did.

The First Step: Owning the Problem

Something motivated you to open this book. Perhaps a counselor, minister, rabbi, imam, friend, or family member suggested it. Maybe you are recognizing the pain you are causing your family. Or perhaps you are concerned about behavior that is scaring those around you—and yourself. What you read in the chapters ahead may be hard to accept, and it may cause you to become defensive. The first step is acknowledging the problem and taking responsibility for doing something about it, and it's never easy

When I asked Andy what motivated him to change, he said, "It was a combination of things: getting arrested, spending a night in jail, going to court, having my name in the paper, and being forced into groups. Even more it was the fact that the secrecy was over. The lies about the black eyes, the cover-up on both our parts were over. Everyone knew—now the secret was exposed."

If there is hidden violence in your relationship, the first step toward change is deciding to be honest about what's happening in your life. In fact, it's more than likely that people already know about your violence and abuse. It's difficult to keep that kind of secret from children, friends, family members, and neighbors, whether they acknowledge it or not.

Not too long ago people who had alcohol or drug addictions or mental health problems were regarded as dysfunctional or as failures. Today, celebrities, sports stars, business leaders, and politicians come forward and acknowledge their mistakes, addictions, or struggles with inappropriate behavior. They talk openly and honestly about wanting to get healthier. Today friends, family members, employers, and society in general are far more accepting when someone genuinely seeks help.

The Next Step: Getting Help

I encourage men who physically abuse their partners to talk to other men, friends, family, clergy, and professionals about what has been happening in their lives. While some people will defend or support your abusive actions because they think that's what you want to hear, those who truly care for you will help you find ways to change and will support your efforts.

Many communities have domestic abuse programs. If you have battered or are abusive, you may feel reluctant to go to such a program. You may be embarrassed or uncomfortable talking about such personal issues in a group setting. I urge you to take the risk and join. The other men in the group will have had similar experiences, and you will feel less alone.

If you are a person of color there may be culturally specific programs that you would feel more comfortable attending. In my hometown of Duluth, for example, the Native American community has designed groups for Native American men and women. If you are a gay man, specific programs and resources are available for you, too. If you have trouble locating the services you need, call a mental health agency, community center, domestic abuse program, or an information and referral number for help. Don't wait. Do it now.

Counseling programs vary from community to community. In Duluth the Domestic Abuse Intervention Project works with men in groups, rather than individually. We find a supportive environment in the group process as we struggle together with sometimes uncomfortable issues. Discussing our beliefs and attitudes about women, masculinity, entitlement, and violence is not easy. In fact, it takes courage.

I've never met a man who has battered his wife or girlfriend who can honestly say he's truly happy with his life and the choices he is making. Ultimately each man in the groups needs to decide whether his beliefs are helpful or harmful to having a healthy intimate relationship. We take the position that battering is intentional behavior and its purpose is to control another person—shut her up, stop her from doing something, or punish her for something she has done. The groups focus on ending not only violence but also other abusive behavior.

Most men in the groups are court ordered to attend. About 10 percent volunteer. I'm always saddened by the men who volunteer but then drop out after a short time. Many men come on their own because their partners have told them to either get help or get out. Sadly when things get a little better they quit, thinking they have a handle on their problems. But there's no quick fix. When a man drops out of counseling after a few sessions, he almost certainly hasn't learned what he needs to learn to change his behavior. Frequently the relationship worsens and his partner leaves. This can reinforce a sense of failure. Moreover men who don't get help for themselves often repeat their abusive behavior in new relationships.

Many men say they would prefer to go to couples or marriage counseling. They insist that the relationship cannot change unless both people get help. Avery, a participant in one of my groups, described his feelings:

> I was so angry at the people at that program. We have a marriage problem, and they wouldn't let us see a marriage counselor. Well, I told them, how the hell are we supposed to work on our problems if we're going to separate groups? They were adamant. I understand their reasoning today. To be honest, after I got out of jail I don't think I was ready for marriage counseling, and I know Kelly wasn't. We finally did end up going to marriage counseling after I completed the men's groups.

Unfortunately some practitioners in the mental health community provide marriage counseling upon request, even when they know about domestic abuse in the relationship. Unless the violence has stopped and your partner feels safe with you, marriage counseling is inappropriate.

I asked Cassie, one of the women I interviewed for this book, about marriage counseling:

> We went to marriage counseling and it was a terrible experience. The counselor said I needed to be more accepting of him. I was angry because Antonio was drinking a lot. The counselor

said that on his days off, if he wanted to drink a case of beer in his own house, I should accept that.

I was reluctant to bring up the violence and abuse, because I wasn't sure how he would react. That was the part of our problem he didn't want known. The one time I did mention the abuse, it was basically discounted. When that happened he felt totally validated. The counselor even said I needed to be more sexually receptive to him and not be so critical of his faults.

The idea of marriage counseling is to sort through problems in the relationship. The goal is to heal and problem solve. However, if a woman can't talk freely, how can the sessions be successful? Many practitioners believe they can tell if the violence has stopped or if one party is reluctant to talk. These assumptions are not only naïve but also potentially dangerous to battered women. For survival purposes victims must be very good at hiding what's actually happening in their relationships. The cover-up is used with parents, friends, coworkers, and even therapists. Disclosure of violence in the home may result in more violence or even an escalation. A battered woman knows she will be blamed if she talks about private matters. Despite the seemingly safe environment of a therapy office and the reassuring statements by the marriage counselor, a victim knows her partner. She knows when it's safe to talk and when it's not.

Most communities have shelters, safe homes, and advocacy programs for battered women. They provide temporary, safe lodging and may help women get protection orders from the court. These programs usually provide education and support groups. They are a way to help women understand what's been going on in their relationships and to help them realize that they're not responsible for the violence. Then they can sort out their options. I strongly encourage women to participate.

Some men feel threatened when women attend these support groups. They think the groups are antimale or that group members are plotting to get women to end their relationships. This is not true. The groups are antiviolence. Many battered women experience confusion, pain, fear, and rage as a result of being battered. Other women who have had similar experiences are there to offer them support. Men who batter should encourage this as a healing process and not ask or expect their partners to reveal what happens in the groups. Respect your partner's need to get help for herself. If you want your relationship to survive and change, you have to trust.

Using the *Violent No More Workbook*

In the following chapters you will read examples of things you can do, or do differently, to avoid situations in which you might be abusive. In the workbook there are a number of exercises that correspond to the chapters in this book. They are designed to help men understand, monitor, and change abusive and controlling behavior.

I invite you to complete them. You may be surprised at what you learn about yourself. Use them to explore where you have been and to set goals for the future. By writing down your thoughts and feelings during this time, you can track your own change process. And by remembering and writing down in detail your past experiences, you will develop deeper insights into your decision making.

Some of the exercises in the workbook are for men who have stopped battering and are in relationships. They are designed for couples working through basic issues such as negotiating, communicating, and arguing fairly. For women, check with an advocate or a therapist skilled in domestic abuse dynamics to determine if there is any risk in doing the exercises with your partner if you are still afraid of him. What seems harmless may be dangerous if he is still using violence, threats, and intimidation. Counselors can be helpful in deciding when and how the exercises should be used.

Finally, whether you are a man or a woman, you may disagree with points I make. This book will expose you to some new ideas, and your initial reaction might be to slam the cover shut because you don't like what you're reading. Or you might feel what's being said doesn't apply to you. My analysis of the roots of men's violence may make you uncomfortable. But please—give it a chance. Read on. If you complete the book I'm confident it will guide you toward truly ending domestic abuse in your life.

Please complete Exercise 1, "How I Got to This Place," and Exercise 2, "What Do You Hope to Accomplish?" in Chapter 1 of your workbook.

The Roots of Men's Violence Against Women

Children have never been very good
at listening to their elders,
but they have never failed to imitate them.
They must, they have no other models.

▶▶ JAMES BALDWIN ◀◀

Mark's Story

Mark is an environmental engineer who lives in an upper-middle-class suburb of St. Paul. He is divorced from Jody, the woman he battered. Mark was nearing the end of his domestic abuse group when I conducted this interview. Unlike the other men who told their stories for this book, he is still sorting through the past and the hurt. His abusive behavior was relentless and punitive after Jody's affair. For five years he made her pay—and they both suffered.

> My parents never fought. Throughout my childhood I only re-
> member one incident when they had a verbal confrontation.
> We lived in a nice neighborhood and had a beautiful home. My
> parents rarely hit us. I think I was spanked on one occasion.
>   I'm not sure what influenced my violent tendencies. I guess
> it had something to do with my size; I'm not very big. I would
> get picked on in school a lot, and I started to fight back. I got

into a lot of fights, and I think that shaped my attitude about violence.

I felt powerful when I got into fights. It also got me acceptance from the guys I wanted to hang around with. At the time I liked that tough-guy image. I thought it might impress the girls, but in retrospect I think they thought we were being childish.

Jody and I got married right after high school, and we were together for about ten years. Looking back I don't think I really wanted to be married. I was young, and all of a sudden I was married and had a kid on the way. I resented the responsibilities of marriage. I got a job that required a lot of traveling, and that caused conflict. I liked being on the road because I didn't want to be that involved with Jody, and I liked the freedom.

One time Jody called me at a hotel and told me I had to come home right away. When I got home, she told me she wanted me to find a job close to home and that she couldn't stand my traveling anymore. A couple of weeks later the bombshell dropped: She told me she'd had an affair. It hit me like a ton of bricks. She said she only slept with the man once and the relationship was over, but the incident changed everything.

After her affair I started treating her differently. What I said went. I'm sure some or most of my behavior was punishment. Even though I tried to put it behind me, I couldn't. I started making all the decisions in the relationship, from what movie we saw to what groceries we bought.

I wanted to get back at her, so I started lying to make her suspicious. Sometimes I wouldn't come home at night to piss her off. I would interrogate her when she got home from being out. She had to account for her entire evening, including who she was with and where she went. Sometimes I would check the mileage on the car to see if she was telling the truth.

The first time I was arrested for a domestic assault we were driving home and she wanted to get something to eat, but I refused to stop. We argued all the way home. She kept saying how I always got my way. We got home, and she said something derogatory to me. I grabbed her and pushed her into the wall. I was in a rage, and she was totally shocked at what I had done.

She called the police. I really went off—I took the wedding pictures off the wall and smashed them on the floor. I was swearing and breaking other things in the house. She went to another room hoping that I would calm down. I grabbed a couple of knives from the kitchen and threw them at the wall, partly out of just being pissed and partly to scare her.

When the cops came, I started to fight with them. I had one of the cops pinned on the floor; another cop maced me. By that time there were several officers at my house. My daughter saw the entire incident, and I know it had a big effect on her, especially when the police arrested me. For some time after that, whenever she saw a police car she would say things like, "Remember when the police came to our house and took you away? I don't like police." I didn't talk to her about the incident and would change the subject whenever she brought it up.

I spent the night in jail, and my lawyer picked me up in the morning. When I got home, I could tell that Jody was nervous. I apologized for what I had done, and we talked for a while. I told her I would go to counseling, but I never did. I didn't want to go to a domestic abuse program because of the stigma of saying you've beaten your wife. With my circle of friends, it would be better to have been arrested for bank robbery than for domestic assault.

Both my lawyer and I asked Jody to write a letter to the court stating that the incident was exaggerated, and she did. By the time the case went before the judge, our relationship was going pretty good. I was on my best behavior during that time because I didn't want to go to jail. I think the fact that Jody wrote the letter and both of us stated that we wanted to make the relationship work influenced the judge. The assault charges were dropped.

I never thought the violence was that bad. My friends, family, and lawyer all supported me. I would bring up the affair she had had, and they would side with me. I guess they felt I was justified in what I was doing, and they really believed that some men would have done a lot worse. My lawyer would say there's nothing wrong with throwing things around in your own house.

With everyone defending me, I felt like the victim of this bitch and of the police, who were overstepping their authority.

I was never intoxicated when I abused Jody. In fact, I rarely drank very much. Jody and I went to a marriage counselor a couple of years later. The issue of my violence rarely came up. When the counselor asked specific questions about the violence, both Jody and I would minimize the abuse.

If I became upset at something she'd said, I would step on her foot and put all my weight on her. She would always cry when I did this because it hurt, but I felt justified because I thought she was hurting me by yapping and embarrassing me in public. Sometimes I would pinch her really hard—usually under the table if we were out with people—to get her to shut up. I would tell her I was going to kick her ass, and sometimes I would threaten to kill her.

I think the emotional abuse was the worst part of it. Jody was very sensitive about her weight even though she really wasn't that big. I'd call her "fat ass." Sometimes I'd get in her face and say, "You fuckin' bitch, I'm so sick of you!" I'd tell her I hated her, and she would go into the bedroom and cry. I would say anything I could think of to hurt her.

I hated the way things were going in my life. I knew what I was doing was wrong, but at the time I couldn't see alternatives. I got into this pattern of being really abusive to her. I mean, it got to a point where I felt almost funny when I was nice to her.

I don't know why we stayed together so long. I guess we both hoped things would change. The last incident occurred about a year ago. Jody had decided to leave. She wanted me out of the house while she was moving out. I came home after work and wanted to talk with her about whether we were actually going to split up. She didn't want to talk and asked me to leave. She was sitting on the floor folding laundry with her back to me. I came up behind her and grabbed her by the hair. I pulled her up off the ground and started shaking her, demanding that she tell me whether we were ending our relationship.

She was scared because I caught her by surprise. I screamed in her face, "I ought to kill you, you goddamned fuckin' bitch."

I pushed her down on the floor and left. She called the police, and I was charged with assault. The charge was subsequently dismissed. My lawyer got me off again.

Even though our relationship ended, I continued to be abusive to her. Jody started seeing another guy after we split, and I would question the kids about what she was doing. It made me feel bad that she was already seeing someone else, so I still wanted to hurt her.

My trust in women is pretty low. But I know I need to get on with my life, and I'd like to get involved in a new relationship. I may need to continue in counseling for a while, and I'm certainly not going to rush into a relationship until I'm ready. I guess I've really seen the light since being in the program. I don't want anyone else to experience the pain that Jody experienced from me, and I don't want the pain myself. Relationships don't have to be like this.

I'm not sure I want to tell a new partner about my past violence. I don't believe I'll ever be violent with a woman again. If things aren't working I'm confident I'll leave or get help before things ever get to that point. There might come a time when I can talk freely about it, but it's too fresh right now.

I feel better today, and I'm starting to get my life together. Despite Jody's affair I really believe I caused the marriage to break up. I'll always be mad about that. I'm trying not to get into a pity thing about where I'm at—you know, the poor-me syndrome. Living alone has not been easy. I'm often lonely, but I'm dealing with it. I know this is going to sound weird, but I wish I would have been sent to a domestic violence program after my first arrest five years ago. I'm convinced we'd still be together today, because my whole attitude would have changed.

Mark didn't witness domestic abuse in the home, as so many men who told their stories did. He told me that he slapped his girlfriend because he wanted to fit in with his friends, and they were doing it. So when he saw his girlfriend talking to another boy in high school, he slapped her, and she started crying. He said that on the one hand he felt bad, but on the other hand he felt good—punishing his girlfriend gave him a sense of power.

The Superman Myth

These are confusing times for men. Society's expectations of men—and men's expectations of themselves—are varied and in many ways unrealistic and unhealthy. Regardless of certain positive changes that have occurred in society, men still get conflicting messages about what it means to be a man.

Movie star John Wayne was the quintessential tough-guy male. He was big, he swaggered, he fought, and he never let his emotions get in the way. He was a cowboy, a soldier, a real man. The characters he played expected women to be submissive. In two of his movies he actually spanks a woman.

John Wayne types can be found in many of the roles played by Clint Eastwood, Sylvester Stallone, Charles Bronson, Arnold Schwarzenegger, Samuel L. Jackson, Bruce Willis, Russell Crowe, Denzel Washington, and Robert Downey Jr., to name a few. Their characters are tough and fearless and usually get their way. Their strong exteriors are portrayed as attractive to the female lead, whom they usually save from dangerous situations. These supermen are so courageous that they fight or kill scores of bad guys single-handedly.

Today, mainstream pornography is filled with scenes of men humiliating and using violence against women. And in "professional wrestling," the largely male audiences chant and cheer as male wrestlers put female wrestlers over their knees for a demeaning spanking, much to the delight of the fans.

While the media regularly plays up male superheroes, other social institutions perpetuate the superman myth as well. Up until recently the Marines advertised, "We're looking for a few good men," aiming to recruit young men who were trained to be disciplined and unfeeling, ready to act as killing machines if ordered into combat. In our cities boys and young men join gangs, wear colors, and are ready to kill each other at younger and younger ages. Gang members are expected to be fearless. Fighting the enemy and being willing to kill proves their loyalty and manhood. Corporations look for audacious, bold leaders to watch the bottom line and defeat the competition. Sports teams demand gutsy participants who will, if necessary, play while injured. Men must win at any cost.

If being a man means strength and toughness, then what are you if you fail to meet those expectations? You're a failure, a sissy, or a coward. I was recently at a playground and listened to some young boys as they played and roughhoused. One of them was being picked on. The others called him a "faggot" and a "woman." Analyzing the put-down was easy. If you aren't a man then you're gay or—even worse—a woman.

Boys are taught to rid themselves of anything that society regards as feminine. I remember being with a group of my junior high friends at a local hangout. I crossed my legs, but not in the traditional male way of legs apart, one ankle on the other knee. One of the boys ridiculed me, saying I was sitting like a woman. I was humiliated. After that I became very conscious of how I sat, so that I wouldn't be considered feminine by my male peers.

Men are socialized to view so-called "feminine" characteristics—sensitivity and the expression of feelings—with hostility. These qualities are perceived as the opposite of what is required to be a real man, or a superman. At an early age boys begin to reject their gentler feelings or any characteristics that may make them seem vulnerable. Failure to live up to the male persona may bring the scorn and ridicule of their peers, so boys quickly learn to adapt. By the time they are adults, men have learned to deny sensitive feelings or have lost touch with them altogether. This "real" man now enters into a relationship with a woman, often bringing with him suppressed feelings and unrealistic expectations of how men are supposed to behave. What a recipe for problems and conflict!

Our socialization as boys and the impact it has on us as men is evident in an exchange between group leader Maryann and one of the men in our groups. Maryann cofacilitated groups with me when I was working at the Domestic Abuse Intervention Project. She is a formerly battered woman who always brought important insights to our groups. Her interactions with men in our groups appear throughout this book.

> **Maryann:** Rick, you mentioned an argument you had with your son and how your wife, Sheila, was angry with you because of the way you handled it. How did things finally get resolved?
>
> **Rick:** I'm not sure they did. She thinks I push him too hard in sports. I coach his hockey and baseball teams, and I can't show favorites. I push the kids, sure. But I think discipline and drive are what it takes to win. I think it's important for boys to learn certain qualities at a young age.
>
> **Maryann:** Perhaps. Any reactions to what Rick is saying?
>
> **Jason:** I don't know. I remember my father screaming from the sidelines when I played football in high school. I hated it. It was like winning was so important to him. He was kind of a football star in high school, and he talked about his playing days all the time. Even though he thought he was helping me, you know, giving me encouragement, I just felt like a failure. I'll never forget the time I sprained my ankle in practice. I told him I'd told the coach I didn't think I could play in the tournament game. He just looked at me with disgust and said, "You goddamned sissy." I'll never forget that.

Ironically, on an interpersonal level some men also perceive women as powerful. They assert that women get their power through manipulation and really want to dominate men. Both in the workplace and in the home, some men try to suppress women's power, whether real or perceived, because it threatens their need for control and challenges their belief that men should be in charge.

Today many men are finding ways to discard the tough-guy armor and redefining what being male is about. This is partly a result of women's frustration with being controlled, and partly men's own recognition of the emotional, spiritual, and physical destructiveness of trying to live up to the superman image. These men are not

threatened by equality with women, because they have found benefits in it they never imagined. They are beginning to enjoy intimacy
in their relationships, discover their children, and live healthier lives.
These men are joining women in seeking a world where both sexes
are equal.

It will be easier to shed our unrealistic expectations of maleness
and the negative beliefs men have about women when society as a
whole begins to reject the superman myth. As parents we can help to
dispel our children's false perceptions of masculinity and femininity.
We can model and communicate the importance of boys and men
living more complete, emotionally varied lives, rather than being
trapped in the cold, controlled, one-dimensional tough-guy image
that, in reality, is neither real nor healthy—nor tough.

How Our Culture Encourages Violence

How do disagreements get settled in relationships? Who makes the
final decision? Who gets the last word? Many men in intimate relationships believe the decision should be theirs. They believe there
cannot be two bosses and that someone has to settle conflicts about
children, money, social events, and the host of other issues that are
part of any relationship. In order to justify taking this power, many
men rely on tradition: Being the man in the house means getting to
call the shots.

Dave related the following story during a discussion about using
money as a way to control his wife, Leslie. Without consulting her
he had cut up their credit cards and closed their checking account.

> **Dave:** I told her I was going to do it. Man, she'll be the first to
> admit she has no self-control when it comes to money. We just
> can't continue to get further into debt, so I took some action to
> change things around our spending.
> **Michael:** Don't you think that what you did is controlling? I
> mean, now she has no access to money without asking you.
> **Dave:** It might be controlling, but someone had to put a stop

to it, and I knew it wouldn't be her. When we get caught up, maybe we can change.

Michael: So she gets an allowance from you.

Dave: I worked out a budget for food, the kids' expenses, and some basic spending money. If you want to call that an allowance, fine.

Michael: And how does Leslie feel about this?

Dave: She's a little pissed, but she'll get over it.

The group had a lengthy discussion about who gets to decide issues such as handling the family finances. Some men in the group agreed with Dave, believing the man should take charge. Others saw this as patronizing and controlling. Dave himself saw nothing wrong with his actions.

It's difficult to say what lasting impact Dave's behavior will have on Leslie. She may feel powerless to challenge Dave and may lose self-esteem, because she's being treated like a child. She may become dependent and fearful. Or she may feel resentful and angry about his controlling behavior. Any of these will damage their relationship.

If Dave wants respect, love, and mutual trust in his relationship with Leslie, his behavior is unlikely to help him get it. Yet many men share Dave's belief that they should make the "important" decisions, even if they don't come right out and say so. Some feel it is their right; others feel it is their responsibility. In both cases they are responding to traditional forces in our culture.

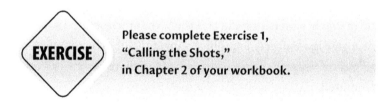

Please complete Exercise 1, "Calling the Shots," in Chapter 2 of your workbook.

The History of Gender-Based Violence

As men it is important that we look at the historical roles and expectations of men and women. With this knowledge we can better understand why and how men's violence in intimate relationships was expected and condoned in the past, which helps us understand domestic abuse today.

In past generations the roles of men and women seemed etched in stone. Social expectations were fairly clear: Men were the bread-winners, and women took care of the house and family. In most marriage ceremonies, both civil and religious, the woman vowed to "honor and obey" her husband. Her role was to serve him, and this social arrangement was for a long time reflected in the legal system.

In their book *Violence Against Wives,* Rebecca and Russell Do-bash note that the first laws relating to marriage were implemented by the Romans. These laws obliged women to conform themselves entirely to the wishes and demands of their husbands. Roman men were allowed to chastise, divorce, or even kill their wives for engaging in behaviors deemed unacceptable.[1]

Throughout medieval times Christianity sanctioned the hus-band's authority over women. The church's marriage manuals ad-vised Christians on the importance of the subordination of women and prescribed the use of flogging so that husbands could maintain appropriate moral order at home.

European culture and English common law were the original basis for the legal standing of a wife in the United States. Until the end of the nineteenth century, state laws gave husbands the legal right to beat their wives for various indiscretions. Even after the laws were repealed, domestic abuse was widely accepted as a pri-vate matter between husband and wife. Not until the late 1970s did states give law enforcement officers greater authority to intervene and make arrests when they had grounds to believe a crime had been committed.

Russell Dobash explains how these long-standing beliefs about wives affected the law even in recent times:

> In the United States up until the 1970s, there were special im-munity laws for men who killed their wives who they caught in

a sexual relationship with another man. The last state to strike down these statutes was Texas in 1974. In England there was the idea of the actions of the reasonable man. And the actions of the reasonable man were associated with a husband who might find his wife in a sexual predicament with another man. What would the reasonable man do? Obviously he would get angry and might kill his wife. Under the reasonable man argument, which lasted well into the twentieth century, murder was considered a lesser offense—it wasn't complete immunity. And that reasonable man belief has permeated the responses to killing of women for a long time and still does in many countries.[2]

Although wife beating is illegal in most countries, in practice women are continually abused by their husbands. To understand why this is tolerated it is instructive to examine the status of women around the world. In many countries and cultures the position of women seems to have changed little since the Middle Ages.

In some Islamic countries women still must cover their faces or entire bodies with the traditional veil or risk punishment for not complying with religious customs. Islam teaches that women and men should dress modestly. But for women certain interpretations of the Qur'an go much further: The face and the body must be seen only by their husbands. The traditional burqa covers a woman's body completely, with just a slit for the eyes. Some believe that such a covering is necessary to protect women from the uncontrollable sexual urges and advances of men. While this may be a culturally accepted norm in many countries, it is hard not to recognize the strong patriarchal (male-controlled) intent behind this practice. When predominately Muslim countries have liberalized their laws, or when the yoke of theocracy has been lifted, some women reject the practice of wearing face-covering veils, although many Muslim women voluntarily choose to wear a hijab (headscarf) consistent with their cultural beliefs and practices.

Oppression of women is not limited to one religion, race, or ethnicity. In some Orthodox Jewish communities a wife cannot get a divorce without the agreement of her husband. Although the practice is illegal, women in India are still burned for not bringing big-enough dowries to their new families. In Afghanistan the Taliban forbids women to work outside the home, attend school, or even leave the house unless accompanied by a male relative. In some Latin American cultures men are excused for having a mistress, while women are ostracized for similar behavior—and if a man kills a woman in a jealous rage, in some Latin American countries he can successfully use his emotional state as a defense in court. Thousands of Southeastern Asian women and girls are virtually enslaved in brothels, coerced into providing sex to local men and "sex tourists," men who are primarily seeking young women and children. In many European countries the police won't intervene in a domestic assault case unless the injuries are severe.

In 2002 I conducted a professional training on domestic abuse in Tajikistan, a small country in Central Asia. I was told by advocates that there was an epidemic of battered women committing suicide by self-immolation, because the violence was so severe and they didn't believe they had any options. The police would never arrest a man unless he'd killed his wife. There were no shelters or safe homes for abused women. A battered woman's parents would not accept her back if she were to try to escape her husband's violence, because doing so would bring dishonor to the family.

In our groups we often talk about sexism as a contributing factor to domestic violence. Sexism is similar to racism in that one group believes in its superiority over the other. With the belief in superiority comes a devaluing and stereotyping of the dominated group. Sexist beliefs and attitudes are a key factor in a man's decision to use violence and abusive acts as a means to control women in intimate relationships.

While domestic abuse has declined in the United States, the number of women killed by husbands and boyfriends has remained static over the past three decades. In the United States over sixteen hundred women are killed every year by their husbands and boy-friends, and a woman is raped every five minutes by a stranger, ac-quaintance, or husband. Women are killed by their intimate partners at twice the rate as males.[3]

In an interview I conducted with Michael Kimmel, author of *Manhood in America,* he said:

> I always think it's important to have a historical perspec-tive. It's not just our personal history or our family history. It's not a question of whether our family at some time in his-tory owned slaves or whether I have ever personally raped or beaten a woman. It's really the cultural legacy that I carry with me without even knowing it. It's sort of like an invisible knap-sack of privilege—you walk through the world and you don't even know you're wearing it. But everybody else can see it. We move through the world with this kind of cultural historical legacy.[4]

You may not see yourself as sexist or as someone who believes in male dominance, but many men feel entitled (as though they have privilege or power) in their relationships with women. This can be as subtle as the man always being the one who drives the car or as blatant as ending an argument with an intimidating scowl that lets his female partner know the discussion is over.

An individual man may not perceive himself as having power. Most men in my groups didn't see themselves this way. Many men I work with have low-paying jobs, dead-end jobs, or no jobs at all, and would question the notion of male dominance. Despite a man's position on the economic ladder, the influence of our sexist society still allows him to feel entitlement with women.

On some level all men benefit from male violence, whether we want to or not. Even though I try not to be sexist, my experiences are shaped by a sexist culture. When the sun goes down, my mother, sister, and female friends can't walk downtown or even walk in their own neighborhoods without some legitimate concern that they could be assaulted by men. I do not experience that fear and consequently have more mobility in our streets than women do.

One night a female friend called and asked me if I would walk her to the store. She was afraid because a number of sexual attacks had occurred in her neighborhood. I remember feeling strong and confident and even a little chivalrous in my traditional protective role. She had chosen me to protect her from all those other men. What was I, as a man, gaining from this situation? A feeling of personal power in relation to her and her dependence—however momentarily—on me. The situation boosted my sense of self-esteem.

Violence against women will only begin to diminish when men renounce the thinking and practice of sexism. We can do this on an individual basis at home, at work, and in our community. When we begin to speak up, other men will listen, and the seeds of change will be planted. Men should take the initiative and work with other men to confront sexism and violence—not to get approval from women but because it is the right thing to do for women, men, and children.

When it comes to the human condition, despite a history filled with slavery, war, genocide, and persecution, some groups of people still maintain their superiority over others. As I write this chapter a new law in Uganda has been passed that calls for life imprisonment for "homosexual behavior." By breaking through the walls of ignorance and prejudice we can start to change the beliefs that one gender, race, religion, ethnicity, or sexual orientation is superior to another.

The Struggle for Equality

Working toward an equal relationship—and dealing with the changes it brings—raises profound issues for men and women. We are sometimes unsure how to relate to each other in a world of evolving norms and expectations. For many people, personal experiences with marriage and relationships have been confusing. Only a generation ago few questioned the traditional arrangement of male and female roles, but now men and women often send and receive conflicting messages about who they should be and how they should interact with each other.

Women are demanding equality in the workplace, the family, and our societal institutions. Men can support this effort, yet many don't. Some resist the prospects of equality because they think there are certain "natural" reasons for men to be in a dominant role. Even those who profess to support equality between the sexes sometimes experience confusion, fear, and distrust in their relationships with women. Why are we afraid of equality with women? Why are we so resistant?

The following discussion occurred in one of our groups:

Michael: Terry, you say you believe in equality between a man and a woman but that the man gets to make the decision when the two together can't.

Terry: Yes. The Bible's clear about this. It basically says the man should treat the wife with respect, but the wife should submit to the judgment of the husband.

Michael: You may think the Bible is clear about this, but there are other interpretations of the scriptures that would say otherwise. Anyway, please go on.

Terry: Fine. But it's not just the Bible. Men think on a rational basis, and women react on a more emotional basis, and that's just a plain fact. So it makes sense that in certain situations the man should make the final decision.

About half the men in the group agreed with Terry.

Michael: Well, I don't know about your relationship, Terry. From my experience, unless someone wants to be in a submissive position, there will always be conflict. You will be imposing your will on your partner based on your belief that you have the right to have power over her because of her gender.

Terry: I'm not imposing my will, because she also believes it's her role in the family.

Variations on Terry's beliefs are numerous. In order for you to justify having power over someone else, you must on some level believe there's a reason you're in a superior position.

The reality is that people or groups of people who are dominated usually resist their oppressors. No one likes being hurt or treated unfairly. No one likes being silenced. However, this is what a man who batters does. He robs his partner of autonomy and equality in the relationship, and he imposes his will through violence and other abusive behaviors.

This does not mean that all women are oppressed. Most women experience discrimination and sexism, but not all are necessarily individually oppressed. In *Ain't I a Woman,* author and social activist bell hooks contends that it has been inappropriate for white women in the women's movement to compare their experiences with those of people of color. She asserts that in the hierarchy of American society, white men are at the top and white women are second.[5]

Additionally not all women are oppressed in their relationships with men. In many relationships there is an equal distribution of power, and in some, women may exert more control in the household than their partners do. And clearly, women of economic means have many more options open to them than some low-income men have. While all women live within the framework of a sexist society, their experiences and reality are not all the same.

Regardless of class, race, religion, and sexual orientation, however, when violence is introduced by an individual or group of people, it changes everything. Violence is the weapon of those seeking and attempting to maintain power, and it works. When a man who batters uses violence, he may initially get what he wants: He ends an argument and prevails in a power struggle with his wife or girlfriend. But at what cost? He may get to call the shots, but his partner is most likely alienated and resentful, and for both partners the relationship is unsatisfying.

What Men Expect from Relationships

When men and women begin a relationship, they bring certain expectations with them. Although these expectations are changing, many men and certainly some women maintain what we might define as a "traditional" relationship.

In such relationships the woman takes on the role and responsibilities of a "traditional wife." She is responsible for the majority of household and child-care responsibilities and agrees to some form of subordinate relationship with her husband.

Some women say they still find satisfaction with this arrangement. However, society increasingly undervalues the traditional "stay-at-home" mother, perceiving a woman's work in the home, including child rearing, as less important and far less prestigious than her husband's work outside the home. Yet in some households, men are becoming stay-at-home dads, and this role is typically not considered subservient. It is no wonder that women resist traditional roles that once were the norm and are now demanding something different. The following discussion about the roles of men and women took place in one of our groups:

> **Maryann:** We've been discussing what it means to be in a traditional relationship these past couple of weeks. My mom and dad had a traditional relationship, and some of you may have had similar childhood experiences. Do you see any problems with this kind of relationship?
>
> **Carl:** I don't think today that it's possible. It's pretty rare that your wife can stay at home and do the traditional wifely things, just because of economics.
>
> **Bill:** Even though the traditional family like I grew up with isn't very commonplace, if I had the opportunity, that's what I would want.
>
> **Maryann:** What do you mean by that?
>
> **Bill:** If I had the money, I would want my wife to stay home, rather than work. Sometimes I feel like I've failed as a husband and a father because I can't make that happen.

Maryann: You would want your wife not to work and stay home with the children?

Bill: You bet. I don't think it's a good situation for kids to be in day care. I know this sounds old-fashioned, but I think a woman should be in the home, at least until the kids have grown.

While some men in the group did not share Bill's beliefs, others expressed confusion about what women, other men, and society expect of them. For many men the inability to make enough money on their own creates a sense of failure. This was particularly true for men who had traditional expectations of the roles of men and women. These beliefs may be shifting, but our internal concept of masculinity continues to influence our self-worth—are we man enough?

According to a 2013 study in the *Journal of Personality and Social Psychology*, researchers who conducted a series of surveys in the United States and the Netherlands concluded that men's self-esteem was lower when their female partners succeeded than when they failed. But whether men failed or succeeded, their female partners did not have the same loss of self-esteem. The authors suggest that men may feel a threat to the relationship if they feel they have been outperformed. One of the authors wrote, "Having a partner who experiences success might hurt men's implicit self-esteem because ambition and success are qualities that are generally important to women when selecting a mate. So thinking of themselves as unsuccessful might trigger men's fear that their partner will ultimately leave them."[6]

I have heard men say they would not mind staying home during the day, sheltered from the demands of the workplace with no worries about making money. After further discussion, however, most men admit they would feel isolated and in many ways powerless if they had to rely solely on their partners for money; they would not feel equal or comfortable in the role of a traditional wife.

For a long-term relationship to function in a healthy way—in fact for it to function at all—inequality must be chipped away at and finally eradicated. This doesn't mean a man and a woman can't construct their own roles in their relationship. I know couples who take turns working so that one person can spend more time with their children, go back to school, or become involved in community or social-change activities. They make financial agreements and don't place a higher value on the person who is providing most of the income. For many couples economic realities make this difficult, but some do manage and don't have a conflict with the arrangement; in fact, it releases them to do other things they believe are valuable.

While many people don't embrace the traditional relationship roles of the past, there are couples who agree to all or part of this arrangement. The traditional relationship in various iterations fits with the couple's values and doesn't seem oppressive. Some make this choice on the basis of strong religious convictions. Fortified by religious and cultural beliefs, a relationship can become problematic when the woman is coerced into submitting to her husband's belief in male authority. In this kind of relationship, domestic abuse is frequently viewed as a marital problem caused by the woman's failure to accept her subordinate role. This was the case for M'Liss:

> I believed Chuck had the authority in the household based on our religious orientation. It was in the scriptures, or at least the way they were interpreted. We went to church three days a week for eleven years. When members of the congregation would see me battered they would say, "What did you do to make him so mad that he would beat you like that?" We finally quit the church after Chuck was ordered into counseling for battering me.

Understanding the roots of your violence as oppressive or sexist may reveal striking contradictions in your thinking. A relationship doesn't have to mean that one person is in charge. Men don't have to be threatened by equality—a partnership can be yours. It is your choice.

You will read about egalitarian relationships, in which men and women develop true partnerships anchored in trust and mutual respect. In this kind of relationship you make decisions together, affirm each other emotionally, share in parental responsibilities, support each other's goals, and resolve problems through negotiation and compromise. Before you can embrace this kind of relationship, you need to fully understand domestic abuse and the steps you need to take to make changes. You can get there if you read on.

A Note about
Religion and Domestic Abuse

Religion provides a personal and spiritual foundation for many people. It can serve as a means to understanding the nature and purpose of the universe; guide personal, ethical, and moral choices; provide meaningful rituals; and offer a basis for faith in an afterlife. Your religion may be a central part of your life, and certain ideas in this book may conflict with your religious doctrines.

For all of the good that religion has done in the world, it has also been a source of persecution and extremism. Some religious doctrines are full of repressive and punitive rules that have led to the oppression of others. Literal interpretation of commandments, laws, and rules has sometimes resulted in women being placed in subordinate roles. There have been men in my groups who have justified their abusive behavior by citing religious decrees dictating that righteous women obey their husbands.

It is not my intent to criticize any religious practice. Calling upon spiritual resources in the journey to nonviolence can provide inspiration, solace, and support. If you are a religious man, I hope you are able to rely on your faith for help in making changes. I also hope you will explore and reject religious assumptions of male superiority and any justification for intimate partner violence. Seek out people in your faith to help you explore the contradictions in religious teachings. Beliefs about the roles of men and women in most religions can be interpreted in various ways. I urge you to choose love, mutual respect, and gender equality.

If this chapter conflicts with your convictions because of your interpretation of religious teachings, I encourage you to examine the resources produced by the Faith Trust Institute. The Faith Trust Institute is a national multifaith, multicultural organization that works with many religions and diverse communities. For more information about the religious response to domestic abuse, I recommend you visit their website at www.faithtrustinstitute.org.

Please complete Exercise 2,
"Who Makes the Rules?"
in Chapter 2 of your workbook.

3

How We Learn to Be Violent

Although the world is full of suffering,
it is full also of the overcoming of it.

▸▸ HELEN KELLER ◂◂

Cassie's Story

Cassie and Sylvie lived with abusive men. Their accounts of what they experienced offer a perspective that men don't often hear. Throughout this book you will hear their stories.

> Antonio and I lived together for eleven years. We were both in the armed services when we met. When we got out of the service, we moved to the Virgin Islands. The physical abuse started almost immediately. I was taught that you stay in a relationship no matter what, so I was determined to make things work.
>
> I left him for a while because of the continued abuse and went to live with my family in Michigan. He followed me to Michigan, and we started to work on our issues. I moved in with him again. He wasn't violent during that year, but when we'd argue he would throw stuff close to me. He'd throw an ashtray a few inches from my head, and then he'd say, "I didn't hit you." At the time I thought, well, that's true, he didn't hit me.
>
> We moved back to the Virgin Islands, and the violence

started again. After hitting me, he would say if I just hadn't done this or said that, he wouldn't have hit me. So I stopped doing or saying things that apparently were setting him off. He told me not to yell, so I stopped yelling. He told me he wouldn't hit me if I got a job, so I got a job. He told me he wouldn't hit me if I didn't drink, so I quit drinking. But the violence didn't stop. He always had a reason. I kept trying to change my life so I wouldn't get hit.

I think the worst time was when he punched me so hard in the face that it split my head open. On another occasion he kicked me in the stomach and broke three of my ribs.

I got a restraining order against him, and he left the island. I have limited contact with him today except for visitation with the children. I think he could have changed if he had gotten some education or been confronted with his behavior early on. We didn't really know what to do or where to go. We went to counseling once, but the counselor didn't want to address the abuse that was going on.

I know that he knew what he was doing wasn't right. Once he introduced me to a female friend of his who was being battered. He was outraged and concerned and wanted to find ways of helping her. Ironically he couldn't make the connection between what he was doing to me and what was happening to this woman. That's why I think if there had been some direct intervention by a counselor or someone he might have been forced to look at his own behavior.

Healing for me is a long process. I thought when I left him everything would be okay, but it wasn't. It wasn't until I started going to women's groups and sorting through everything that had happened that I started to heal. I never thought I was a battered woman. But I'm gaining self-confidence. I don't know if I'll ever marry again. It's strange that after all that happened, I still have feelings for my ex-husband. I mean, we spent eleven years together and had children together. Yet I don't think I could ever go back. My trust level with men is pretty low, and I'm not sure I would want to take the chance of another relationship.

Sylvie's Story

I lived with Tyler for three and a half years. When we first started dating, I liked the fact that he had claimed me. It made me feel good that he found me attractive and wanted me. At that time he was very supportive and bought me a lot of presents.

Tyler was an up-and-coming public official, and looks were important to him. He wanted me to dress a certain way so we looked good together. I went along with that, but he became more and more controlling. I had mixed feelings about his controlling nature, but I grew up believing that men were supposed to have the power in the household, that the man was master in his home. I believed a woman's role was to maintain a neat home, be well organized, and make good meals. I thought these domestic things were a reflection on me as a person, as a woman.

He insisted that I make the bed right after we got up in the morning. After dinner, especially if we had company over, I had to clean the dishes immediately after we ate. He would give me a certain amount of money each week, and if it wasn't enough he made me show him the receipts. At the time none of this seemed unreasonable. Of course, today I recognize how controlling he was. I know his expectation that a woman should be subservient was wrong.

The first time he hit me was after we got home from a political event. Some of the men were talking and putting women down. They were saying things like the only way women get ahead is by sleeping their way to the top. I got into an argument with them, and my partner pulled me away and said, "Who the fuck do you think you are? Don't you ever talk that way in front of my friends again!" He was upset with me because he believed what these guys were saying, and he didn't want me speaking my mind and embarrassing him. All the way home he berated me, telling me I was stupid and worthless. When we got home, he slammed me up against the wall and punched me several times. And though he apologized later, he told me he wouldn't tolerate his woman asserting herself.

The violence continued, and I finally told him if it didn't stop I was leaving. He said the only way I would leave would be in a body bag. I stayed because I was afraid of him, but I finally made the move. We were arguing about my leaving, and he hit me in the face with a pop bottle and knocked out most of my teeth. He waited five or six hours before he took me to the hospital. There I was, dazed, with my teeth hanging out and my face completely swollen, listening to him apologize. I left after that happened.

I'm not sure this man is capable of change. I'm sure he's battering another woman today. His whole existence revolved around having power over women. And in a strange way I think he got off on the violence.

I'll never forget how he treated me. Because of him, I see all men as a threat. Sadly even my sons are a threat because of their size and the way boys and men are socialized. As long as men have power over women, I'll be resentful. I'd like to be in a relationship at some time, but it's something I can't visualize because of those experiences.

Women and Violence

Both Sylvie and Cassie were devastated by the violence they experienced: hitting, slapping, punching, yelling, knocked-out teeth, split-open heads, broken ribs, angry stares, death threats, flying ashtrays, domination, and control.

Both women changed to meet their partners' demands. They adapted to survive, yet the violence continued. Finally, both women made the decision to get out.

These women were battered severely. Your violence may not have escalated to the levels described in their stories. You may even be inclined to measure your behavior against the actions of Cassie's and Sylvie's ex-partners and think that what you've done isn't as bad. It is important to remember that in both cases, the first incident was not severe. Apologies and promises followed. But in both cases the violence escalated, and both men became criminally abusive.

In an attempt to understand the reality of a woman living in an abusive relationship, researchers Rebecca and Russell Dobash interviewed 109 women who had been battered. They found that the women's experiences and responses to the violence were fairly similar.

The Dobashes found that when the first assault occurs, most women think the act is an aberration; in other words, they believe the behavior is not normal. The man usually apologizes, and the woman accepts his promise that he will never be violent with her again. When the second assault occurs, the level of violence increases, and most women leave. They go to a parent's or a friend's home or a shelter. But the Dobashes found that when a woman leaves at this stage, her motivation is to teach her partner a lesson, not to end the relationship. If the woman believes that her partner has learned a lesson, she returns.

After the third assault the violence escalates further, and the woman usually leaves again. If she returns it's not because she wants to; it's because she doesn't have the financial resources to live on her own or she fears she will lose the children or she fears for her safety, not because she thinks her partner will change. She may begin abusing alcohol or drugs to anesthetize herself in the face of an unbearable situation. She may become physically or emotionally sick.[1]

Like Cassie and Sylvie, some women try to adapt. They placate their partners to lessen the chances of being hit and try their best to live with the situation. They abandon any hope of salvaging the relationship. The love they once felt vanishes, and they prepare to leave.

I advise women to get out of an abusive relationship after the first assault. That may sound harsh, but my experience working with men who batter is that the violence simply continues unless there is intervention.

As the Dobashes concluded, women often go back initially because they want to believe the relationship can be saved. I ask women who return to their partners to talk to women's advocates at their local shelter. Battered women need to understand the dynamics of battering and to be aware that if their partners do not get help, they will probably use violence again.

Any woman who has been battered should develop a safety plan so that when she needs to get out, she can do so with relative security. Creating such a plan includes gathering emergency phone numbers, lining up people she can call for help, and finding places to stay if she senses her partner becoming abusive again. She should also insist that her partner get help, which does not mean just a couple of counseling sessions. If he is truly motivated to change, he will make a commitment to counseling or a domestic abuse program. If he's willing to get help and be accountable for his behavior, the relationship can mend. Only when a woman is fairly certain that her partner will not use violence again can the couple work on their problems together.

If you have been violent, your partner may be willing to give you another chance. Make use of the opportunity: Get help. However, she may want to end the relationship. This is a familiar consequence of domestic abuse. If that is the case, you cannot undo what has occurred, but you can begin to make changes for yourself. You will probably enter into a new relationship at some point, and you should get help now to avoid becoming abusive with a new partner.

The Violence We Learn at Home

Boys who witness domestic abuse when growing up are more likely to use violence as adults. Researchers estimate that 50 to 70 percent of men who batter either witnessed battering at home or were themselves abused by a parent.[2]

Many researchers conclude that men learn to use violence as children. They see their fathers use violence with no negative repercussions for their actions, and they get the message that this kind of behavior works and is an acceptable response to conflict.[3]

Another message the children get is that the father is boss. He has the right to discipline not only his children but also his wife. He seems all-powerful. Sometimes a child may sense there is something wrong with the behavior; at other times he or she may conclude that their father has a rational reason for becoming so angry and abusive.

Either way, the messages etched in the minds of children who observe violence are indelible. Men in our groups have said they vowed not to repeat the domestic abuse they saw as children. However, for most of them, when conflicts arose with their partners and they felt they could not win or control the situation, a green light from the past would start flashing. With a hit or a punch they could change the situation, just like their fathers did. And if there are no consequences for the violence—such as getting arrested or losing the relationship—the behavior is reinforced.

Many men have had unhappy childhood experiences. Some were abused or mistreated by parents; others watched their fathers abuse their mothers. Some did not experience physical violence but were verbally abused or received little emotional support at home.

If you were hurt or neglected as a child, it is important that you not blame your childhood trauma for your actions today. For one thing, holding on to painful childhood experiences might make you distrust intimacy; you may get easily defensive because you're in a survival mode. If this rings true for you, get help from a counselor. You can work through these feelings and painful memories. Regardless of how and where you learned about violence, you must address your current way of reacting to women in relationships. That is something you *can* change. We make a personal choice to become violent regardless of what we've been exposed to in our childhoods.

Please complete Exercise 1, "Learning about Violence," in Chapter 3 of your workbook.

The Violence
We Learn from Society

Many men who choose to use violence did not grow up in households in which their fathers hit their mothers. In a society in which negative attitudes and violence toward women are commonplace, boys and men may experiment with behaviors that conflict with the values they learned in the home.

Our attitudes about women, men, and relationships can frequently be traced to childhood experiences, to what we learned and observed in school, church, neighborhoods, and our families of origin. Together they become a blueprint for living, a foundation for how we respond to situations throughout our lives.

Boys learn a great deal of violence from the culture in which they live. They play imaginary games of war, compete in violent sports, read violent comic books, watch violent movies, play violent video games, and are exposed to violent pornography. Boys are taught at an early age that violence is an acceptable way to handle conflict. If they refrain from using violence, they may be ridiculed by other boys and feel they don't measure up.

I interviewed Jackson Katz, author of *The Macho Paradox,* about his thoughts on how culture influences boys and men. This is what he had to say about the rise and impact of hip-hop artists like Eminem:

> In terms of numbers, the primary consumers of hip-hop music are white suburban males. We might ask, why do so many young white men and men of color feel attracted to and identify with the hypermasculine posturing and homophobic and misogynistic [women-hating] lyrics? When Eminem emerged on the music scene, he wasn't the first rapper to be misogynistic, but as a white man who is very talented, he certainly got a huge platform for his art. He's been celebrated widely, winning multiple Grammy awards and an Oscar for best song in a motion picture.

If you look at the lyrics of his music, he's taken homicidal misogynistic [messages] to new highs (or new lows). So a culture that embraces Eminem as a cultural icon can't say it's serious about reducing men's violence against women. You can't on the one hand embrace an artist who's made a career of verbally attacking and assaulting women and gay people and then say that we want to do something about rape and domestic violence.

What would happen if Eminem were to change the objects of his aggression from women and gays to, say, African Americans or Jewish people—do you think he would be winning Grammy awards? Do you think he would be winning Oscars?[4]

Hip-hop music is not to blame. It's just the reality of the times. I was recently listening to some of my favorite 1960s music and was struck by the lyrics of so many "classic" songs that were all about conquering and possessing women. While not as overtly violent and misogynistic as music today, the messages were nonetheless clear.

As changing men we must counter the notion that men's violence against women is an individual problem committed by a few troubled individuals. We have an obligation to challenge a society that produces violent music, violent pornography, gratuitously violent movies, and violent and sexist video games that objectify and devalue women. Whether or not this exposure *causes* violence may be legitimately debated. But when boys and young men are constantly exposed to such messages, they are desensitized to violence against women and confuse fantasy with reality.

In Chapter 2 you read Mark's story. He explained that when he was growing up his father treated his mother with respect. He rarely heard an argument and saw no violence between them. In school, though, his male friends had a strong influence on him, and he began putting girls down to become accepted within a certain group. Like his friends, he wanted to be in charge when dating. And like his friends, he learned that slapping a girl was something a boy was entitled to do if his girlfriend flirted with another boy, ignored him, or talked back. Using violence against women was not something Mark learned at home. He developed these attitudes among his peers, and his behavior was reinforced by his male friends.

The following discussion in one of my groups focused on what influenced our beliefs about violence and women:

> **Lewis:** You know, it's strange. Seeing my father kick the hell out of my mother all those years, and the way he treated us kids, I promised myself that when I became an adult I would never be that way to my wife or kids. And here I am in this damn group.
>
> **Phil:** I guess it's something we just learn.
>
> **Michael:** Are you saying that if you see and experience this stuff as children, then you automatically become abusive?
>
> **Phil:** No, but this is what I apparently learned from my childhood. I used to think my dad hitting my mom was somewhat justified, because I could tell what would set him off and I couldn't understand why she couldn't.
>
> **Randy:** My father was never violent with my mother. In fact, all I saw was the two of them being very affectionate.
>
> **Michael:** So, Randy, you didn't observe violence in the home, yet you battered your wife. Phil just said he thought he learned violence from watching his dad. Why do you think you started to be violent with women? Where do you think you got your messages about women and relationships?
>
> **Randy:** I suppose just living. Some of my friends in high school would talk about slapping their girlfriends if they got out of line, and everyone would laugh. My friends meant a lot to me, and they had a lot of influence over decisions I made. When I played on the football team I started developing this tough-guy image because I thought it would impress people. Getting into fights and slapping up your girlfriend was all just part of it.

Why We Use Violence

Violence produces immediate results. It's effective. Except in cases of real self-defense, I've never met a man who battered who would dispute the fact that his motive was to stop his partner from saying or doing something he disapproved of, or to punish her for doing something he didn't like.

Participating in a domestic abuse group can help some men understand how growing up male in this culture has influenced their beliefs about women and relationships. Others, especially those who grew up in violent households, may need to see a counselor or therapist to unravel some of the past and finally say good-bye to it. Regardless of how you got where you are, you alone are responsible for what you do next. It is helpful—sometimes even necessary—to understand your past, but it is completely up to you to take charge of your future.

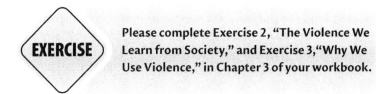

EXERCISE   Please complete Exercise 2, "The Violence We Learn from Society," and Exercise 3, "Why We Use Violence," in Chapter 3 of your workbook.

Sexual Violence and Male Entitlement

Strangers and family members have assaulted and raped girls and women for centuries. In times of war, invading soldiers rape civilian women as part of their conquest. Few countries and cultures have been immune to these crimes. As Iris Chang states in her book *The Rape of Nanking*:

> Chinese women were raped in all locations and at all hours. An estimated one-third of all rapes occurred during the day. Survivors even remember solders prying open the legs of victims to rape them in broad daylight, in the middle of the street, and in front of crowds of witnesses. No place was too sacred for rape. The Japanese attacked women in nunneries, churches, and Bible training schools. Seventeen soldiers raped one woman in succession in a seminary compound.[5]

The systematic rapes that take place in most wars tell us much about male thinking about women and violence—rape is the ultimate form of dominance and humiliation.

In some countries if a woman reports a rape, her husband and family may ostracize or stone her. She conceals the sexual assault because she would be considered unclean and unacceptable for marriage. Many girls and women do not report rape because they fear they will not be believed or will suffer the anguish of a public trial and media exposure.

Males are also the victims of sexual abuse, but in far smaller numbers than females. Boys have been sexually abused by women, and some men are considered rape victims of women. However, most male victims of sexual assault are abused by men and other boys. The recent revelations about the long history of clergy sexual abuse of boys has shocked the Catholic Church and society. In some countries boys are being trafficked in the same way that girls are: groomed by traffickers and coerced into prostitution, primarily for adult male clients. There are 1.5 million people in our federal and state prisons and county workhouses, and most are boys and men. In many of these institutions they are raped or coerced into sexual acts. For some perpetrators the acts are for sexual gratification, but often they are used as punishment and as a tool to ensure their domination. As James Gilligan states in his provocative book *Violence: Our Deadly Epidemic and Its Causes*, "The rape of males is one of the most widespread—indeed, virtually universal—features of the penal system as I have observed it, and as many others have confirmed." Gilligan claims that prison authorities simply look the other way as the practice of rape occurs, with few inmates daring to report the offenses. The short- and long-term effects on males who have been sexually violated are generally parallel to the effects on females.[6]

Whether women or men are the victims of sexual violence, the statistics are clear: Men are the primary perpetrators of rape. It's only fitting that men challenge the culture that supports this act. We need to speak out—we *can* and *must* teach our sons a different way. Men can't just assume this is a woman's problem, because it is very much our problem. We must confront the tacit acceptance that sexual coercion and rape are inevitable realities at parties, college campuses, in the military, and in the home.

Aggressive and even abusive sexual behavior is sometimes excused as an inherent, uncontrollable biological urge that is part of the genetic makeup of the male. According to this line of thinking, men supposedly have a sexual appetite that is produced by testosterone, so their desire for sex must be satisfied. This argument, however, is simply another excuse. Rape and sexual coercion are minimized, and no one questions the culture that supports this behavior.

The language many men use reflects these common, exploitative sexual attitudes. "Hitting on" women, "scoring," and "getting laid" are terms that have little to do with love, intimacy, or even acknowledging another person and have much more to do with sexual conquest. With this language men reduce women to objects they can acquire and use.

According to the Domestic Abuse Intervention Project, 50 percent of women who have been physically assaulted have also experienced sexual abuse or sexual coercion by their partners.[7] Many men believe that sexual access is their contractual right after marriage, and so if they force or coerce their wives into having sex, they consider the behavior normal. Many women do not define forced acts of intercourse in a marriage or long-term relationship as rape because of confusion about their perceived obligations to their partners.

We have all been affected by societal messages about sex. Human sexuality gets categorized into right or wrong, proper or dirty. We grow up with guilt, confusion, and anxiety about sex and have few outlets to talk frankly and ask questions about our feelings and experiences. As adults, we often don't—and can't—communicate about sex with our partners. And for better or for worse, both sexes engage in dating practices that we learn from the culture. Expectations and miscommunication from these encounters can result in unacceptable and sometimes criminal behavior.

In one of my groups I described the following scenario: A man takes a female friend out to dinner. He pays for the dinner, and then they go dancing and have several drinks. She invites him into her apartment. When he attempts to have sex with her she refuses and resists. He pursues her and forcibly has intercourse with her.

When I asked the group members whether they thought the man had raped the woman, many said no. Several men in the group believed there is an expectation that men are entitled to sex, given certain conditions. If a man buys something for his date, if she dresses a certain way, if they've been drinking, or if she is demonstrative, some men believe they have permission to pursue her. If she resists or says no, he may not believe her or may not care.

I then described another scenario in which a man pressures his wife to have sex. He tells her it is her duty and that if she doesn't have sex with him, he'll "get it" elsewhere. She submits. Again many of the men in the group did not see any problem with this kind of pressure.

Sexual abuse is not limited to coerced sex. One woman told me how her husband would consistently make derogatory comments about her body, particularly about the size of her breasts. Sometimes he would make these statements in public or in front of their children, despite the humiliation it caused her.

Another woman related how her husband would bring home hard-core pornographic videos. He would make her watch the films and act out what they had viewed. Many of the sexual acts were violent or painful, yet she felt she had to submit.

As men we can untangle the negative cultural messages that all males have been exposed to about sexuality. We can speak up when the media, friends, and coworkers trivialize sexual abuse through comments and jokes. When men joke about rape (they still do), most women become understandably angry, while men, especially in social settings, are usually silent, even if they feel uncomfortable.

It does not have to be this way. Men can refuse to participate in the sexual objectification of women. We can teach our sons not to use women and help them understand the importance of sexual respect in relationships. In your current or future relationship, your sexuality can be based on mutuality and respect for each other's needs.

The Impact of Violence on Sexual Relationships

My discussions with men who have battered and women who have been battered show that the sexual relationship usually changes after violence occurs. Intercourse after a violent episode is common. A man often believes that if he is sexual after being violent, his partner will see how sorry he is or how much he really loves her and will forgive him for the violence. He may believe that the tenderness he expresses makes amends for his abuse. For some men the violence also provides an erotic charge.

For many women, having sex after an assault can be a way of calming her partner down, and women will frequently submit out of fear of further violence. The experience, though, is often degrading and devoid of tender or intimate feelings. Other women are confused by sexual expression following a violent episode. They hope for the relationship to be made right. They want to be intimate and feel loved.

As Sylvie explains, her sexual relationship with her partner was a mixture of violence and confusion:

> To me it's the ultimate in control when a man has sex with you after he's beaten you. I think Tyler had this strange way of equating sex with negative attitudes about women—basically a woman's function was for the sexual pleasure of men. It was all very confusing for me. Here this man beats me, and then he's making love to me.
>
> Tyler raped me many times, although I'm not sure he saw it that way. Sometimes when he had friends over he would make

derogatory sexual comments about me. I felt humiliated and violated.

When we were making love and I responded in a certain way to a position we were in, he would become abusive and beat the hell out of me. He would accuse me of sleeping around and practicing these positions, because of the way I responded. This was especially traumatic—to get beaten right after making love.

Since I left him, I haven't been sexual. I was dating this one guy and the issue of sex came up, and these old memories came up and I got frightened. That part of me has really been damaged.

Cassie also experienced sexual abuse throughout her marriage, especially after a violent episode:

I learned very early that I had no choice. Sometimes he would force himself on me. I told him I wasn't going to respond sexually, but he didn't seem to care. That really reinforced this whole thing that he didn't care how he was getting sex. It didn't matter to him if I participated or not. It was the ultimate in objectification.

I either had sex or I got beaten up. I never saw it as sexual abuse at the time. Whenever we had a fight it was never completely over until we had sex. Even when I was feeling rotten I had to submit, and for him everything was supposedly okay.

The sexual abuse both Sylvie and Cassie experienced has stayed with them years after their relationships ended. They have been robbed of something precious: the ability to trust another human being in intimate, loving contact.

If you are still with someone you have abused, it is important that you listen to your partner's concerns and respect what she needs. She may feel distant or may not feel like engaging in sex because of what has gone on in the past. If she needs time, honor her request without making her feel guilty or pressuring her. These can be confusing times for her, and wounds can take a long time to heal. Guilt or pressure will only reinforce her pain and distrust.

A Note to Men

We need to address this issue squarely. We cannot assume that being in an intimate relationship provides a license to sexual access. Acknowledging sexual abuse in counseling, or even with your partner, may make you feel ashamed or guilty, but like all aspects of being accountable, it is a part of taking full responsibility for your actions. When you hear how your behavior was experienced by your intimate partner, the remorse you feel might be a necessary step on your road toward making real changes in your life.

When we examine our sexual behavior, whether it was as young men or as adults, most of us have done things that we now wish we hadn't. We may have taken advantage of women or used them simply for sex. We may have gone to a strip show, paid for sex, or viewed pornography. We may have pressured a partner to have sex. Maybe you still think that some of these activities are okay. For me, when I step back and look at my own past behaviors with the knowledge I have today, I more fully understand how much influence our culture has had on us. I now understand that because I *could* do certain things doesn't make them right.

Many men have at some point bought into false assumptions: that prostitution is a victimless crime, that stripping and pornography are choices women make of their own free will. The majority of women being trafficked (prostituted) don't choose this profession. They are being exploited, and many are being coerced. As men we can make the decision not to be consumers of the sex industry.

Cordelia Anderson, author of *The Impact of Pornography on Children, Youth and Culture,* put the issue of pornography into perspective in an interview:

> People often say that pornography has always been around. Prostitution has always been around. Just because oppressions have always been around doesn't make them okay. Just because it's the way it has been, doesn't mean it's the way it should be. And so this whole issue of the expectation that men are sup-

posed to want women as sexual objects for their use and abuse is completely supported by the pornography industry. Since porn, stripping, and prostitution have become mainstreamed, it feeds the sense in men that they are entitled as the user to "get off" at somebody else's expense. This is your right. This is your need. I think it's very damaging to our boys and men, not to mention the women who are being used and exploited.[8]

This analysis doesn't mean that we should be moving into some new Puritan age in which sex is taboo, sexual imagery is forbidden, and sexual freedom is sinful. Nor do I condone censorship. But we need to have the courage to reject any activity that misuses women and children, and we need to have a more critical discussion of what it means to have healthier sexual imagery and positive sexual experiences—experiences that aren't predicated on physical harm and exploitation.

Please complete Exercise 4, "Being Sexually Respectful," in Chapter 3 of your workbook.

It's More than Physical Violence

When elephants fight, it's the grass that suffers.

►► AFRICAN PROVERB ◄◄

The word "battering" refers to the systematic use of abusive behaviors, including physical violence, to establish and maintain control over another person. Ending your use of physical violence is the first step in your process of change. But you must also commit to ending other abusive behaviors.

Jim's Story

Jim grew up in a middle-class neighborhood in a small community in California and moved to Minnesota in his twenties. He was arrested for domestic assault and was ordered to attend our program. He was thirty-four at the time of this interview and had been married three times. Jim describes the brutal violence he used in his relationships. He also discusses how he used other abusive behaviors to intimidate and control his partners.

> I came from a very violent home. One night my dad was really drunk, and he was trying to force himself into the house. I knew either he would do something to my mother or she would do something to him. The next thing I knew they were fighting outside the doorway of our apartment. He was beating on

her, and she grabbed a knife and stabbed him in the side and pushed him down the stairs. My father survived, but the relationship didn't.

There were many times when I hid under a table to avoid the violence around me. I was always afraid, because I was constantly witnessing my father and mother hurting each other. It's strange—as a kid it all seemed kind of normal to me. I thought all families were like mine. When I started assaulting women, I never made a correlation between my actions and my upbringing, but I think now that it must have had an impact.

My stepfather also battered my mother. He punched her in the mouth, pulled her down, and kicked her when she was on the floor. I would try to stop him, but I would get thrown aside. Sometimes when I would intervene it would slow the fight down, so every time they got into a fight I'd try to stop it. I remember many times I would be upstairs and I would be listening to their fights for hours. I would take the pillow and cover my head and cry for the longest time. I really was afraid they would kill each other.

My stepfather would discipline us kids with a belt that had studs on it. I remember actually feeling the welts on my rear end. Many times my parents would go to a bar and leave us in the car while they went in to drink. In the winter we would be freezing. My brother would go into the bar and tell our parents we were cold, and then they would finally come out. If we ever said anything in the car, my stepfather would hit us.

My mother was also abusive to us. When I was a teenager, I had come home late, and as I rode my motorcycle into the driveway, my mother hit me on the back with a broom handle. I fell off the bike, and she began hitting me on the head and on the back with this broom handle. At the time I didn't see this as abusive, because all the violence in our home seemed normal.

All through my childhood I was very rough. I would beat up on my younger brother, and my older brother would beat up on me. One time in the seventh grade I got into a fight with a kid at school. I remember being scared of him because he was kind of a bully, but I couldn't back down. When we fought, I smashed his face into the brick wall of the school. I remember feeling very powerful, especially with all the kids around me saying how great I was. And to have beaten up this kid who I perceived to be so tough felt good.

I was violent with girls from the time I started dating. My first steady girlfriend was Terri. Once we were at a party and everyone was drinking. I wanted her to drink and have fun, but she didn't want to. We got into an argument in the car, and I grabbed her by the throat and pushed her up against the door and told her she was going to do what I wanted her to do. When I let go of her, she slapped me. I slapped her back especially hard and went into a total rage. I punched the window and broke it and left her crying in the car.

The messages I got growing up were that women should be submissive to men. The man had total say. I believed that if women crossed the line, you had to put them in their place. I grew up believing that women were to be used, and so that's what I did.

I was nineteen when I met Cathy. She was seventeen. I had just entered the armed services. I didn't hit her until after we got married. After I had that marriage license, things changed. I felt like I owned her. Later on, when we were divorced, she told me that when we were living together I treated her like a queen, but as soon as we got married, I changed. Before marriage I guess I felt that I could lose her, but once I had that piece of paper, she was mine.

Of all the women I physically abused, Cathy got the worst of it. I can remember having parties and getting extremely intoxicated. I would get into an argument with her, throw her around, and punch her in the face. She cooked, cleaned, and took care of the children. When I wanted sex, we had it and there was to be no flak about it. In some ways I'm surprised she stayed as long as she did.

One time when she was three months pregnant with my daughter she went to a high-school football game. She wasn't home when I thought she would be. I was in a total red rage and went looking for her. I came home and she was there.

She was scared when she saw how mad I was, and she tried to leave. She screamed, "I'm not going to get beat up by you again!" I grabbed her and threw her fifteen feet; she landed on the couch. I went over to the couch and put my left hand on her throat and began backhanding her with my other hand numerous times. She lay on the couch crying and bleeding. Even though I felt bad for what I'd done to her, I thought she'd brought it on herself. I was convinced she was out looking for another guy. The way I saw it, she shouldn't have been gone so long and she should have been home with me, case closed. I really believed she asked for it.

Some years later I was up for a promotion at my job. Cathy had prepared a big meal that night with candles and everything because she knew we would find out about the promotion that day. She was all positive and in a really good mood. Well, I didn't get the promotion and was in a terrible mood when I got home. I took it out on her. I was mad because she had this meal all fixed up. I started yelling and screaming, and then I threw the dinner off the table.

When I beat her, I'd feel very powerful. When I would see the terror in her eyes, I knew I had won. Sometimes, though, I would feel guilty. I would tell her how ashamed I was for what I was doing, that I would get help for my drinking. I would apologize. I would usually want to have sex after my violence, and she would agree. I thought it was because she loved me, but I think now she agreed to sex to pacify me.

Our neighbors out in California used to call me the green-eyed monster because I was always exploding in a jealous rage. Cathy is a very pretty woman, and I felt she got a kick out of men eyeing the way she walked. I thought she showed off her beauty and her body. I felt since she hurt me by making me jealous, I would hurt her by being violent. We were having a party one night, and I became jealous of a male friend of ours who was talking with Cathy. I'd been drinking a lot and was doing a lot of PCP. I started to slap her up. I made a big scene and told everyone to leave. That night I destroyed the apartment. She left me after that incident.

Eight years after Cathy left me, I was still hanging on to the relationship. I would call her, write her, and go to the town where she was living and try to see her. I would beg her to take me back. One time I got very high on PCP, put a gun to my head, and told her I would kill myself unless she took me back. I would tell Cathy that our daughter needed a father in her life. I tried everything, but she was through with me.

I married Gretchen two years later, after a very short courtship. We moved to Duluth and stayed married for seven years. My violence toward her was mostly grabbing her by the arms and pushing her down. I think I only hit her once. I really didn't have to be very violent with her, because she was submissive, and I could make her afraid by just yelling at her. I would give her a certain look, and she would know I was upset. In that marriage I was the ultimate ruler. I don't believe I was ever in love with her, but I stayed with her because it was convenient.

One time I came home really drunk and demanded she make me a steak. I went into the kitchen and there were all these dirty dishes in the sink, and I flew into a rage. I started throwing the dishes at her and then I hit her in the face with the back of my hand. I started breaking everything in the house. It was Christmastime and I smashed all the presents. The kids were watching this. I threw the Christmas tree through the window. Our neighbor called the sheriff, and they took me to the detox center.

Toward the end of this relationship, Gretchen and I got into an argument about who was getting custody of our child. I punched her several times in the face. She tried to leave, but I was determined not to let her take our daughter. Gretchen called the police. I attacked the police officers and was charged with assault. The court ordered me into outpatient treatment for my alcoholism and the Domestic Abuse Intervention Project for my violence.

While in treatment I continued to drink. When I went into the Domestic Abuse Intervention Project, I was in total denial. I didn't feel I needed any help and was very angry that the court had ordered me into counseling. But after several weeks, something touched me in the group, and I realized I had a problem. The program was helpful for me because I heard the other men's stories and realized I wasn't alone. I started to see that the abuse was really wrong and that it was my responsibility to change. After completing the program and probation, I stayed on as a volunteer.

In my current relationship with Toni, things are dramatically different. When there are problems we sit down and talk, and I explain how I feel. When we have conflicts today I'm able to express my feelings, and, perhaps more important, I listen to her rather than just flying off the handle. I still take time-outs. When I have visitation with my children from my past marriages, they don't see the anger and the abuse that they used to. I know they see the difference.

When I think back, I know I was dependent on women, emotionally, financially, and sexually. I felt I needed a female partner in my life to make me whole. I had very low self-esteem and a lack of love for myself. I'm not jealous with Toni like I was in past relationships. I'm more secure with myself.

I'm proud of where I'm at today, because I made the changes to stop drinking and stop the violence. I hope that in my family the abuse stops here. My parents never recognized the abuse. I got the help I needed because I got arrested and because I went through the program. I'm dedicating myself to being a positive role model for my children and for other men.

I call myself a recovering abuser. I do something similar to the twelve-step program for alcoholics. I try to do positive things in my life, analyzing myself when I need to and associating with positive people. You have to get to know yourself and love yourself, and then you can love others.

Using Intimidation to Control

Many men use physical violence infrequently but abuse women by resorting to other coercive behaviors, including intimidation. They learn how to threaten people without physically touching them. Some men use body language. They glare, tower over their partners, or block their physical space. Some slam down their fists, punch walls or doors, or throw things. Such behavior is frightening; the person being intimidated is never sure if physical violence will follow.

Andy, who told his story in Chapter 1, said, "If we were at a party and my partner was talking to another man, I would just look at her, and she would be at my side. No one knew what was going on. It was just a look or a crooked smile and she knew."

As Sylvie explains, intimidation creates immediate fear:

When Tyler was angry at me, he would walk around me while he was talking or yelling so I never knew what to expect. I'd try to maintain eye contact with him because he had hit me in the back of the head before. He wouldn't necessarily have to be talking angrily, but the fact that I had to turn around and watch him was very intimidating. He knew exactly what he was doing.

Getting what you want this way, or just simply venting your anger, may be temporarily satisfying. You may get what you want at the time. But if people you say you love are afraid of you, how can intimacy, trust, and caring exist? Because you have behaved like this for a long time, you may not be aware of your family's fear, but you can be sure that your partner and your children are afraid.

In one of my groups, Ben was coming to terms with his past intimidating behavior. He did not want his family to be scared of him. He acknowledged that his abuse affected his family, and he wanted to change.

Ben: Ever since I started coming to this group, I'm really becoming aware of how much fear I instilled in Holly and the kids. It doesn't feel very good to know they're still afraid of me.
Michael: That fear may be there for a while, and you're going to have to be patient. You can't expect them just to forget what happened.
Ben: I know. But it bothers me. I can tell when I walk in the door that things change. I don't want them to be afraid of me anymore.

Michael: Ben, what are you like when you come home? Are you smiling and cheerful or angry and tense?

Ben: Well, I'm usually pretty tired. I have a stressful job, and it takes a while for me to unwind. I wouldn't say I'm overly cheerful, but I'm not always angry, either.

Michael: Well, when you're feeling a certain way, sometimes your body language projects that emotion. So if you're tense, your body language may project a message like "Stay *away* from me!" What do you think?

Ben: Well, it's certainly possible.

Michael: Are you willing to try something?

Ben: Sure.

Michael: For the next week, do this: When you get home, take a forty-five-minute walk before you go into the house. As you walk, think positively about yourself and your life. Put the day out of your mind. Every time something from work enters your mind, push it out and focus on something pleasant and enjoyable. Take deep breaths while you walk, and try to relax. When you enter the house, be positive.

The next week Ben reported to the group that he'd noticed a change. People in the house seemed less anxious. He was really surprised that after only one week of doing things like taking a walk, using positive self-talk, and making an effort to change the way he presented himself, he'd achieved so many positive results.

Men who use intimidation, whether deliberately or not, need to become aware of how they respond to conflicts and problems that arise in the home. Self-monitoring and feedback from others may be necessary. If you are upset or in a bad mood, let your partner and children know that your mood has nothing to do with them. For example, you can calmly say, "I'm in a bad mood, it has nothing to do with you, and I need some time to be alone."

Sometimes men are not aware, or choose not to be aware, of how scary they can be when they're angry. In a relationship in which there has been no abuse, anger is not so frightening. But partners and children who have been abused have vivid memories of violence, and anger will elicit fear in them even if violence doesn't follow.

Sometimes men in our groups will say that punching a wall or door is better than hitting their partners. That is true. But punching an inanimate object in your partner's presence can produce the same results as hitting her. A punched wall or a thrown object may give your partner the impression that she is next.

Men who batter can use their voices to terrify and control others. A common way that men do this is by shouting. Some get right into their partners' faces and yell. The purpose is obvious: Most people are unnerved by it. As Lisa told me, her husband's yelling was particularly frightening:

> Justin's biggest weapon was his voice. He had an extremely loud and deep voice. I remember one time when he was yelling at me, I could actually feel the sound waves hitting my body. It was extremely intimidating—like I was being slapped in the face with his voice. It was always hard to hear after he had one of those tirades.

If you are serious about changing, you have to stop using this kind of intimidation. Monitor yourself by making a commitment not to shout and to lower your voice during times of conflict.

If you are angry or upset, find another outlet to deal with your emotions. Talk with a friend, walk away from upsetting situations, and practice restraint. All of the men I interviewed for this book said they continue to take time-outs when they are angry. They also said they consistently need to monitor themselves. They have learned the importance of responding to conflict in a nonintimidating manner, and they do what it takes to be nonviolent.

Change takes time. Each family member's perception of whether you have actually changed will vary. You must give people time to observe your behavior. It's only when your family begins to feel safe that trust can be restored. If you have battered, you probably have many ways of using intimidation. Some men have said they like having the power and "respect" in their households, and that intimidation is a way to get it. But at what cost? Do you really want your partner and children to be afraid of you? Do you want your family to walk on eggshells whenever you're home?

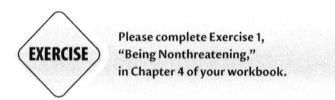

Please complete Exercise 1, "Being Nonthreatening," in Chapter 4 of your workbook.

Using Threats

Sometimes men who batter threaten further violence. Naturally women who have been beaten in the past take these threats seriously. Several men in our groups have said that their partners know they wouldn't actually do what they threaten to do. But how can their partners be sure? And if the men have been violent in the past, why wouldn't their partners think the threats were real? Why did the men make threats in the first place?

Threats are used to elicit a response or to get your way. Whether you intend to carry out the threat or not, your partner has a reason to be afraid.

Some men threaten to take away or gain custody of the children. They know women feel particularly vulnerable in this area, and they choose to exploit it. Other men threaten to harm themselves. In one of our groups, Al discussed his threat to commit suicide.

> **Al:** I don't know why Emily put that stuff about me wanting to commit suicide in the court affidavit. She knows I would never do something like that.
> **Michael:** How would she know that for sure?
> **Al:** She knows.
> **Michael:** In the statement it said you took the gun from the basement, went upstairs, and told her that you were going to

kill yourself, and then you left. Why would you make those
threats?

Al: Well, she had been real cold to me after I hit her. You know,
real unforgiving. I thought maybe the threat of losing me would
shake her up a little and things would change. It was a stupid
thing to do, but she knew I'd never really kill myself.

Some men who batter do threaten suicide, usually when they
think they are losing their relationship. A man threatening suicide
may believe his partner will rethink her decision and stay with him.
But destructive relationships are rarely saved by threats, and intimidation may only make the breakup harder and longer. To understand your use of threatening behavior, do the following exercise.

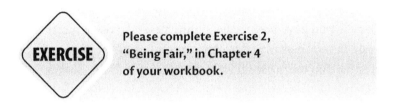

EXERCISE

**Please complete Exercise 2,
"Being Fair," in Chapter 4
of your workbook.**

A Note to Women

Take all threats seriously. If your partner is threatening you in any
way, get advice from a battered women's program in your area. You
may need to use the legal system or stay at a shelter to protect yourself. A man who is threatening to commit violence, kill himself, or
take the children is dangerous, and his behavior is illegal.

Isolation: Blocking Her Freedom to Decide

In a relationship in which there is battering, men often attempt to
isolate their partners. They do this by sabotaging, manipulating, or
making demands that their partner end her relationships with certain friends or family members. In Sylvie's case her partner cut off
her relationships with friends for a specific reason:

When we first started dating I had a lot of friends, and Tyler seemed okay with that. But things changed, especially when the physical violence intensified. He started to devalue my friends. If a friend of mine gave me clothing as a Christmas present, he would use it as a rag to wash the car. He'd say, "I don't know why you want to hang around her, she ain't no good."

He wanted the power to make me feel bad and to make me feel good. So my having friends was a threat because they could make me feel better, and he wanted to be the only one who could do that.

Another form of isolation is pressuring someone to give up activities that she enjoys or placing obstacles in the way of interests that give her personal fulfillment or professional enrichment; for example, applying for a better job, taking classes, being involved in a community group, playing on a sports team, or joining a book club.

For Cassie her partner wanted her to better herself, but only up to a point:

Antonio encouraged me to go back to school, and I did. But as I got close to graduating from college, he made things very difficult. I don't think he ever thought I'd get to that point, so when I did, he said I was neglecting the house and the kids. It was literally a fight for me to get out the door to attend my classes.

After I graduated, he encouraged me to get a job. He'd say, "You're a smart woman, you've got a degree, and you can get a good job." So I got a job, but I had to start at the bottom. Everything was okay and he was supportive until I started to work my way up the ladder. He got threatened by the people I worked with. And I think he felt inadequate because I was making more money than him. That's when the beatings started getting real bad. I think he felt like less of a man.

Why does a man who batters try to inhibit his partner's relationships with others? Here are three reasons:

First, he may be afraid his partner's friends or family members will help her get out of the abusive relationship. He is usually aware of the pain he is causing and knows the abuse will make her think about leaving. He identifies her friends as a bad influence because he suspects them of plotting with his partner to help her leave.

Second, he may be, and often is, very jealous of others—especially other men. If his partner goes out with friends, he fears she is seeking the company of another man. He is insecure, and because of his past treatment of her, his insecurity about the relationship increases. He asks himself, "Why would she want to stay with me after the way I've treated her?" He is particularly suspicious of divorced or single women, because they are independent and he worries they will give his partner ideas about leaving.

Third, he may believe his partner does not need friends and needs only limited contact with her family. "Anything she needs emotionally or intellectually she can get from me," he thinks. He wants her world to revolve around him, and by keeping her isolated he encourages her dependence on him.

In one group we discussed isolating behavior and some of the beliefs and expectations men have when they enter a relationship:

> **Michael:** Allen, you were talking last week about how you told Stephanie not to associate with a certain friend she'd known since childhood. Do you believe men have the right to decide who their partners are friends with?
> **Allen:** I didn't decide anything. We've been having this argument for a long time, and I think she knows I'm right. Kate, this friend of hers, is in the bars constantly, and she has a reputation. I think as her husband I have some say in this. After we talked, she agreed with me, so it wasn't like I forced her.
> **Michael:** What do the rest of you think? Should Allen have a say in who his partner can be friends with?
> **Bob:** I think both people in a relationship have a right. My wife criticizes my friends all the time.
> **Toby:** Yeah, if his wife's friend is loose, it reflects badly on him.
> **Michael:** So when you marry you have the right to give the thumbs-up or thumbs-down to your partner's friends if you think they reflect badly on you? The marriage contract gives you that authority?

Bob: There has to be compromise and give-and-take in the relationship. And I think if your partner makes a bad decision, you have an obligation to protect her.

Toby: I think it's more an act stemming from mutual consideration than an authority or control thing.

Michael: It seems very controlling to me. I wouldn't like my partner to have that power over my friendship decisions, and I don't believe I have the right to interfere in hers.

We spent the entire session discussing this issue, with no resolution. Most, but not all, of the men believed it was perfectly acceptable to tell their partners not to associate with certain people. They were either protecting their partners or protecting their reputations. Most believed this was a marital responsibility. The next week we took up the theme again, and I asked Allen to participate in a role-play with me. I would play him and he would play his wife, Stephanie. He reluctantly agreed.

Allen [as Stephanie]: Allen, I really don't think you're being fair about Kate. Yes, she's divorced, and yes, she dates men, but so what?

Michael [as Allen]: She's a bad influence. I don't trust her.

Allen [as Stephanie]: It sounds like you don't trust me.

Michael [as Allen]: I know what it's like when you're with those women. How do I know you won't get tempted being with her, listening to the things she's saying to you and getting worked up? And I know she thinks I'm an asshole.

Allen [as Stephanie]: We just have a drink and talk.

Michael [as Allen]: I told you, I don't trust her, and I don't want you to see her anymore! No more discussion!

I ended the role-play and asked for feedback from the group.

Bob: Well, if it happened that way, I wouldn't think it would be fair.

Michael: Why?

Bob: She seemed like she was telling the truth.

Others nodded in agreement.

Michael: But earlier you guys said he had the right to decide what friends she could have if he thought they were a bad influence. Allen, how did it feel being in that position?
Allen: Not good. I didn't mind it so much until you ended it the way you did.
Michael: What did that feel like?
Allen: I felt kinda like a kid.

If you have battered and are still in your relationship, remember that healing takes time—and sometimes it never happens. Back off. Let her have her own life, and allow her the time to sort things out. Isolating her may give you what you want in the short term, but ultimately you will drive her away.

Many of the men I interviewed for this book said that understanding why they had isolated their partners in the past was important for their future relationships. They needed to let go and they needed to trust. Perhaps more important, they needed to get to a place in which they were truly supportive of their partners' goals. In their current relationships they encourage their partners to have friendships. They support their partners' plans to go back to school, get a job or change jobs, or pursue other independent activities that make their lives more whole. And as their partners' lives become more satisfying, their relationships improve.

From time to time you might feel threatened. Change can be scary. But people need space to grow independently from one another, and they need to have their own lives. Then they can support each other's goals, because their union is based on love, concern for each other's happiness, and trust in the relationship.

**Please complete Exercise 3,
"Being Trusting and Supportive,"
in Chapter 4 of your workbook.**

Using the Children to Get to Her

A man who batters often uses the children as weapons against his current or former partner. He may belittle and undermine her in front of them. He may threaten to take them away or gain custody by claiming she's an unfit mother. He may threaten to harm the children. Some children are injured when they try to protect their mother from a man who is abusing her.

Not all men who have battered use their children as weapons, and many men are loving and devoted fathers. Yet all too often, because of the bitterness of the failed relationship or as a tactic to get what they want, men who batter make custody threats. Some do it under the guise of love for their children, and others base it on their rights as fathers.

For most women the thought of losing their children is extremely distressing. Men who batter have told me they exploited those fears in order to get their partners to drop domestic assault charges or restraining orders. Many women have told me they stayed in abusive relationships rather than risk losing their children.

As Sylvie explains, the threat of losing her children was powerful and made her stay—but the effect on her children was negative:

> I think my children lost confidence in me because I stayed in an abusive relationship. I think they felt they couldn't trust me to protect them since I couldn't protect myself. The worst thing was that when I threatened to leave him, he said he would kill one of my kids if I did, and I believed him. I stayed longer than I should have because of those threats.

Cassie knows that what her children saw when they were very young has long-term effects.

> My kids saw the violence from the very beginning. I was breast-feeding Sammy, and Antonio and I got into an argument. He punched me in the nose and blood was flowing all over and Sammy was screaming. I see the impact of the violence on my children all the time. When they get into arguments with each

other, they get violent. They had to learn that stuff somewhere.
My oldest boy never takes responsibility for any of his actions.
I know his exposure to his father's constant denial and blame
has affected him.

If you have battered, consider the effects your violence has had
on your children. Well-documented studies show that children's exposure to domestic abuse increases the risk that they will develop an
attitude that aggression is the norm, especially boys.[1]

While you may not be directly abusive to your children, seeing
your violence has a profound impact. Children witnessing domestic
abuse can develop behavioral and health problems, depending on
the level of violence they observe. They may have difficulty con-
centrating in school, become disruptive, or get into fights. Children
from abusive situations have a difficult time trusting people and
establishing intimacy in relationships. Some children blame their
mothers for "letting" the violence occur, while others assume responsibility for the violence themselves. They are confused and feel
guilty.[2]

Children are influenced not only by the violence they observe
but also by the breakup of the family. Their stress level increases
as they observe the continued hostility between their parents. And
they are often put squarely in the middle as their parents struggle,
often in court, over custody and visitation.

If your relationship has ended or is ending, try to be fair and reasonable with your ex-partner, even if you're angry. If you are thinking
of seeking custody of your children, think also about your motives.
Are you pursuing custody as revenge on your partner or as a way of
maintaining some control over her life? Do you want the responsibility of raising your children? Can you fulfill it? Would it be in the
children's best interest to live with you—or with their mother? Is
there some middle ground that works best for your children?

The following discussion about custody took place in one of our
groups:

Grant: Angela let me know that she's filing for divorce. I told her fine, but I'm going for custody.

Maryann: Are you going to seek joint custody or full custody?

Grant: Full custody, for sure.

Maryann: You're working full-time, right?

Grant: Yeah, but she's working too. I'll find a way to manage. I think a man can be just as good a parent as a woman.

Maryann: I think men can be wonderful parents. I'm curious though—do you know where Angela is going to live?

Grant: Well, her plans are to live with her mother for a while. I guess her mother will take care of the kids while she's working.

Maryann: I am asking these questions because I wonder whether you've been thinking about what would be best for the children. Your children have been through a lot. I'm just wondering if you've considered what would be the most supportive environment for the kids.

Grant: Well, in some ways it would be better for them to be at their grandmother's house. She really loves them, and it would be better than day care. But if Angela gets custody, pretty soon they won't even know they have a father. She'll meet some guy, and then he'll be in their lives.

Maryann: Not having full custody doesn't mean you give up being their father. You have to decide what kind of father you want to be, how you want to spend your time with your children, and, ultimately, what is best for the kids.

Even if you have no custodial relationship, you can be a loving and responsible parent. You can take your children to a sports event, the zoo, a concert, or a movie. You can explore a city park or take them camping or hiking or hunting or fishing. You can encourage them and participate in their activities such as music or sports. You can be supportive and help them resolve problems. Get involved in their schools. Show them your love, and be the kind of caring father who makes a difference in his children's lives.

Whether you or your ex-partner has custody, don't make the children suffer for the problems in your relationship. You may be angry and hurt, but you don't have to poison your children. You and your partner can make decisions that are in their best interests even if working out custody and visitation is hard.

In one of our groups Jack and I had the following interaction about using his children in a manipulative way during visitation:

> **Michael:** Jack, you said last week that your ex was angry with you because of things you said to the kids when you had visitation. Do you understand why she was angry?
>
> **Jack:** I know that last week I was defending my questioning of the children. I know that puts them in the middle. But I still don't want my children exposed to an unhealthy environment. I mean, I think any of the men here would be pissed if their kid's mother was having men overnight. What kind of example is that for the kids?
>
> **Michael:** It sounds like you're still defending what you did.
>
> **Jack:** I know I shouldn't have used the kids that way, but I still believe I have the right to be concerned. I'm not the only guilty one here. The kids tell me the rotten things she says about me.

Christie, Jack's ex-partner, called me about these incidents. She said Jack repeatedly asked the kids questions about her, and they felt they were being interrogated every time he had visitation. She said he implied to them that she was immoral because she had a boyfriend, and that it was her fault the relationship had ended. She also said her oldest boy was always hostile toward her after spending time with his father.

Obviously Jack and Christie's children are emotionally affected by their parents' behavior. It's true that you can't keep things from your kids. You can't hide what is happening in your relationship. However, you should not attempt to make them side with you against their mother. When Jack questions his children, they feel guilty if they give too much information and are afraid of what their father will say about her. They may try to avoid allying themselves with one parent or internalizing the negative comments that are made, but this is a terribly unfair position to put them in. This scene gets played out in various ways in far too many families. If you have children, it's important to look at whether you're using them to get back at your partner or ex-partner.

Regardless of the anger and resentment you may feel toward your ex-partner, think about the effect your actions and words could have on your children. Be honest with them, but don't abuse their trust. Your children are also victims of the situation. Yet they are resilient and will heal if you make a commitment to put care and effort into your relationship with them. Be a good father. Keep your issues with your ex-partner separate—from your children.

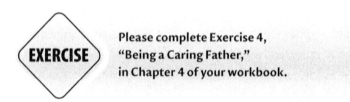

EXERCISE Please complete Exercise 4, "Being a Caring Father," in Chapter 4 of your workbook.

The Pain of Emotional Abuse

Author bell hooks has said, "In order to thoroughly control, you have to tame the spirit." Emotional abuse can be used to establish that kind of control.

I'm sure you can remember a time from childhood when a parent, teacher, or sibling put you down in some way. You can probably still feel the hurt. If someone said you were stupid, you may have questioned your abilities. If someone said you were no good, perhaps your self-esteem was diminished. We are all sensitive to the opinions others have of us.

Both men and women can be emotionally abusive. Even in the healthiest relationships people occasionally reach down into their personal bags of known vulnerabilities, past disagreements, and unresolved issues, and fling harsh comments at their partners. Usually when we do this we're reacting defensively; one partner may inadvertently say something hurtful, and the other responds in kind. However, in healthy relationships, partners usually don't deliberately make such comments, and if they do there's usually an honest explanation and apology for what was said. The confrontation may be painful but probably not destructive.

Emotional abuse within the context of battering takes on an entirely different dimension. In the arsenal of battering, emotional abuse is a powerful psychological weapon designed to depersonalize the victim, cause pain, and increase power. Men who batter are almost always emotionally abusive before assaulting their partners. It is easier to rationalize your behavior when you are negatively labeling the person you are hurting. When you call a woman "bitch" or "slut," you have reduced her standing as a human being entitled to consideration and respect.

For Sylvie, emotional abuse usually accompanied her partner's physical violence:

> I hated being called a bitch. I'd tell him, "I'm not a bitch; a bitch is a female dog." One time during a bad assault he made me get down on all fours. He said, "See, you *are* a bitch." He never totally broke my spirit despite the things he said and did, though if I'd stayed with him, he probably would have.

Cassie started believing the things her partner was saying:

> Antonio told me I was ignorant and incompetent. When I first got my job, I thought the people who hired me must not realize I'm incompetent. And when he told me that no judge would give me custody of the children because I was a bad mother, I believed him.
>
> When we were intimate, I would tell him personal things. But I was always sorry I did because he would use them against me. It was almost like he was recording them and just waiting for the right time to bring them up. When he called me names, it made me feel like I wasn't even human.

Language is a prime tool of emotional abuse. What happens to people when they are called derogatory names based on their race, ethnicity, gender, religion, or sexual orientation? What does it do to our psyches? Not only do we feel direct, immense emotional pain; we also internalize the emotional abuse—we begin to believe what is being said.

I grew up in a community that had its share of anti-Semitism. As a young Jewish boy in a primarily Christian neighborhood, I heard the taunts of other children as they called me "kike," "Christ killer," and "dirty Jew." The children did not make up those words; they heard them at home or at the playground. Whoever said "Sticks and stones may break my bones but names will never hurt me" was wrong. Those derogatory names made me feel that I was a bad person, that I did not belong in "their" neighborhood, and that there was something wrong with being Jewish.

My mother encouraged us to watch films about the Holocaust. These films show the ghastly details of the extermination camps in Europe. She wanted us to be aware of that history. The humiliation, destruction, and confiscation of property, the yellow star, the beatings, cattle cars, gas chambers, and ovens all became images etched in my mind. Why were these people—my people—so despised that something like this could have happened? At my age I couldn't comprehend.

During the Christmas season I felt utterly isolated. Every year our school put on the traditional Christmas program. The school choirs sang religious songs. In junior high the entire student body attended the program—except for the few Jewish students who were forced to sit in the principal's office because our parents would not permit us to go. The office was enclosed in glass, and as other students walked by on their way to the auditorium they could see us, the outcasts, sitting in the office. Their taunts and my embarrassment made me resent being different and, of course, resent my Jewishness.

As I got older I refused to acknowledge that I was Jewish. If someone made an anti-Semitic remark, I pretended I didn't hear it. I hated being a Jew.

My hatred of myself as a Jew began to consume me. I left the United States as a young man and, ironically, moved to Germany, where I lived for almost a year. I remember driving down the auto-bahn (freeway) and seeing a sign that read "Dachau—Next Right." I never stopped at the concentration camp where tens of thousands of my people had perished. Why? Because I had internalized the opinions of anti-Semites. I did not want to be associated with "those people." This form of self-hatred, based on what I had experienced in my youth, stayed with me for a long time.

I began to change when I came back to the United States. I read books and reflected on this subject and realized that other Jews shared similar experiences. Some years later, when I was back in Europe for work, I visited Poland. While in Krakow I knew I had to see Auschwitz, the infamous death camp where millions of people were worked to death, shot, tortured, and gassed. I bought a bus ticket to the camp. The bus from Krakow ran parallel to the very train tracks on which the Jews and other "undesirables" had been transported. Everyone on the bus was absolutely quiet, absorbed in their thoughts about what had happened during that shameful time in our history. As I stood in the remnants of the death camp, tears rolled down my face. How could so many German people and Polish accomplices dehumanize others to such an extent that they became "vermin," as the Nazis called Jews—something that must be destroyed?

When I started working in the domestic violence field, I found some interesting parallels between my denial of being a Jew and the lack of self-esteem and feelings of worthlessness that many battered and emotionally abused women experience.

Most of the men in our groups have admitted that, when angry, they would make the one comment or put-down they knew would hurt their partners the most. Frank said the emotional abuse he used was cruel, but at the time he felt justified:

> I was always into my jealousy stuff with Leila. Whenever she came home I would really give her the third degree about where she'd been and who she was with. If I didn't like the response or didn't believe her, I'd grab her by the hair and say, "You fuckin' slut, you goddamn whore!" I'd call her sexual names because I knew that hurt her. I was so jealous at that time. I thought, if she hurts me then I'll hurt her back.

Name-calling and put-downs are designed to hurt, to chisel away at confidence, to erode self-esteem. Many women have told me that they started doubting themselves because of the terrible things their partners were saying about them. "Why would he say these things if they weren't true?" some of them thought. They began to believe they were bad mothers or inadequate wives. They questioned their physical appearance, their abilities, and their competence.

The combination of insults and violence can be devastating. A man who batters can use both to destroy the independence and spirit of his partner—qualities he was once attracted to but now finds threatening. They are threatening because he needs her to be dependent on him. If he can make her feel ugly, stupid, or incompetent, she begins to be unsure of herself and her worthiness. With low self-esteem she may stop resisting the abusive attacks. Resigning herself to the control of her partner becomes her reality.

The behavior described here doesn't occur in all abusive relationships. But all of us have said something in anger that we wish we hadn't.

Throughout this book I talk about the long healing process women often must go through after being abused and why, if you are still with the partner you have abused, you need to be patient. A deeper understanding of the impact of emotional abuse will not only increase your empathy but also keep you aware of how painful words can be. That old saying "You can't take the words back" is true.

Please complete Exercise 5, "Being Respectful," in Chapter 4 of your workbook.

Understanding and Stopping Battering

You have learned in this chapter that domestic abuse is more than physical and sexual violence. At one point, some of the women in the education groups at the Domestic Abuse Intervention Project made a list of the abusive behaviors used by the men who had battered, silenced, scared, manipulated, confused, and controlled them. These actions are represented by the Power and Control Wheel, which can be found on the opposite page and in Appendix A.

You might be asking, "Is everything I do considered abusive?" Of course not. But like a basketball player trying out new moves to get to the basket, a man who batters reflexively shifts his behaviors to control or influence his partner. The more you know about what motivates you to be insulting or controlling, the easier it will become to catch yourself before you say or do something abusive.

Men who batter frequently try to minimize their conduct with comments such as, "I only hit her once." That may be true. But whether you hit your partner one time or fifty, once you use violence, everything changes. The other behaviors on the Power and Control Wheel take on deeper significance, because despite your assurances, your partner never knows when you might use violence again. Many men fail to recognize the impact of the abusive acts identified on the Power and Control Wheel; a man is still battering unless he stops using *all* of those behaviors.

If you are in a relationship now or are contemplating getting involved with someone, pay attention to your reactions to your partner, especially when you are having conflicts. Catch and stop your-

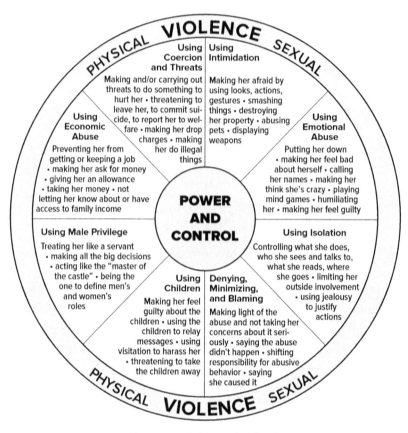

Power and Control Wheel

self every time you start using abusive behavior to hurt, control, or punish your partner. When you become abusive you are making a choice. You have the personal power and self-control to *choose* not to be abusive.

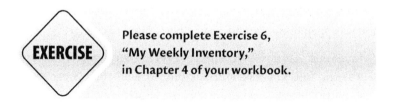

EXERCISE

Please complete Exercise 6, "My Weekly Inventory," in Chapter 4 of your workbook.

5

Getting Past Denial

Self-pity in its early stages is as snug as a feather mattress.
Only when it hardens does it become uncomfortable.

▸▸ MAYA ANGELOU ◂◂

Seeing the difference between self-defense and retaliation is hard for some men. Confusing the two allows them to avoid taking responsibility for their actions, as do minimizing their abuse, blaming their partners or alcohol for their violence, and claiming that uncontrollable anger caused their behavior.

Ron's Story

Ron grew up in Cleveland. He experienced domestic abuse firsthand by observing the actions of his father, stepfather, and mother. He developed a substance abuse problem when he was young, traveled from city to city, joined the United States Marine Corps, and subsequently went AWOL. When he left the service, he ended up in the Midwest. He battered the woman he was living with and was ordered into the Domestic Abuse Intervention Project. Ron was in one of my early groups. Unlike a lot of court-mandated offenders, Ron was open to examining his life. He wanted to change.

> My father was a very violent man. He left our family when I was only four. I have painful memories of this period of my life in spite of how young I was. One time my dad was angry at me

because I'd turned on our gas stove. So, I guess to teach me a lesson, he put my hand on the fire of the stove top—I have the scars to remind me of him. My parents divorced shortly after that, and my mother remarried a few years later.

When I was around eight my mom became a binge-drinking alcoholic. It was at this point that the domestic abuse between my mom and stepdad began. The trouble usually would start when my mom would come home, or sometimes when she wouldn't come home, from the bars. There was a lot of violence. I would lie to my stepdad on her behalf so she wouldn't get beaten. As a child I was confused. I would alternate between blaming my mom for her behavior and then blaming my stepdad for his actions. It was a difficult spot for a kid to be in.

Sometimes I would hide in my bedroom with a baseball bat hoping my stepdad would come in so I could nail him. He was a huge guy, but I don't remember being afraid. There was one occasion when I thought he was going to kill my mom because this time a knife was involved. From my bedroom I heard him say, "Pick up the knife, you cunt, and I'll cut your fuckin' throat." I came out of the bedroom and got between them, and they actually stopped fighting.

One time we were all sitting at the kitchen table eating, and my parents start arguing again. The table got knocked over and the legs were sticking up. My stepdad grabbed my mom by the hair and was slamming her face against a table leg. Her jaw broke and her eyes were blackened from this incident. The police were called, and they arrested my stepdad. Whenever she fought back, she really got it, and that's what happened that night.

I felt like I was living in a dream world. The strange thing is I never thought anything was really wrong with our family, because despite the violence, most of the time things around the house were very peaceful. My stepdad was a good provider, and Mom was a great housekeeper. We had a lot of family outings. My parents could be very loving, but about every four months there would be a blowup. When my mother's alcoholism got out of control, the violence got more frequent. When I was around thirteen, I started to understand that things weren't quite right in our family.

We lived in the inner city of Cleveland. I was really a big kid, so I didn't get messed with, but even though I had physical size, I was afraid of violence and avoided it. When I was sixteen I left home and became a full-blown alcoholic and drug user. Oblivion was my goal. I lived with various family members for a while, but that didn't work out.

I needed to do something with my life, so I joined the Marine Corps and was stationed at Camp Lejeune, North Carolina. I was drinking a lot and soon went AWOL. When I was apprehended, I was forced into substance abuse treatment, but I didn't buy the program and continued to drink. I started to get into fights with men, usually in bars. I fought because I was frustrated and because I didn't like being fucked with. I was very opinionated and bullheaded. If I got into an argument with someone and I felt threatened or challenged, we'd be fighting.

When I was released from the service I hitchhiked through the Twin Cities on my way to Seattle. The police picked me up because I was intoxicated. I decided to go into treatment since a program was offered. When I got out of treatment, I met Jess, the woman I would live with and batter.

Jess was afraid of me right from the beginning. I would scream in her face and terrorize her. We would usually fight over little things, but when I wanted the upper hand I would punch holes in the walls or slam things around the house to scare her. One time I put her over my knee and gave her a spanking. This wasn't just a spanking; it was a beating. I was stone-cold sober when I did that to her. I thought of Jess as almost childlike, and if she fucked with me, she was going to get it.

I would usually apologize after I assaulted her, and then I would tell her how much I loved her. During my apologies I'd minimize the incident and blame her for getting me so upset. It was really easy for me to turn things around and then say to her, "You're lucky I don't leave you."

Even though I felt Jess had it coming, I did feel bad when I was abusive. Because of my experiences as a child, I had sworn I wasn't going to abuse women, but like so many men who grow up in violent households, I became a batterer. I don't believe alcohol was a factor in my behavior, because I battered Jess when I was sober. When I hit her, I actually experienced an adrenaline high. There's a certain feeling you get when you have that ultimate power over someone—it's difficult to describe.

My worst incident occurred when I got home from a fishing trip and Jess wasn't at the house. I had a feeling that something was up. I thought she might be at her mother's, so I drove to her mom's house, and sure enough she was there. I demanded that she get in the car, but she refused, so I put her over my shoulder, carried her out, and forced her into the car. Her mother was screaming and asking Jess if she wanted her to call the police. Jess yelled back that she did.

When she said yes, I flew into a total rage. I felt betrayed that she told her mom to call the police, and I hauled off and punched her several times in the face. We argued in the car, and when she threatened to leave me, I stopped and punched her in the face some more. I drove away again, but she continued to argue with me, so I again stopped the car and started to beat her. I felt I could scare her back into her place—that she would tell the police everything was okay. I thought this strategy would work, because she'd covered up for me when I had beaten her in the past.

But this time was different. A car drove up behind us and Jess jumped out. She ran to the other car, and the people let her in before I could really react. She was badly beaten up, and they took her away. It didn't appear there was anything I could do about the situation, and I knew I was in trouble, so I just decided to go home. I went to bed, and the next thing I knew the police were in my bedroom. I was charged with a felony.

I had no idea Jess was going to leave me. I found out later that she was in contact with advocates at the shelter and they had helped her figure out a plan for leaving me. I was given three years' probation and ordered into substance abuse treatment and the Domestic Abuse Intervention Project. I thought of myself as sort of a tough guy when I came into the group, but when I think back, I was far more open than most of the other men. From the very beginning I wanted to discuss my violence—I wanted it to stop. I knew I needed help, and being forced into counseling gave me the opportunity.

At about this time I enrolled in college and befriended people at the school. Ironically I started dating an advocate from the shelter. I was honest with Anne about my past use of violence and my experiences in the group. I talked with a lot of my friends about what was going on in my life. I wasn't ashamed that I was in the abuse classes; in fact, it seemed the more I talked, the freer I became.

Early on in my relationship with Anne, I did become abusive. Most of the abuse was of a threatening nature. I would scream at her; I never hit her, but on one occasion I restrained her. She wanted to leave an argument, and I wanted to finish it, so I grabbed her by the arms and held her. I know she was afraid of me during the early years of our relationship. Anne stuck with me at that time because I think she saw the progress I was making and she knew I was working on my issues. Still I was unpredictable, and I knew I was capable of reverting back to using violence. One time Anne was late and I was furious. I wasn't sure what I was going to do when she got home, so I called this guy I'd gone to group with in the past. I told him I was feeling really upset and kind of crazy. We talked about what was going on, what I was feeling, and why my thinking was mixed up. That conversation and his support really helped calm me down.

I'm committed to not being violent or abusive with Anne. I'd like to believe all my abuse is in the past, but I still don't totally trust myself. Fifteen years after getting ordered into counseling, I know I still have issues with women and relationships. A few years back I went into therapy for a long time to work on my childhood stuff. It was hard and painful, but I learned a lot about myself. That experience was important to me.

I think about my violent history and the kinds of struggles men and women have in relationships, and I try to understand how my past has influenced me today. As long as I continue to talk about these issues and as long as my thinking is challenged,

I know I'll be okay. It's about awareness and remembering where you were, and, of course, how you want to live your life in the present and in the future.

Taking Responsibility

Somehow it just seems like human nature to make excuses for ourselves when we screw up. We do it all the time. If we make a mistake at work, we blame others or the nature of the job. If we respond inappropriately to something at home, we blame our children or our partners. If we're in a bad mood, we blame the world.

It isn't easy owning up to our mistakes. We know that "to err is human," yet hardly anyone has an easy time admitting to being wrong. What a difference it would make if parents, teachers, politicians, professionals, bosses, coworkers, friends, and family members were to stop blaming others and take responsibility for their own actions. And that is exactly what men who batter need to do: own up to and take responsibility for their violent behaviors.

Outwardly society takes a dim view of men beating women. Most boys are taught never to hit girls. Men who are arrested or in some other way publicly confronted with their violence find it difficult to face their friends, family, and society. Some men feel ashamed of their actions, and some just feel bad that they were caught.

Still others feel justified. They can't get beyond the idea that the violence would not have happened if their partner had acted differently. They see their violence as the logical result of a certain situation, and they find it difficult to see any alternative. They are full of rationalizations, blaming statements that provide an excuse for the violence such as if she had only stopped bitching, not come home late, understood what I was feeling, not put me down, been a better mother, not drunk so much.

In one of our groups Rod explained an episode that led to his arrest. Rod's wife, Nicole, had come home late from an office Christmas party. She had tried calling home but couldn't get through. Rod was supposed to be at his pool league. He couldn't get a baby-sitter, so he had to wait for Nicole to get home before he could leave, and he was furious.

When she got home, Rod began insulting Nicole, calling her a goddamned bitch, threatening to beat her up. She responded by telling him to grow up, which further enraged him. He pushed her down the hallway, screaming at her all the way. She attempted to stop his pushing by kicking him. He punched her twice in the head and was subsequently arrested.

Maryann asked Rod to describe his behavior in more detail.

Maryann: Rod, you've just explained the incident to us. You outlined how you felt, how angry you were, and why. Looking back at the way you handled things, can you envision yourself doing things differently in light of everything that has happened?

Rod: Well, not really. I mean the kids were home, she had been drinking, and she knew I was supposed to be at the pool league.

Maryann: So pushing and punching her resolved that dilemma?

Rod: I wouldn't have punched her if she hadn't tried to kick me in the balls. The way I look at it, it was self-defense.

Maryann: I'm concerned about how you chose to react to her. Are you saying that you had no other options?

Rod: Well, I suppose I could have not gone to my league or blown it off. But pool is important to me, and she should have been home.

Maryann: What about *not* pushing her down the hallway and *not* hitting her?

Rod: I hit her on the side of the head, not in the face, and believe me, it wasn't that hard or she would've been out. The cops had no reason to arrest me.

Rod had difficulty seeing other choices. He could have left the house and cooled down when Nicole returned. He didn't have to call her names or push her. And when she tried to kick him, he could have attempted to deflect her. He certainly didn't need to respond by punching her. Instead of taking any responsibility, he blamed her and downplayed his violence by claiming that he hadn't hit her that hard.

Men seem to have a more difficult time acknowledging personal faults and mistakes than women do, perhaps because of the ways in which we are socialized. We are brought up to be strong, in control, and "right." Men often think they'll be seen as failures if they admit to being wrong or to having problems. As a result some men lie, downplay, or blame others during and after conflicts. For them, blaming the one they have harmed is even more common. On some level they know that hitting and hurting others is morally wrong, so they go to great lengths to rationalize their actions. If Rod were honest, he would have to be accountable to Nicole for what he did. He doesn't want to be held responsible, so he rigidly holds on to the lie that his violence was justified.

Honesty is valuable. If you are honest, even if you have done wrong, people will judge you far less harshly than you might think. You are less alone, and people tend to trust you and respond honestly in return. Rather than seeing you as a failure, people respect the fact that you are taking responsibility for your actions and are doing something concrete to make amends.

If you are—or have been—violent in a relationship and you're serious about changing, taking responsibility for your behavior is critical. Being accountable is a sincere acknowledgment of harmful behavior and an acceptance of responsibility for it. It isn't easy, and it is often humbling, but it must be done.

Minimizing Violence

When explaining your violence to others or to your partner, you may have heard yourself making comments like these:

- "It wasn't that bad."
- "I only hit her once."
- "I only slapped her."

- "I would never punch her with a closed fist."
- "She bruises easily."
- "I didn't hit her that hard."
- "I was drunk."
- "This is the first time I've ever done something like this."
- "I just lost it."

These statements may make you feel slightly better, but they minimize the seriousness of your violent and abusive acts against your partner.

Men who batter often downplay an incident to get those who are confronting them—police officers, counselors, friends, or a partner—to believe that the abuse was not that bad. The more you downplay what you did, the more difficult it will be to come to terms with your behavior.

Max described the following incident in one of our groups:

> I came home after having a few drinks after work. I'd had a really bad day, and I was upset. Paula hadn't made supper, and I told her I was hungry. She said she wasn't going to make me dinner because I came home late and because she was watching TV. I started screaming at her. I kicked the TV off the table, grabbed her by the hair, and told her that I should beat the shit out of her. I slapped her, and she started screaming because I think she really believed I was going to beat her up.
>
> I felt that she cared more about that stupid TV show than me. I guess I wanted to let her know I was hurt. I did feel kind of guilty about slapping her later. The next day I apologized and told her I'd been upset about things at work. I also told her I'd been drinking on an empty stomach and that when I felt rejected by her, I just lost it. I mean, I would never really hurt her.

Note how Max starts his explanation by saying he'd had a hard day. When he apologized to Paula, he said he'd been drinking on an empty stomach. Then he says he "lost it" when it was quite clear he was angry because Paula was not doing what he wanted her to do. Max made a *choice* to become abusive.

Saying "I lost it" or "I lost control" are common ways of describing a violent episode so it appears it wasn't really you doing the hitting. The message is that when you get angry, something unavoidable happens to you—and you become violent.

When a man claims he "loses control" when he's pushed to the limit, I ask why he doesn't "lose control" at work and hit the boss when he gets angry. One reason is that he'd probably lose his job. If he's upset, depressed, or mad at the world, why doesn't he "lose it" on the subway, on the bus, or in a store? He'd probably get arrested. Bosses, friends, and strangers are usually not the targets of men who batter, in part because of the potential consequences.

Claiming that the violence was "not that bad" also minimizes it and denies the reality of the person being hurt and abused. Not only does Max attempt to justify his behavior, but he downplays his violence by saying, "I slapped her and she started screaming, because I think she really believed *I was going to beat her up*," as if grabbing her by the hair and slapping her weren't violent. He says in group, "I would never really hurt her," as if what he did wasn't hurtful.

Denying or downplaying an abusive incident or blaming it on your partner only delays your accepting full and total responsibility for your use of violence. If you want to change your behavior, you can't put off this vital step.

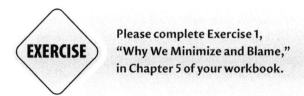

EXERCISE

Please complete Exercise 1, "Why We Minimize and Blame," in Chapter 5 of your workbook.

Self-Defense or Retaliation?

A common theme we hear in our groups is that a man's use of violence is an act of self-defense. There are many variations on this

explanation, but in most cases the story is similar to Eric's excuse
for beating up his wife, Kristen:

> **Michael:** Eric, will you explain your situation again? I'm having
> trouble hearing you take any responsibility for your actions.
>
> **Eric:** Well, like I said before, I was trying to leave the house. I
> guess I was trying to teach her a lesson about not bringing in
> her share of the money. Anyway, she stands in the hallway and
> tells me I'm not going anywhere.
>
> **Michael:** She's blocking the doorway?
>
> **Eric:** Yeah, more or less. So I get my coat and tell her to get the
> fuck out of the way.
>
> **Michael:** Did you say anything else to her?
>
> **Eric:** I probably called her a bitch. You know, like, "Get the fuck
> out of the way, bitch!"
>
> **Michael:** Then what happened?
>
> **Eric:** She slapped me, so I nailed her. I mean I told her, you ever
> hit me, you're going to get it. You know it's this double stan-
> dard, like women can hit men and we're not supposed to hit
> back. Well, I think that's bullshit. She hits hard. As far as I'm
> concerned, a man or a woman hits me, I hit 'em back.
>
> **Michael:** Do the rest of you agree with Eric? If a woman hits
> you, does that give you permission to hit her back?

Many in the group agreed, nodding cautiously, though Tim was
not quite convinced.

> **Tim:** Well, I guess it would depend on what you did. I mean,
> men are a lot stronger and more used to fighting than most
> women I know. I suppose if you slapped her back that would
> be okay.
>
> **Michael:** What did you do, Eric?
>
> **Eric:** I already told you, I nailed her!
>
> **Michael:** You punched her? Kicked her?
>
> **Eric:** I punched her.
>
> **Tim:** How many times?
>
> **Eric:** This is bullshit. I don't know. A couple of times. And I
> only hit her once on the side of the head. I mean there were
> no black eyes or broken bones. She told the cops I kicked her

in the stomach and they believed her and now I'm here. Look, I warned her.

Many men who batter feel the way Eric does. He defends his actions by emphasizing that his partner hit him first and then by saying the lack of bruises or broken bones means he used reasonable force given the situation. He repeatedly uses her slap and his past warnings to justify his violence. In order for Eric to change he will have to ask himself some hard questions: "Was my use of violence really justified?" "How much physical force did I really need to defend myself?" "Was this really self-defense?" "Did I have alternatives?"

The legal definition of self-defense helps determine what is and is not acceptable. According to the law, self-defense is the use of force reasonably necessary to prevent imminent (about to happen) injury. Self-defense does not authorize a person to seek revenge or punish someone. And self-defense does not permit retaliation. In other words, if your partner throws something at you or slaps you, that does not give you the right to punch her.

Some women do use violence. If you have battered your intimate partner, chances are she has fought back or resisted your violence; this is not mutual violence. And some women do initiate violence. Some men have told me they were glad when their partner hit them, because it gave them permission to beat her and feel justified. After all, they think, "she hit me first."

As Cassie explains, there is a distinct difference between her violence and her partner's:

> Not that my violence was right, but the impact was totally different. One time I was furious with him. I broke every window in the house with an iron pan—and I mean every window, upstairs and downstairs. I know he must have been scared at the rage he was seeing because he just stood there. That was violent and wrong of me.
>
> But on one occasion when we were intimate I told him I loved water. I loved rivers and the feel of water on my body. It

was my solace. I never thought he would use that against me, but he did. When he was angry with me, he would wait until I got in the shower and then he would come into the bathroom and beat me. One time he hit me so hard, he split my head open. There I was when the police came, naked and bleeding in the bathroom.

After all these years I am still terrified when I take a shower. I tell the children not to come into the bathroom. I have a clear shower curtain so I can see the door. And to this day I'm still afraid. When he hears glass break, though, do you think he shudders because of that evening when I broke the windows? You can't tell me what I feel is the same as what he feels.

In the documentary *With Impunity: Men and Gender Violence*, Ellen Pence talks about the difference between men's and women's violence:

Let me give you a hypothetical situation. Let's say in whatever state that you live that for the next ten years not one man will beat or rape a woman. Not one man will be incestuous with his children. There will be no battering. There will be no frat parties where women who are intoxicated will be sexually assaulted. There will be no use of date rape drugs. You are able to completely eliminate men's violence against women. What would be the social consequences of ending men's violence against women and girls over that ten-year period? The impact would be enormous. The difference in social costs for the community, law enforcement, the courts, prisons, social services, mental health treatment, substance abuse treatment, and productivity would be staggering.

Now if you were to take the same hypothetical example and say that in your state for the next ten years not one woman will beat or rape a man. Men are going to be able to walk the streets freely. Women aren't going to gang rape a man on a college campus or military installation. Men aren't going to be beaten up at home. Men aren't going to be trafficked. What would the social consequences of that be? It would be almost negligible.

Why? Because women's violence against men is not a social problem.[1]

When men in the groups would claim that women are just as violent as men, I would ask them to answer the following questions:

1. Do you ever get tense and anxious when you hear your partner coming home, wondering what kind of mood she'll be in?
2. Does she ever strike you for absolutely no reason that you know of?
3. Are you ever afraid that you'll be pressured to have sex with her after she's beaten you?
4. Do you flinch when she's angry and makes intimidating gestures? Are you afraid that her actions are a sign she's going to hit you?
5. Are you afraid that if you decide to leave her, she'll break into the house and beat you? Or try to kill you?
6. Are you afraid of her?

Men almost always answer "no" to all of these questions. Some even chuckle when I ask them. A woman's use of violence usually differs from a man's because of the power imbalance. A man is usually larger and stronger than his partner, and his violence is often accompanied by other battering behavior, which increases his power. He may threaten to kill her. He may hurt or kill a pet or display weapons in a threatening manner.

This is not to say that men are never battered. While the number of men who fit the description of being battered is extremely low when compared to the number of women being battered, violence is always dangerous. If your partner uses violence, threatens to harm you, or makes you afraid for your safety, please get help. Domestic abuse programs and counseling centers can help, as can using legal remedies like getting a civil protection order (sometimes also called an order of protection, an order for protection, personal protection orders, or protection from abuse orders) or calling the police.

Guidelines
for Remaining Nonviolent

Most men who claim they acted in self-defense will later admit they had alternatives to using violence. To remain nonviolent many formerly abusive men have committed to the following principles:

---

1. Violence is not acceptable unless I am truly in fear of being hurt, and then I should use only as much force as I need to defend myself.

2. In the future I will be aware of flash points—situations in which I become agitated or very angry—that in the past have prompted violence by me or my partner.

3. I will leave situations—take a time-out— rather than use violence.

4. I will accept the fact that my use of violence is based on my desire to control a situation. I do not always need to be in control, to be proven right, or to win.

5. I will strive toward respectful resolutions of conflicts without being abusive.

Do you believe there are conditions to making these commitments? Exceptions? Do you feel a resistance to accepting them? Committing to these principles is not just an intellectual exercise. These five principles are the foundation for your efforts to remain nonviolent and nonabusive. If you can agree to them only if certain circumstances exist, then you have more work to do.

A Note to Women

If you are a woman who uses violence against your partner, you should be clear about whether you are responding to your partner's violence, defending yourself, or initiating the violence. Talk to friends or an advocate to help you decide which it is. Don't take the blame if the violence is your partner's; say no to it and get away from it. Work with an advocate. If you think the safest course is to leave your relationship, either temporarily or permanently, an advocate can help you develop a safety plan or obtain a civil protection order. You can also call the police.

If you find that you are clearly initiating the violence, get help. I often tell women using violence in an intimate relationship that their use of violence is dangerous—your male partner's retaliatory response could cause you substantial injury. This is not a double standard; the reality is that most men are physically stronger than women and are socialized to fight.

Some women justifiably fight back when they are being battered. But the consequences for using violence, even in self-defense, can be serious. In some low-income communities and communities of color, battered women may be reluctant to call the police because of tensions between law enforcement and the neighborhood. The police response may be one of indifference, and the criminal justice system is often harsher on men of color than it is on white men. Women of color want the battering to stop but are sometimes unwilling to involve the criminal justice system when the consequences to their partners (and thus to themselves and their children) might make the situation worse for the family.

For a battered woman who uses violence, calling the police may also result in negative consequences if she is a new immigrant. She may have to contend with police officers' and the court's ignorance of her culture, ostracism from the broader community for involving the authorities, threats of deportation, and the involvement of child protective services.

If you find yourself in a situation in which you are using violence, regardless of your circumstances, seek help. Whether you've initiated violence or are using violence in self-defense, it typically won't stop unless there is an intervention. Talk to an advocate and get the help you need.

Letting Go of Blame

It may be difficult to stop blaming your partner for your violence. The following group discussion illustrates this:

> **Michael:** Why do you think it's so hard for us to get beyond blaming our partners for our violence?
>
> **Julio:** Well, for me, it's just recently that I've seen I could have acted differently. I mean I still want to hold on to all the things that Anna did or said.
>
> **Michael:** So you still believe she shared responsibility for the violence?
>
> **Julio:** In my head I know I'm responsible. But when I think about the times I was violent, it's hard to let go of her part in it. I mean there were times when I thought she was egging me on so I would hit her. Our fights were totally outrageous. I had told her not to push me, and she knew I would hit her if she kept going. So when she kept on pushing, I kind of thought she knew what the consequences were going to be. It doesn't justify what I did, but that's the way I saw it.
>
> **Michael:** Are you saying you think Anna wanted to get hit?
>
> **Julio:** No. But I couldn't understand why she wouldn't just shut up when I warned her to stop. She would say shit that got me so pissed off I would just lose it.
>
> **Michael:** So if someone says something I don't want to hear or says something that hurts or offends me, then it's their fault if I hit them?
>
> **Julio:** When you say it like that, I would say no. But there are two people in an argument. Are you saying she didn't have any responsibility in this? I mean I'll own up to my use of violence, but she needs to recognize when she's pushing my buttons.
>
> **Michael:** I'm not saying Anna hasn't done or said things that might be inappropriate or hurtful. What I am saying is that regardless of what she says or does, your violence is yours and yours alone. I think it's really important to stop blaming her.

You say you've acknowledged your violence, but all your comments have this qualifying statement that says she shares responsibility. Until you come to terms with that, I'm afraid you'll remain stuck.

Julio: I hear you. I don't know why I'm having such a hard time letting go of that.

Julio's comment about Anna "pushing his buttons" makes him sound like a robot whose buttons are being pushed on and off. The whole notion that words can provoke us into using violence is an argument that we have to set aside. If our response to words is violence, even if the words are hurtful or seemingly offensive, our violent response is a *choice* that we make.

A man who batters frequently believes his partner should be a mind reader, knowing when to approach him and when to leave him alone. Failure to approach him in the "correct" way results in his getting angry and rejecting his partner or hurting her feelings. This can lead to an argument, which can escalate to violence.

As Cassie states, men who batter often have twisted perceptions of what provokes violence:

> There were times when I would start arguments that resulted in fights. I mean we had a lot of issues that caused problems, from money to the children—a lot of stuff. And I know there were times when I said hurtful or mean things. When I would bring up a problem we were having, he would say I was provoking him. But I wasn't starting a fight so I could get beat up. Nothing I said gave him the right to do that. He would take any form of communication that made him feel uncomfortable as an excuse to become abusive. Later he would blame me and say I had provoked him.

Letting go of the idea that your partner provokes the violence is difficult. Men who batter often believe their partners are intentionally pushing them into conflict. But if they were being honest with themselves, they would acknowledge that the conflict usually has more to do with their own anger and resentment over their partner's wanting something or having a different opinion. When their partners assert themselves or disagree, men who batter see this as a provocation.

Andy describes his resistance to seeing the truth and accepting responsibility for his behavior:

> I'd hang on to my position tight and try to convince other people that my partner brought the violence on. I'd say, "I'm not to blame here. Yeah, I did some stuff, but it's a two-way street. There are two people in this relationship." I hung on to that. I hung on to that for dear life. I finally started to change when I let go and realized she didn't have to change for me to change. And she wasn't to blame for my behavior. I was responsible for my violence, just me.

Alcohol, Drugs, and Violence

Being under the influence of alcohol or drugs is a common explanation for violent behavior from men who have assaulted their partners. Fifty percent of men who enter the Domestic Abuse Intervention Project have chemical dependency problems, which is consistent with research on substance abuse and intimate partner violence.[2] The research also indicates that men who batter are more likely to use violence while under the influence of drugs and alcohol and are more likely to commit more severe acts of violence when impaired. Despite the co-occurrence of substance abuse and domestic abuse, the use of drugs or alcohol isn't an excuse.

Russ, a former police officer from Chicago, met with me to enroll in one of our groups. He was upset as he told his story.

> **Russ:** Last night I punched my wife and began to choke her. I was totally drunk and just lost it. I've never done anything like that before.
> **Michael:** Is she okay?
> **Russ:** Yes. I mean, I think so. She's at the women's shelter. I've been trying to get in touch with her.
> **Michael:** What happened last night?

Russ: Well, I was really drunk and I just flipped out when she got home. I don't remember everything, but I was on top of her and was choking her. Then she lost consciousness and I let go. When she came to I tried to apologize. I mean I would never ever do something like that if I were sober. I'm not that kind of a person. I must have been in a blackout or something, because I was totally out of control. Anyway she was crying and upset and wanted to go but I wouldn't let her. I must have passed out, because when I woke up, she was gone.

Michael: You say you were totally out of control. Why do you think you didn't kill her? I mean you stopped choking her. As drunk as you say you were, as out of control as you say you were, you stopped choking her.

Russ: I don't know. Something snapped, I guess. I'm very confused.

For Russ alcohol is an excuse, a way for him to try to explain away his violence. There are two problems with this. First, some men deliberately drink too much or get high to give themselves permission to be abusive, especially when they are going to bring up issues that are hurtful or unresolved. Getting drunk or high with the intent of entering into a confrontation with a partner is a setup for abuse. After the violence, the man can chalk the situation up to being drunk or high and tell himself, "It wouldn't have happened if I'd been sober." Some men who batter and have substance abuse problems are in relationships with women who also have substance abuse problems. Again many of these men blame their violence on their mutual use of drugs and alcohol. While having two people impaired can be a recipe for problems, it still is not a justification for your choice to use violence.

The second problem is that society, friends, and family—and often the mental health community—may view alcohol or drugs as the primary problem. Many people assume that if a substance abuse problem is resolved, the abuse and violent behavior will end. This is a dangerous assumption for the partner of an abusive man. People who abuse alcohol or drugs and act violently have two problems, not one. They need to address both.

Unfortunately substance abuse treatment usually does not address the reasons for a person's violence. In many cases men will continue to batter when they are sober.

If you think you have a substance abuse problem, take immediate short-term steps—whatever's necessary—to ensure you will not be in a position to act out violently. Then get a substance abuse assessment and follow the recommendations of your counselor. This may mean going into inpatient or outpatient treatment, followed by aftercare or AA. After this you can begin a domestic abuse program dealing specifically with the issues of your violence. The two programs have two very different functions, even though some of the issues you will deal with overlap.

A Note to Women

Some researchers have concluded that a battered woman stays in a relationship with a physically abusive man for a much longer period if he has a substance abuse problem. In many cases she is reluctant to leave a dangerous relationship because she feels compelled to make excuses for her partner's behavior. She accepts the rationalization that his use of alcohol or drugs is a contributing factor to his violence.[3]

If your partner is both violent and under the influence of alcohol or drugs, you are at risk. Call a shelter or domestic abuse program in your community and get help.

Some battered women medicate themselves with drugs and alcohol to deal with an abusive partner, and some simply have a substance abuse problem. Admitting that you have a problem is never easy. Getting sober may be an important step to making healthy choices about your future and how to deal with the abusive man in your life. There are many resources in your community that can provide help.

Anger

Anger is a common human emotion. Someone cuts in front of us on the freeway, our children do something wrong, a coworker screws up, things don't go our way—there are countless reasons why we might get angry.

This is a normal feeling and not necessarily a negative emotion.

However, men who batter often cite anger at their partners as the reason for their violence. This discussion that took place in one of our men's groups shows how Calvin uses anger to justify his violence:

> **Calvin:** I decided to come to this group to get a handle on my anger problem.
> **Michael:** What do you mean by "anger problem"?
> **Calvin:** Well, when I'm in a relationship with a woman and she does something that pisses me off, sometimes I get violent. I want that to stop.
> **Michael:** Are you saying that anger causes the violence?
> **Calvin:** If I wasn't angry, I guess I wouldn't be violent.
> **Michael:** Does that mean that if you get angry with me right now you're going to hit me?
> **Calvin:** No. You don't understand.
> **Michael:** What don't I understand?
> **Calvin:** There are certain things that get people angry, and then that triggers a violent response. My ex-girlfriend would say things that got me so angry I would become violent. I suppose if you said certain things I could get that angry with you.
> **Michael:** It seems to me you're making a choice about who you're going to be violent with and when you're going to do it.

People in relationships get angry with each other all the time—we make mistakes, we disagree, we're insensitive, we fail to meet expectations. While anger does not cause violence, it precedes violence, and many men know that their anger produces fear in their partners. Men who batter use anger as a way to control their partners and show displeasure. Most women will resist being controlled, yet a man who batters tries to impose his will anyway. He perceives her refusal to shut up or to stop doing something as defiance, and he gets angry. His expression of anger is followed by threats, intimidation, and violence—and then he blames the violence on his anger.

A woman who lives with an abusive man quickly learns to watch for mood swings and either accommodates his demands or resists them. There are consequences for both. Men who batter often believe they need to express their disapproval through angry words or actions. Lashing out can bring an initial and often exhilarating rush and an immediate outcome. Screaming in your partner's face, slamming a table, throwing an object, punching a wall, or breaking things lets off steam and gets everyone's attention. But venting anger in such an intimidating way is threatening, abusive, and unfair to others.

Some people walk around angry at the world, expecting someone to cross them. Then they can vent without taking responsibility. I am not suggesting you should never get angry. But do find an appropriate way to express your anger. As with other emotions, you can feel and express anger in a healthy, nonhurtful manner. You need a clear understanding of the patterns that occur when you get angry before you can change them. If your usual response after getting angry is to explode at someone, remove yourself from the situation before you say or do something abusive.

It's important that you not confuse the emotion of anger with your choice of becoming abusive. Explaining your violence by saying, "She made me so angry that I _____" is a convenient but dishonest excuse.

As you address the ways you deny or downplay your abusive behavior, and as you stop blaming others for your violence, you will begin to see more clearly what you do when you become violent. Then you can begin to move ahead and make real changes in your life. In the chapters that follow you will read about concrete ideas and suggestions to help you change and heal.

6

Letting Go
of Relationships

O, beware, my lord, of jealousy!
It is the green-eyed monster which doth mock
The meat it feeds on.

▸▸ WILLIAM SHAKESPEARE ◂◂

In this chapter you will read about the importance of letting go of a relationship that has ended. Many men in my groups realize that their violence had severely damaged their relationships. Usually it was their partners who left, but some men had ended the relationship themselves; for others, the decision was mutual. Not all relationships harmed by violence end, but often the emotional strain of repairing the damage is just too much.

If your relationship has ended or is ending, you will learn about ways to control your jealousy, the danger of being obsessed with your current or past partner, and the importance of letting go and moving on with your life. Both men and women have a hard time letting go. They may be angry and feel isolated and even scared about the future. Men who batter frequently tell me that they feel betrayed, even though *their* violence was the reason their partner left. As painful as your life feels right now, it's okay for you to feel sad. You can learn from your mistakes, make changes, and find a healthy new relationship when you are ready. The important thing is to move on and let your partner move on too.

In Matt's story, which appears below, he reflects on his life and describes his relationships with women. He then explains what happened the night he put eleven bullets into his wife, Briana, who was trying to end their relationship. He is in prison for life. Matt's case may seem extreme, but these types of murders happen all too frequently.

A Note to Women, Families, and Friends

If you are a victim of domestic abuse, you may already have heard or read that leaving an abusive partner can be a dangerous time. But according to Jacquelyn Campbell, PhD, who has done extensive research on danger and risk, women eventually do become safer from dangerous abusers when they leave the relationship. The majority of abused women manage to leave, and the violence ends. Only a very small percentage of women get killed during the process of leaving.

Campbell states that 3.5 million women are abused each year; half of these women leave their abusive intimate partner, ending the violence. About sixteen hundred women are killed annually by an abusive partner, half of them while attempting to leave. This doesn't mean that the risk involved in leaving isn't high, but it does point to the fact that leaving can end the potentially lethal ongoing violence.[1] Leaving is risky, and even occasionally deadly, so be sure to assess your situation with the help of a victim's advocate, and take all the steps necessary to protect yourself when separating. Besides helping a battered woman evaluate risk factors when she's leaving a relationship, a victim's advocate can assist in developing a safety plan if needed.

If you are a friend, family member, or coworker who is concerned that someone you care about might be in danger of being harmed or doing harm, I hope this chapter provides the impetus for you to intervene. You may feel reluctant to get involved, but do it anyway. Encouraging people to seek help is an act of caring. In far too many intimate partner homicides, friends, family members, coworkers, and others in the community say they wish they had been more proactive when they sensed a problem with a couple. "She had broken it off, but she was constantly getting texts and calls from him." "He would park in front of the house." "She told me she was scared." "He was always talking about how angry he was about the divorce." "He didn't seem like himself."

Matt's Story

On a cold November day in 2005 I (Michael) enter an imposing maximum-security prison to interview men who have killed their intimate partners. Built in 1914 the prison has massive brick walls, guard towers, and razor wire. It is the kind of facility that would scare most anyone.

Once inside I'm directed to go through security as the metal doors clang shut behind me. Even though I'm a visitor, it's not hard to imagine what life is like in here, day after day, especially for men who may never get out. I'm aware of the institutional smells as the throngs of inmates, correctional officers, and prison staff go about their business.

I'm taken into a barren meeting room, and I set up my tape recorder for the first of several interviews. A staff member brings Matt into the room. We introduce ourselves, and I tell him about the book I'm writing. I explain that my hope is that his and other inmates' stories will shed some light on the all-too-pervasive occurrence of murder of intimate partners by their husbands and boyfriends. Matt tells me he understands the objective of the book and is willing to help.

Matt was forty-two at the time of this interview. I've changed the names of the parties in this account.

I wasn't abused as a child. My father was an alcoholic, but I really didn't know it at the time. My parents divorced when I was five, and I was too young to realize what was going on. We were poor and lived in low-income housing. There were five boys in the family.

I only saw my dad a few times after the divorce, and they weren't pleasant. He just showed up at the house, as alcoholics often do. I came home from Cub Scouts one day and saw this guy sitting at the kitchen table and realized he was my dad. When I was eleven he showed up again. I knew he was dying because my mom told me that his liver was giving out. Every night his nose would bleed, yet he would still drink. His big thing was letting me carry the six pack into the house—his way of bonding with his son. At the time I still idolized him. I was at my aunt's farm that summer. My aunt came into my room at three in the morning and told me to get up. She said, "Your father's dead." It's hard on a kid seeing your dad in a casket.

I got involved with Erin. We were both sixteen and inseparable. We lived together for two years and then had a child together. I became a heavy drinker and stayed out all night—like father, like son. I would leave her at home because I wanted to party and now we had a kid. We'd break up and get back together. We were too young to be parents.

With Erin I was passive-aggressive. If I was upset (especially if I was drinking), I'd call her abusive names, but the physical violence was limited to pushing her around. She finally ended the relationship and got an apartment. I wanted her back. I'd sit across the street and watch her—you know, trying to intimidate anyone I thought was going to go out with her. She let me in the house to watch our son during the day, when she was working. She was done with me; she was just allowing me to be the babysitter. She'd get home from work and I'd want to stay with her, but she'd have none of it. She finally cut things off, but I didn't leave easily. I broke windows at the house and was very threatening. She got an order for protection and that was basically it.

After that I lived in a lot of places around the country—traveling everywhere and always partying with friends. I tried, but I just couldn't be with other women. After Erin left me, I thought that if I got involved, I'd get my heart broken again. But then I met Meg.

Meg and I dated for a short period and then we married. We were together for about three years. She told me that she had been sexually abused by her brothers and stepbrothers. Meg was very abusive. She was having an affair and we argued a lot. One day we had a huge argument and she threw the cover of a blender at me that just missed my eye. I was bleeding, so she drove me to the hospital. The doctor asked us what happened, and I told him. He said, "You should press charges. If it had been one inch down, you would have lost your eye." The doctor reported the incident to the police.

She was a fighter. She would beat up girls at the bars if they looked at me. She was pretty tough. When Meg was in a rage, I would just hold her down, which usually worked because I was much stronger. But she was violent with me. One time we had a fight in the car and she was yelling and then she punched me in the face and dug her nails into my neck. I called the police. My neck was still bleeding when the police came, but Meg had left the scene. They issued her a summons, and she was ordered to show up in court. As a result we were both required to go to anger management classes. I didn't think this was fair, but I went. We split up after that, and she went to live with her new boyfriend, who threatened to kill me if I ever contacted her.

I started going to church and became a Christian. I met Briana at Bible study. I thought that God was giving me one more chance. Briana was beautiful. I really wasn't looking for anybody, because I was getting involved with the church and just trying to get back on my feet. One night I got a phone call. It was Briana. She asked me if I'd like to go for a walk down by the river, and that's how our relationship started. We'd go to church together, and I just started being with her more and more. She was the kindest person I had ever met. She was a child care worker at the time. We had many long nights together when we would talk about our future—her dream was to have children and live on a farm. That wasn't my dream, but I went along with her because I wanted to please her.

We married the next year, and it was the happiest day of my life. Briana was such a peaceful, loving spirit, and we just loved being together. Things went well for a while. I curtailed my drinking when we were courting. It wasn't until after our marriage that I started drinking a lot again. Our sex life wasn't very good—she wanted to get pregnant, but she wasn't very sexual. She wouldn't even undress in front of me. We were living a Christian lifestyle, and when we had problems in our relationship we would pray. I had a job, and we bought a house that we fixed up.

We didn't talk about our problems very often, and I pretty much held things in. I started doing meth. Briana didn't know about my drug use. I'd stay out all night doing meth and sleep here and there. I would go to a buddy's house and call her and say that I was thirty miles away just so I could get high all night and not have to come home. She wasn't happy when I'd stay out, but she'd say, "At least you're not driving." By this time she was pregnant, and that was the focus of her life.

My meth problem got worse and worse. My brother had recently died, and that had a huge impact on my life. I was gone for days on end, and Briana knew something was wrong. She told me she wanted to end the relationship. She said, "I can't go through this anymore—this staying out all night." I would spend my entire paycheck on drugs. We were supposed to be saving, but here I was staying out all night and draining our bank account.

Our relationship was crumbling. We agreed to separate, but then she let me move back in with her to try and salvage the relationship. During this time she ran into an old boyfriend and started to reconnect with him. She didn't tell me about him. She finally left me and said she was going to live with her parents. She was working at a residential group home and wanted to move on with her life. I stopped doing drugs for a while, but when we talked about our relationship, we both agreed it wasn't working. I totally blame myself for what happened. I really thought that Briana deserved better, but I was miserable.

I was living on my own and started doing a lot of meth. I stayed up for five straight days getting high. When she left,

I felt like a failure again. Then I decided that if I killed myself in front of her, she would see that I wasn't a failure. I called Briana and told her I was going to commit suicide. And she said, "Oh, Matt, you're just like the people I take care of. With your luck, you'll just fail and end up brain-dead, and I'm not going to feed you through a straw for the rest of your life." I then reiterated that I was going to kill myself. I let her know that I had a lot of pills. She sort of blew off my overdosing. I don't think she knew how far down I really was. She was just trying to give me the "tough love" business because she had taken care of many people who'd tried to kill themselves.

I could feel the end coming. She told me she was going to file for divorce. I called her and said, "Briana, this is happening too soon. I don't want a divorce." The next thing I knew, there's this guy at my house serving me papers.

I went to the Wal-Mart and happened to run into Briana. This time she wasn't nice at all. I owed her money for the phone bill, so I went over to give her the money, but she was really pissed off. She yelled, "What do you want?" I said, "Here's the money I owe you." I was trying to calm things down as we started walking toward her car. It was totally out of character for Briana to be so angry at me. I said, "Briana, can't we just work this out?" I never expected the next words that came out of her mouth. She said, "I don't love you, and I don't want you in my life anymore." She then admitted that she had a boyfriend. I never thought Briana would lie to me. I was just numb when I found out about this guy. It was the ultimate betrayal.

I thought, I did it again—I ruined another relationship. She drove off with her girlfriend, and I went back into Wal-Mart and bought the cheapest gun they had. I wrote my address down, but I didn't have my driver's license. They probably could have stopped me from buying the gun, but within ten minutes they sold me it to me, and some shells, without an ID. The gun was a semiautomatic.

I drove to the bar hoping to find someone to talk to because I was in a bad state. The bartender said I ordered about five or six screwdrivers and four or five beers. I sat at the bar not talking to anyone. I just stared and was furious that she had lied to me about being faithful. Finally, I drove home with the thought of killing myself. I got home and took the gun in the house and put the shells on the counter. I left a message on my answering machine saying, "This is the last time you'll ever hear my voice." I wrote a suicide note to my mother. I said, "I'm sorry, Mother, I love you."

I started to write a letter to Briana and then stopped. I fed the dog in case they didn't find my body. I was writing these notes, and then I saw the wedding ring on the table and pictures of Briana and me. And then words came to my mind. You failed, just like Briana said. I thought, no, I won't fail. I'm going to have her watch me as I kill myself, and then she'll have to live with what she made me do. I took the gun, got in my car, and parked right in front of the residential group home where she worked.

She came out of the building and walked right into my path to smoke a cigarette. I thought, she probably thinks I'm there to cry and ask her to take me back. That's all I could think about—how she reacted. I had never hurt her, so she probably wasn't afraid of me. I was hoping that when I told her I was going to kill myself she might have a change of heart. You want someone who cared for you to continue caring; I hoped she would help me out and want to give our relationship another chance.

I didn't go there to kill her. I wanted her to watch me die. If she hadn't mentioned her boyfriend, I think I would have shot myself. She started screaming, "I can't take it anymore. I just got off the phone with my boyfriend, and you need to know once and for all that this relationship is over. I don't love you. I never loved you. My boyfriend is on his way over here, so you better get the fuck out of here."

That was it. I just triggered out on that poor girl. I shot her eight times. I was about six feet away from her. I shot her in the leg, side, and in the back as she was falling. She was screaming. She might have lived if a bullet hadn't hit her artery. All I can remember is hearing her yell. In a situation like that, you just react. It all happened so fast—all of a sudden, boom! All that I heard that night were the words about her boyfriend, and I felt like a failure again. I shot her with a semiautomatic, and it was over in seconds.

I left the scene. I had blood on me, and I'm thinking there's no way that this just happened. I didn't know if I killed her or not. I went back to the hotel where I was staying, opened the trunk of the car, and there was my empty gun, so I knew I did it. I called 911 from a nearby store and said I would like to report a shooting.

I got a life sentence. I have to do a minimum of thirty years. I suspect there's a chance at parole, but that's unlikely with life sentences for murder these days. I've been here for ten years. When I got here, I woke up on the suicide-watch floor. I screamed out for forgiveness. From that day on I vowed that I'd make the best of my life. I took a life.

I graduated from college in here, and I've been clean and sober all these years. I've read every book that I can. I look back at what I did. I read newspaper articles on domestic violence, and my heart has been ready to send letters to Briana's family to say that I'm sorry. But it's too soon, and, you know, I shot her.

To this day I believe if she had talked to me, we could have worked things out. But her reaction that night was, "Get out of my life. Get out of my life for good. I don't want you. I have someone else in my life." All the subconscious memories of past failed relationships and my childhood experiences came out. And the thought that Briana had a boyfriend while we were still married was the ultimate rejection, the ultimate betrayal.

Thinking back, I needed professional help, but when you're in the middle of it all it's not that easy to see. You need a network of people in your life to get that kind of help. I needed counseling. You can't do this on your own.

I see a big connection between jealousy and obsession. It all comes back to those childhood experiences. For me, it was the abandonment by my father and the way all of my relationships ended. The way these relationships ended was painful—the rejection and the feelings that you have that you're a failure as a man.

I killed this poor girl. I'm sorry for that. She didn't deserve it. Her family didn't deserve it. I can't bring Briana back. I can't undo that. I'm just doing the best I can in here.

Red Flags

In considering this tragic story we can only speculate as to whether an intervention might have changed the course of events. Matt was spiraling downward. He was abusing drugs and alcohol and seemed to be crying out for help. He had lost his job and threatened suicide, at least to Briana. I wondered if any of his friends or family members saw this coming. Did they see Matt in a desperate and despondent state? Had he told his plans to anyone? Did anyone know how angry he was at being rejected by Briana? Had anyone suggested to him that he needed help?

Briana never called the police or sought a civil protection order. In many intimate partner homicides the police or the courts have never been involved. It doesn't appear that she sought help from a shelter, a battered women's program, or a counselor. She had filed for divorce, so her lawyer knew that the relationship was over. It's unclear what her boyfriend, family members, friends, or lawyer said to her about the relationship or whether they were concerned about her safety. She was only twenty-five and knew she wanted to get out of a bad marriage.

From my interview with Matt and a review of court documents, Briana didn't appear to take the threat of suicide seriously, but we don't know this for sure. She could have been very fearful but thought that her response at the time was less likely to set him off. She wanted him out of her life. I'm assuming she confided in her boyfriend, because he apparently threatened to intervene if Matt didn't leave Briana alone. She had a friend with her during her confrontation with Matt at the Wal-Mart. Perhaps Briana, like many victims, believed she knew her partner better than she really did. Maybe she thought that even though Matt was messed up, he wasn't capable of murder. If she wasn't overtly afraid, maybe her friends and family didn't feel the need to be overly concerned.

Absent direct knowledge of physical violence, interveners, friends, and family members should be mindful of other red flags.

Matt was seriously jealous, which is clearly a red flag. During his interview with the police he said, "I was, like, in a state of jealousy." How many people who knew Matt or Briana were aware that this was a danger sign?

Matt was having difficult times financially, which can also be a risk factor. He spent his money on drugs and lost his job. This alone might not tell us much; many people are in financial crisis. However, if this were considered along with the other risk factors, perhaps someone with knowledge about red flags could have intervened. When we look at risk factors, several stand out in this case, but if people don't know about them, the potential danger can't be minimized.

Matt appealed his case to the Court of Appeals. The court affirmed the conviction. The court documents in the appeal provide a few details that I didn't hear in my interview. Matt shot Briana eleven times, not eight, as he told me in the interview. Matt's employer offered him his job back if he straightened up, but there's no indication whether he knew about Matt's marital problems or any other warning signs. Matt purchased fifty rounds of ammunition when he bought the gun, but from his version of the story he didn't have an ID. Since he bought a rifle rather than a handgun, a background check wasn't required.

Finally, would Matt have been amenable to getting help had someone intervened? Had he been ordered to participate in counseling or volunteered for it, would he have been open to exploring his beliefs about women and entitlement? Matt had participated in an anger-management class for an assault in an earlier relationship, but it's unknown whether gender issues were even discussed.

Some might analyze the facts in this case and the interview I conducted with Matt and conclude that his decision to murder his wife was influenced by drug addiction, abandonment issues, a traumatic childhood, social isolation, financial problems, or easy access to a gun. Lost in that analysis would be Matt's socialization as a man. Lost in that analysis would be Matt's beliefs about women and the acute sense of betrayal he experienced when Briana decided to leave him.

In the closing minutes of my interview with Matt, he talked about how women hurt men emotionally when they end a relationship. Despite his remorse at killing Briana, which I think was sincere, I also detected a deep-seated resentment toward women that lay right beneath the surface.

Letting Go

Over the following weeks I interviewed several more men at that prison. Their stories varied, but they had a common theme. Most of the men talked about feeling rejected and betrayed, the way Matt felt when Briana left him. While most admitted that they had killed their partner (some claimed they didn't remember doing it), for the most part they clung to their resentment over how they had been treated by the woman they had murdered. Even after many years in prison, they still blamed their partners.

Some of the men, including Matt, said they had intended to kill themselves in front of their partners as a sort of punishment, but they didn't. Others said they had planned to kill their partners and then turn the gun on themselves, but they didn't.

Relationships often involve painful experiences: Communication breaks down; conflicts surface over children, money, sex, and commitment; and people have affairs. Sometimes one partner seeks affection and love elsewhere because the relationship is emotionally bankrupt and intimacy is gone. For some an affair is a one-time thing; afterward they feel guilt and they see the affair as a mistake. An affair in a monogamous relationship can be devastating. Some relationships survive, however, and the partners rebuild their trust and continue to work on the relationship.

Many men in our groups have told me that, in retrospect, they should have ended their relationships much sooner. Love and intimacy were long gone, but they stayed because of the children, out of fear of being alone, or for financial reasons. Violence adds a confusing component to all this; sometimes it prolongs a dying relationship because your partner may be afraid to leave. Sometimes the violence accelerates the breakup—she no longer will tolerate the abuse and doesn't believe you will change.

Of course, a couple shouldn't consider divorce every time their relationship hits some ruts in the road, but they shouldn't hang on when it's time to let go, either. Frequently, at the end of a relationship, one or both parties are ambivalent. Seeing a counselor and being truly honest about your feelings may help clarify whether you want to make the commitment to make your relationship work or not.

If you have physically abused your partner, however, couples counseling is not appropriate unless the violence, intimidation, and coercion have stopped, and your partner feels safe to talk freely without fear of retribution. You should not pressure or coerce her to attend counseling. She may need time and support from outside sources—such as battered women's advocates and support or educational groups—before she's ready to participate in marriage counseling with you. Respect her request. And if you haven't been through a domestic abuse program and made changes, you're not ready for marriage counseling either.

Letting go of a relationship is always hard. Confusion over what went wrong and dwelling on how you might have handled things differently can seem overwhelming. Do not pretend your feelings don't exist. While these emotions may be raw and painful right now, it's important to experience them and understand that they are part of a natural healing process. In time these difficult feelings will slowly pass, and you will be able to get on with your life. Talking with your domestic abuse group, working with a counselor, or having the support of a good friend can not only help you understand your feelings but also provide some needed perspective into why your relationship ended.

Try to let go of bitter feelings about your partner or ex-partner, and reject negative thoughts about getting back at her because you feel betrayed. While you may feel hurt and angry now, attempts at retribution are usually futile and can be dangerous. You know this. Those negative thoughts are not helpful. In your mind you invent different scenarios that you think will somehow make you feel better. They won't. Trying to get back at her won't make your feelings go away, and nursing thoughts of revenge gets in the way of your moving on with life.

Refrain from blaming her. She may have made mistakes in the relationship too, but if she wants to move on, honor her decision. Similarly, try not to let feelings of shame overwhelm you. You've made mistakes, but you've hopefully learned from those mistakes and are now on a new path.

In this chapter you will learn about a practice we call self-talk. You may have already tried this if you're in counseling or a domestic abuse program. You will also learn how to handle jealousy, often an intense and unpleasant emotion.

Even in relationships that haven't been damaged by violence, people sometimes drift apart. They may have different goals from the ones they first had when they got married or decided to live together. People change, and splitting up doesn't mean they have failed. However, if you feel desperate about losing a relationship, seek help from a counselor. Develop a plan to stop focusing on your former partner. Part of it may include finding new activities so you don't feel isolated. You may also try reconnecting with old friends and reaching out to people who will support positive changes in your life. Counseling and support groups can help you let go of negative feelings and move on with your life.

Self-Talk: Learning to Think Positively

Self-talk is that inner voice you use to converse with yourself. We all have it. It is part of an internal thinking process, and in some ways it's like a little recorder in our minds that continually plays positive or negative messages.

If you feel anxious, jealous, insecure, or angry, you are usually thinking negatively about a situation or person. Maybe things in your life seem hopeless. Then the tape starts playing those negative messages: "I'll never get that job; I just don't have the skills." "She doesn't really care about me; I'm wasting my time." "I'm no good; everything I do comes out bad." "I'll never be happy; I might as well stop trying." If you continue to focus on these negative thoughts and don't resolve the problem, you can become seriously depressed. And you may start taking out your negative feelings on others, especially family members.

Positive self-talk is a process of replacing negative messages with positive ones, or at least neutral ones, if overtly positive messages seem too far out of reach at the moment: "I'm a good person." "I know I'll succeed if I keep trying." "I have no reason to be jealous." "This problem—like other problems—will pass." "It's okay if I feel bad and confused right now." "I know I've made mistakes, but I need to get on with my life." You may need to repeat these statements many times to erase the negative thoughts. Learning to use positive self-talk, like most skills, takes time, willpower, and concentration.

The following is an example from our group of how positive self-talk can work. Steve's usual response to conflict was to storm around, swear, and yell. I asked him to practice positive self-talk the next time a conflict occurred and to express his anger in an appropriate manner. He agreed.

In one of the next group sessions, Steve told us about how he had used self-talk to avoid becoming abusive. He said he was angry because his partner got home late with the car, which meant that he was late for his golf game. In the past, Steve said, he would have been "all over her" as soon as she walked in the door.

> I was really mad as I waited for her. I made a couple of calls, but I couldn't locate her. I was getting more and more pissed off,

but I tried the positive-self-talk approach. Every time a negative thought came into my head, like, "She doesn't give a shit about me," I replaced it with a thought like, "There must be a good reason why she's late."

I then called my golfing partners and told them that I'd be late and would catch up with them. When Patricia got home forty-five minutes late, I sat at the table rather than rushing to the door. She was nervous when she came in because of my past behavior, but I didn't look angry—at least that's what she said. I calmly asked her where she had been. Normally I would have been screaming things like, "Don't you know I've got plans?" But I waited for her response, which was apologetic and reasonable. Seeing that she wasn't afraid of me felt good. I guess I don't have to be an asshole every time I get mad.

In another group Jerry had been making it hard for his partner, Joan, to go back to work. Maryann questioned him about this:

Maryann: Jerry, you were talking last week about how you didn't want Joan to go back to work. What's been happening?
Jerry: We've been talking. I told her I would try to be supportive, but she knows I don't want her to go.
Maryann: Did you tell her that you didn't want her to go?
Jerry: I guess I've been pretty indirect and manipulative. I tell her I'm okay with her decision, but then I tell her I make enough money for both of us. I'm sure I come off as suspicious.
Maryann: Why are you so resistant to her getting a job?
Jerry: Well, she used to work at this restaurant a while ago, and there were lots of men there. I remember that when we were dating, she would go out with her coworkers after work and have drinks and a good time. I don't know, I guess I'm assuming I'll be jealous, and we've had some rocky times, you know.
Maryann: My hope is that you would accept her decision and support her. We've been discussing self-talk the last couple of weeks. Maybe the group can come up with some ideas on how Jerry could change the negative messages he has when he thinks about Joan going back to work.

The group came up with the following ideas for self-talk:

• Joan needs to have her own life.
• She'll be happy.
• If I don't control her, she'll respect me more.
• I have my work life, and she should have hers.
• I don't need to be jealous.
• The extra money will be helpful.
• I need to remember what I've learned in the group.
• I trust her.

> **Maryann:** Jerry, when the negative thoughts occur, try to use some of these statements. If you need to, repeat them in your mind and believe them.
>
> **Jerry:** I'll give it a try.

Think about the following when negative self-talk is consuming your mind.

Things will pass: Think of a past situation when you either made a mistake or experienced negative consequences for something you did. Maybe you screwed up big time—made a mistake at work, did something embarrassing at a party, said something to someone that you later regretted. Without excusing what you did, think about how that past negative situation, over time, became less significant. Time does heal. Hopefully you learned something about yourself and won't repeat a similar mistake. When you're mired in negative self-talk, flip the thought switch that is telling you that things won't change. Switch it to a positive thought: Things will change, this will pass, I'll get through this.

Building empathy: Being responsible for your abusive behavior is hard. You've hurt someone physically or emotionally. We all cling to rationalizations for the bad or inappropriate things we've done, but if you genuinely take responsibility for your actions, you can learn from your mistakes and move on. When I've had a disagreement with my partner, I find that I need to listen to what she is saying on a deeper level. For instance, if my partner tells me that what I did or said was hurtful to her, I may need some time to reflect. I ask my partner for a little time. This isn't avoidance, but it stops me from being defensive in the moment. I use this time to think about what my partner has said. I find it helpful to think about how I would react if the situation were reversed. In other words, how would I feel if my partner said something that I felt was disrespectful of me or my values, even if the comment was unintended? This can be powerful. If you screwed up, acknowledge it and learn from the experience. We are all imperfect, but we can change.

We cannot "will" our problems away, but we also don't need to dwell on them and have them consume us. We have no control over certain things in life, but we can control our reactions to them.

EXERCISE Please complete Exercise 1, "Self-Talk and Learning to Think Positively," in Chapter 6 of your workbook.

Handling Jealousy

Both men and women get jealous. It's a very common emotion, and most of us have experienced it. Yet for some men who batter, jealousy becomes life consuming and distorts reality. A jealous man questions everything his partner does and feels: her trust, fidelity, love, and commitment. He gets jealous if she buys new clothes, puts on makeup, or gets a new hairstyle. He gets jealous if she talks on the phone, sends e-mail or texts, writes letters, keeps a journal, uses social networks, or goes out with friends. In our groups these men constantly blame their violence on their partners' unfaithfulness, even though their suspicions are often unjustified.

Especially for men who batter, feelings of jealousy are tied to a belief that they have a claim to a woman: "She's my wife" or "She's my girlfriend." Some men are possessive from the beginning of their relationships. Many battered women have told me that their husbands became extremely possessive right after they both said "I do," immediately growing jealous or suspicious if their behavior did not conform to their husband's expectations. And frequently the women had no idea what the expectations were.

Jeff told the following story in one of our groups:

Jeff: Rose and I had been arguing pretty much all night about her going bowling with this group of friends. I didn't used to mind, but there are these women in this group that I just don't trust.

Michael: Why?

Jeff: Everyone knows they're pretty loose. One of them is single and the other recently divorced, so....

Michael: So what happened?

Jeff: Well, like I said, we were arguing about her going, and I was pretty insistent that she not go. I mean part of it was her friends, but we had also been drinking, and I didn't want her to drive. When she tried to leave, I blocked the doorway. Then she tried to go out the back door, and I grabbed her by the arm and slapped her and took the keys out of her hand.

Michael: Was the real issue the fact that she'd had some drinks or that you didn't want her to go bowling with her friends?

Jeff: Both. But I guess I was mostly reacting to her being with those women. Anyway she was pretty upset. But I think on some level she knew I was right. We talked about it later that night.

Michael: What kinds of feelings were you having about her going?

Jeff: I suppose I was feeling somewhat insecure and scared, and had she gone I would have been worried.

Michael: Of what?

Jeff: That being with those women would give her ideas. That maybe she would find some other man there and sleep with him. I don't really know, except I felt insecure.

Michael: So you hit her and stopped her from going. I'm curious. Did those feelings of being scared and insecure go away by forcing her to stay home?

Jeff: That night I didn't have those feelings. But later I had them again because I knew I was depriving her of doing something she really enjoyed. So I've been thinking that Rose must really think I'm a jerk or something, and then those nervous feelings come back.

In this case Jeff used violence to control his partner and end a disagreement. He succeeded in one respect, because Rose did not go out. But looking at the long-term impact of his actions, we see that the very feelings he wanted to avoid—fear and insecurity—were intensified. He told the group he became even more jealous later. He finally accepted Rose's going out with her friends, in part because he knew she was angry at him for trying to stop her, yet he always made an issue out of it when she was getting ready to leave. Jeff also admitted checking up on her because his insecurity and jealousy were so intense.

As much as Jeff tried to justify what he was doing, he was aware of his partner's unhappiness, and his mind kept conjuring up the worst. Every time he made an arbitrary decision about her life, he imagined her thinking about leaving him for someone who would treat her better. As his insecurity grew, he became more controlling. He used a variety of threats, including the possibility of taking his own life. The abuse became an endless cycle until finally Rose left him.

Handling jealousy is not easy, but it is possible. If you continually have jealous feelings, talk to friends, practice self-talk, talk about it in your group, or see a counselor. The best way to keep from being destructive is to put the situation into perspective. Your partner's right to have friends and spend time as she wishes does not have to make you feel jealous. And if someone finds your partner attractive, it does not have to be threatening. Trust is earned and develops over time; it cannot be imposed by making demands or controlling another person.

Becoming a new couple, whether dating, living together, or married, is challenging. You and your partner may have different expectations about friendships with other people. Is it okay to have friendships with people of the opposite sex? Is it okay if your partner wants to do something socially with friends or coworkers without you? Can you accept these kinds of choices without feeling rejected or jealous? These are important boundary and relationship issues. Being autonomous (having some separateness in your life) and being attached and faithful are strong bases for a good relationship. Friendships outside the relationship are possible when there are no secrets or deception. This kind of honesty requires communication, commitment, and trust.

For men who have battered, and for women who have been battered, getting to a place of mutual trust can be hard. Because of the abuse it is likely that your partner's distrust will linger until she recognizes your changed behavior as real. In the meantime don't make demands on her, manipulate her, or try to control her. Talk about your jealousy in your group, with a counselor, or with a friend. There are no guarantees that your relationship will fully heal, but you know that repeating past controlling and abusive behavior is a recipe for failure.

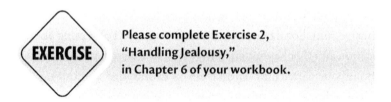

EXERCISE   Please complete Exercise 2, "Handling Jealousy," in Chapter 6 of your workbook.

Feeling Desperate? Get Help

For some men the thought of losing their relationship is unbearable. They become desperate, and their jealousy becomes an obsession. A desperate man may think about his partner all the time. He may try to think about something else, yet images of her with another person slip into his mind, setting off feelings of anger and pain. He cannot imagine living without her.

A man in this situation can be destructive and is often dangerous. We frequently read articles about an estranged husband killing his ex-wife, family members, and then himself. You've just read about a homicide in this chapter. There is a difference between feeling jealous and having an obsession with someone. If you are jealous, you may be concerned or even afraid that your partner is interested in others or that others are interested in her. Jealousy can usually be resolved through honest communication, reassurance, and trust. A counselor and caring friends can help you through this hard time. An obsession, on the other hand, is an intense preoccupation with losing your partner. These compulsive feelings and emotions are usually unwanted but frequently all consuming.

Some battered women are stalked and threatened by possessive ex-husbands or ex-boyfriends who won't let go. These women live their lives in a perpetual state of fear. To escape an abusive partner, some women decide they have to move, leaving their homes, friends, families, and jobs. And for some the terror doesn't end—surveillance occurs long after the relationship has ended. Neither divorce nor court orders seem to stop men who become desperate.

For many men reading this book, these descriptions of obsession don't fit. But for some, feeling desperate has resulted in controlling, abusive, and illegal behavior. If you find yourself obsessing about a relationship that has ended or may end, if you cannot stop thinking about your partner, or if you feel you cannot live without her, get help at a domestic abuse program or a mental health agency in your community. A counselor can help you sort through your feelings, gain some perspective, and move on with your life. Sometimes when a relationship ends, you think you'll never get through the pain. Your feelings of loss are real, and you need to grieve just as you would if someone close to you had died. A counselor can help you cope and get through this, too.

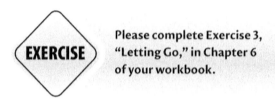

Please complete Exercise 3, "Letting Go," in Chapter 6 of your workbook.

A Note to Women

Men who are desperate about holding on to a relationship can be dangerous. If your partner or ex-partner makes threats such as, "If I can't have you, nobody will" or "If you leave me, I have no reason to live," seek help *immediately.* If he follows you, threatens your friends, checks up on you, sends unwanted letters or e-mails, or calls your home against your wishes, you could be in danger. Seek assistance from a battered women's shelter, obtain a protection or restraining order, or develop a safety plan, which may include going to a safe house or moving to a different area. Call the police and let them know what is occurring. *Never* disregard indications of a desperate man with an obsession, especially if there has been violence in your relationship.

I recognize that leaving an abusive intimate partner is never easy. You may have doubts that you're doing the right thing. You may still hold out some hope that he will change. And if you're a woman with limited resources, the thought of going it alone may seem overwhelming despite the abuse. You might look at your children and wonder how you'll manage alone. I don't underestimate the challenges and barriers that lie ahead for you as you make this decision. Please get help. Develop a safety plan with an advocate. Look at the risk markers outlined in this chapter. When and how you ultimately leave is up to you.

7

Making Changes
and Staying on Track

Our greatest glory is not in never failing,
but in rising up every time we fail.

▶▶ RALPH WALDO EMERSON ◀◀

What Traps a Woman
in an Abusive Relationship?

I first met Chuck and M'Liss Switzer in the 1980s. We had appeared on the *Sally Jesse Raphael Show* and the *Phil Donahue Show*, two national television programs that aired in the 1980s and 1990s, to talk about domestic abuse. The Switzers were there to tell their story, and I was there to provide commentary on the dynamics of battering. At the time awareness of domestic abuse was just beginning to surface around the country.

Audience members asked M'Liss a crucial question that day, one that battered women hear over and over again: "Why did you stay with him?" Battered women's advocates often turn the tables when they hear this question and respond, "The question shouldn't be why does she stay but rather why does he batter?"

Both questions are legitimate. The reasons why a battered woman stays in an abusive relationship are complex, and leaving the question "Why does she stay?" unanswered won't deepen our understanding of domestic abuse. Sometimes I'll rephrase the question by asking, "What do you think traps a woman in an abusive relationship?" People seem more accepting of this interpretation, and it is probably more accurate.

First of all, a woman doesn't set out trying to find a man who will beat her. Girls don't say, "When I grow up, I want to marry a man who will assault and hurt me." The belief that women are masochistic, that they like to be beaten, is simply a myth.

Some battered women will say they should have recognized the danger signs when they first started dating. Violent outbursts, controlling behavior, hyperjealousy, and demeaning attitudes toward women were all indications of potential problems. But for many women these signals got jumbled in with the positive feelings they had about the men they were dating.

Many women who have suffered domestic abuse grew up in violent families. Some of them say they came to believe that violence was a carefully guarded secret and was to be expected in a relationship. In other words, this is just the way families are.

Battered women have told me that when they were first slapped or punched they were shocked. They thought, "How can this be? Why is he doing this? What did I do? What should I do now?" It is this final question that frequently confounds a woman's decision making. Many people will say, "If my partner ever hit me, I'd be out the door in a minute." While some women do leave the first time they are hit, it usually isn't that easy. At workshops I often ask participants to list all the reasons why a woman might get trapped in an abusive relationship. At least forty different explanations will surface. Here are a few:

- She's afraid she'll lose her children because he has threatened to take them or gain custody.
- She has accepted his apologies and promises, and believes the abuse won't happen again.

- She feels pressured to stay married because in her religion divorce is believed to be wrong.
- He has made threats, and she fears retribution if she leaves.
- She still loves him.
- She lacks financial resources.
- Her family has pressured her to stick it out ("You made your bed...").
- She feels she's to blame ("If I hadn't done this..."; "If I hadn't said that...").
- She believes his threats of suicide.
- She doesn't think she'll ever find another partner.
- She believes the negative things he has said about her, so her self-esteem has been damaged.
- She doesn't have a support system and doesn't know where to go or who to talk to.
- She doesn't believe the police or courts will help.
- She thinks abuse is part of marriage.
- She doesn't want to be seen as a failure if she leaves.

Usually a combination of reasons—psychological, emotional, and physical—traps a battered woman in an abusive relationship. Women begin to adjust who they are when faced with abuse; they develop adaptive behavior to survive or to make the relationship function at a level that has some semblance of normalcy.

Then there is the other question: Why does he batter? When discussing a battered woman's reason for staying, we must never lose sight of who has ultimate responsibility for the violence. Many men who batter manipulate and play on a woman's fears of being alone, losing her children, being ostracized, or being further abused. Controlling and abusive behaviors are like strategies men who batter use to win arguments and get their way. Some men who batter use blatant behaviors, and others are more subtle, but the intent is still the same.

In many ways an abusive relationship is like a war in which one country has more weapons than the other. In order to exact concessions from a less powerful country, the aggressor country will make demands and threats. If this strategy doesn't work, it resorts to a show of force, hoping to prove its superiority and accomplish its objectives with minimal losses. If this approach fails, the aggressor country can unleash all its weapons, until the less powerful country capitulates—and it usually does. This doesn't mean the less powerful country doesn't try to negotiate a way out or resist the aggression. Sometimes a peaceful solution is found and the hostilities cease, but the threat of violence always exists when there is a power imbalance and the aggressor country is willing to use force to achieve its goal.

Men who use violence can stop. But battering doesn't end until intimidating behavior, threats, coercion, and the need to control also cease. Repairing a relationship damaged by domestic abuse is hard. Restoring trust takes time and may not be possible. For many battered women the memories are too painful, the anger too overwhelming. They simply don't believe that real change has occurred, or they feel the need for time alone to heal and sort things out. When battering has diminished a woman's trust and caused a loss of intimacy, she may refuse to invest the time and energy necessary for reconciliation.

Staying together and trying to work things out can also be difficult for men who have battered. Being confronted by someone who is justifiably angry about the past, living with guilt, and working to change his attitudes and beliefs create a thorny wall to climb. Some men conclude that it just isn't worth it.

This leads us back to the Chuck and M'Liss Switzer story. Chuck battered M'Liss for twenty years, but against all odds they stayed together. They are a violence-free couple today. Their story exemplifies some of the changes that are necessary for couples to stay together when domestic abuse has occurred in a relationship.

In this chapter we will explore the difficult but not insurmountable challenges for couples who want to work things out. Staying together is not for everyone. Each person in the relationship must decide what's best for him-/herself. Hopefully you will both get feedback from counselors, advocates, family, and friends on whether this is the right path for you in light of everything that has happened. But if you decide to try to stay together, the Switzers' perseverance is inspiring.

The Switzers' Story

The Switzers agreed to be interviewed for this book because of their fierce belief that we as a society must confront domestic abuse at its roots. Chuck and M'Liss have told their story numerous times on national television and in news magazines. M'Liss has published her own book, *Called to Account*.[1] She serves on the board of directors of the Domestic Abuse Project in Minneapolis. Chuck and M'Liss frequently speak to offenders who have been court ordered into counseling programs. They commit their time and energy to telling their painful story because they believe hearing it will help men who batter see that they can change, too.

Chuck and M'Liss met at Minnesota Bible College. At the time M'Liss didn't recognize that Chuck had the potential to be abusive. Chuck battered M'Liss for more than twenty years before she got help.

Chuck's Story

Chuck grew up in a rural area of southwest Missouri. He never drank, was obedient at home, and says his family had "good Christian roots."

> I had two sisters and a brother. My father was very abusive toward all of us. When he became violent, he was unmerciful. He would beat the living daylights out of us. He would allege that he'd lost something and then force us to look for it, sometimes for hours. He did this as a game, as a way to control us.

He had been in the army and must have gotten some of that mind-control stuff there. He actually ran our house like a prison camp, and we were deathly afraid of him. I'm still afraid of him. We really don't have much of a relationship today—we talk only indirectly. I did confront him on his behavior after I completed counseling for my violence, but he denied he ever did any of those things. Strangely my siblings also deny that any of the abuse took place.

My father was also very abusive toward my mother. The first incident I remember was when I was only about three. At this time my mom and dad were roughly the same size. They'd just come home from a family party. Evidently my dad had done some things my mother wasn't pleased with, and there they were, rolling around in the front yard, wrestling and throwing blows. Whenever my mom would confront my dad about issues, he wouldn't even respond verbally; he would just decide the best thing to do was to beat her up. He figured that was the way to get her to come around to his way of thinking. And I saw that happen. I got a very clear picture that violence works. It's the ultimate in control.

I think our family was as violent as a family can get. There wasn't any screwing around. There weren't any threats, they just went right into it. One of them started a conversation, they disagreed, and then they were hitting each other. There wasn't a lead-up time like you often hear about, and there wasn't any alcohol; my dad would just beat the living daylights out of my mom with his fists.

After she was beaten up, I would stay away from her. If I tried to comfort her, she would beat the shit out of me, so I left her alone until she was fully healed. I never felt any empathy for her. Violence was just part of the picture. My mom used to beat me and my siblings, and I never thought there was anything wrong with it. In our cultural stratum this seemed to be normal. The way you dealt with kids when they misbehaved was you simply beat 'em up.

I know this will sound strange, but despite the violence, I did see my parents being loving to each other. I saw them kissing and hugging. I really thought they loved each other. My parents prayed together, went to church together, and had Christian people over to the house.

The violence was part of our life. And it wasn't just my parents. My grandfather beat my grandmother. I remember one time at the dinner table at my grandparents' house, my grandmother questioned my grandfather on some farm issue, and she raised her voice. He jumped up from the table and hit her so hard she flew into the next room, and that was the end of it. I wasn't shocked by this at all—not the least bit surprised. It seemed like it was part of the culture. My cousins who lived a few farms down the road were constantly coming over to mend their wounds from beatings. That's the way things were.

I beat M'Liss from the day we were married and didn't stop until I was charged with assault. All that time I didn't think there was anything wrong with what I was doing. To be honest I got off on the violence—it was like a sugar high. My adrenaline would increase and when I was whaling on her it was really like I was intoxicated with a feeling of power. Sometimes the violence was premeditated. I mean I would actually think about being violent on the way home.

I could easily be sitting in prison for killing M'Liss—it was that close with some of the incidents. When I think back, most of the issues I beat her for were trivial, and some incidents I don't even remember why I hit her. One time I was dragging M'Liss around the house with a belt around her neck because she burned the toast. After the beating I just went off to work.

Despite what some people say about losing control, I was clearly in control of my actions. I knew exactly what I was doing. I could turn it on, and I could turn it off at will. One time I had beat M'Liss pretty severely. I mean I was in a rage, but just as I was finishing with her, I saw the neighbor come to the door. When I answered the door and talked with the neighbor, I was totally calm. I'm sure he couldn't tell that anything had happened in our house.

M'Liss fought back only once that I remember. I was disciplining our son, and she hit me on the head with a pan. I turned to her and said, "Don't you ever do something like that again."

I was giving her the clear message that if she ever hit me, I would most definitely raise the ante—implying that I might kill her, and I might have.

I was very critical of her friends. I was smart enough to know that when she started talking to other people, it brought a new dimension into our lives. I didn't want her to change. To put it crudely I bought this horse and I didn't want anyone messing with its training. The more she associated with other people, the more she would know, and I thought she would be less dependent on me. I didn't like that at all.

When M'Liss charged me with assault, I was furious and scared. I didn't believe that what I was doing was criminal behavior, but on some level I started to realize that I had a problem. I didn't want to lie about the police report in front of the judge. I went to an attorney. He told me I should plead innocent and that a jury would never convict a disabled vet on a domestic abuse charge. However, I was guilty, and I plead guilty. Being on probation was a humiliating experience. Having to report to the probation officer weekly was hard for me to accept because I'd never been in trouble with the law before.

I was ordered into domestic abuse counseling. At first I just wanted to get it over with—you know, meet the requirements of the court. Again at this point I wasn't totally convinced that I had a problem, except that I got tangled up with the courts. But after about four months into counseling and after listening to the other men, I started looking at myself. First I was in groups with just men, and then M'Liss and I went into groups with other couples. It was in the couples groups that my eyes were opened. Listening to other people's stories, especially from the other women who'd been abused—that had a real impact on me. Coming to grips with the fact that my behavior was criminal was very humbling. At about this time M'Liss had also gotten an order for protection, so I ended up living in a rat-hole apartment. I was all alone, and I wanted my life back. In order to get it back, I knew I had to take a serious look at myself.

I was in groups as a participant for years. I had stopped the violence and was working to end the other ways I was controlling and abusive. Because of my progress, they let me cofacilitate a group with a counselor. It's still difficult for me to hear about my past violence. I still feel guilty. When M'Liss reminds me of my violence and her pain, it's like digging up the garden in my head. I think the reason most relationships with violence don't make it is because men who batter can't acknowledge what they've done. When they stop using violence, they immediately want their partners to forget about it and basically forgive them. That just doesn't happen. So even today I have a hard time hearing about what I did to M'Liss. I feel like she brings up the past too much. She says she rarely does, but it's still hard for me to hear. The change process is hard and long and never totally over. It's a mind-set—that's how you change.

M'Liss's Story

M'Liss was born in St. Paul, Minnesota, and her parents divorced when she was one. After her mother died she was reared throughout much of her adolescence by her older sister, who was abusive and domineering.

My mom remarried when I was ten. My stepfather was really nice—never abusive to my mother or us kids. Two years later my mother died, and my sister became my guardian. She was really nasty to me. She ruled the roost. She abused me both physically and verbally for the next ten years.

I converted to a fundamentalist church when I was twenty-one and ended up going to Minnesota Bible College. That's where I met Chuck. We dated for about a year, but he wasn't abusive until we got married. He was in the Marine Corps and came back to Minnesota on leave so we could get married. I quit my job, moved out of my apartment, said my good-byes, and was ready for a married life with the man I loved. We were going to drive down to Missouri to see his folks and then head to Tennessee, where Chuck was stationed.

We spent our honeymoon night in a motel in Iowa. We made love for the first time that night, and I didn't have an orgasm. Chuck was furious. While he was still on top of me, he started hitting me around my shoulders and head with his fists.

When he got off, I went to the bathroom and got cleaned up. He was standing at the bathroom door apologizing and saying it would never happen again. I wanted to believe him, and I really didn't have anywhere to go, so I just let it go. I distinctly remember thinking this must be the way marriage is—so we moved on. It's clear to me now that when we got married I became a thing, something he owned.

The violence was very frequent at first—about once a week. We lived off base, and I never thought about seeking help or talking to anyone about it. You simply didn't talk about things like that back then, and there wasn't any help available. And with Chuck being in the service, I didn't want to get him in trouble. Sometimes Chuck's violence wasn't even related to me—he was just taking it out on me. Any time I was critical of Chuck or I didn't agree with him, he would beat me until I did. It got so bad that if I didn't cook the eggs right, I got beat. I even got beat for dropping a fork one morning. I took the car to the car wash and the fender was damaged, and I got beat for that. One time we went down to Sears, and he wanted to buy a lawn mower, but I talked him out of it. That night he beat me up because of what had happened at the store. Whenever he was unhappy, I got it.

Chuck is a big guy, so he was careful to abuse me in ways people wouldn't notice. He would choke me with a belt or with his hands, kick me in the stomach, or drag me around by the hair. One time he followed me into the bathroom and threw me through a glass shower door. Another time he hit me on the side of the head, which made my inner ear bleed. I went to the doctor for it, but I lied about what happened.

I know this will sound strange, but I was always afraid Chuck would leave me. He knew I was threatened by the thought of being alone, so he would use that as a weapon. He didn't use a lot of emotional abuse or put-downs that a lot of battered women experience. He would simply say I deserved the beatings because of my actions.

We were faithful churchgoers at the time—three times a week. I never talked to the pastor about the violence. I had learned that if you were getting beat you must be doing something wrong. "What are you doing that makes him so mad?" At the time I felt enough shame and blame that I believed I must have been doing something wrong. Why else would he be hitting me?

My self-esteem had always been really low. My sister—my guardian—was abusive. She had me convinced I wouldn't amount to anything, and, of course, no man would ever want me. So when Chuck wanted to marry me—well, I just held on, violence and all. Somehow I worked it out in my mind that this was the way it was going to be. I was determined to be a better wife to avoid getting beat up.

We went to a psychiatrist about ten years into our marriage. The psychiatrist didn't really understand domestic abuse. One exercise he had us do was to plan times when we would be together and tell each other exactly how we felt. Well, telling Chuck how I felt was dangerous. If he didn't like the way I felt, he'd beat me up. One time the psychiatrist told me he didn't think Chuck would kill me. That just shut me down, because I didn't feel he understood anything about my feelings or experiences. This other time Chuck was beating me, and I managed to get the car out of the garage. He came running after me, bounding over a chain-link fence after the car. I was just desperate. I went to a phone booth and called our psychiatrist at his home. I told him Chuck was beating me up, and I didn't know what to do. All he said was to call him at his office in the morning.

I warned Chuck that I would call the police if he assaulted me again. For a whole year after I made that threat, he didn't hit me. That summer we went to Canada for a vacation. We were only twenty minutes across the border when Chuck beat me up in the car. After we returned to Minnesota, we went another whole year without any violence. Then we took a trip to Missouri to see his family, and he beat me up again when we were out of Minnesota.

It was at about this time that I could see things were really deteriorating. I started getting really scared that he would hurt me even worse or maybe kill me. He'd stopped apologizing for the violence, and his self-esteem was going down the drain. He just didn't seem to care anymore.

I'd had enough. Finally, I went to the police and reported the assault. When we went to court, Chuck was getting more and more upset, worried that he would lose his job if the assault charge became public. The night before we went to court for the sentencing, he took a loaded Winchester into the bedroom and threatened to kill himself. I tried to reassure him that everything was going to be all right. I told him he needed help. He blamed me for pressing charges. Things were out of his control now, and he didn't know what to do.

In counseling we were in separate men's and women's groups, and both of us learned about battering and techniques to use like the time-out. We were both taught to take time-outs whenever we felt we were getting agitated. Whenever I started to feel uncomfortable, I would take a time-out, and we both would agree that we would come back to the issue at a later time. He'd usually respect my wishes to have that time alone.

Things were going pretty well when we were in counseling, but then there was an incident. Chuck wanted to have sex with me, and I refused. He hit me in the face. My women's group at the Domestic Abuse Project really encouraged me to get an order for protection, and I didn't want to, but I agreed. The advocate said that Chuck had to see there were going to be consequences for his continued violent behavior, even though he had been making progress. Looking back I guess she was right.

I wouldn't let Chuck back in the house until I was pretty sure I'd be safe. At first if I had an issue, I'd only go to restaurants with him to work things out, because I didn't think he'd go off on me in public. I didn't trust him for a long time. I would challenge him from time to time just to see if he would honor the time-out, to see if he would listen to me or threaten me.

I've had to let go of a lot of the pain. At some point for me, I had to make the decision that the relationship was more important to me, and I had to let go of the resentment and anger. Chuck would have to tell me he was sorry again and again to get it all healed. I didn't know if he could do that. I don't think

Chuck has been able to fully forgive himself, but we've continued to work on our issues. For me the important thing is that Chuck values my opinion, we can compromise, and he treats me respectfully. I'm happy today. I loved Chuck despite the violence. I wanted the relationship to work, and it's working.

It May Always Be a Struggle

When an individual or a group of people have been oppressed or persecuted, healing and regaining a sense of normalcy may be difficult. Resentment and anger at being harmed and humiliated are normal human responses. Yet restoration of the mind and spirit can and does occur; forgiveness is also a part of the human condition.

Reconciliation

In 2013 I attended the International Association of Women Police in Durban, South Africa. While I was there, I had numerous conversations with South Africans, both black and white, about life during and after apartheid. Apartheid was a system of racial segregation, enforced from 1948 to 1994, under which the rights of the black majority of South Africa were denied. The white Afrikaner minority maintained rule through a series of laws.

Blacks lost their land and were forced into segregated townships, prohibited from traveling freely without work passes, denied legal rights, humiliated, jailed, and persecuted. Demonstrations and resistance to this oppression were similar to those of the civil rights movement in the United States. Many people lost their lives fighting apartheid. International pressure, internal strikes, and grassroots resistance finally led to collapse of the system when white President F. W. de Klerk agreed to negotiate an end to apartheid. In 1990 Nelson Mandela, an anti-apartheid activist and arguably the most revered leader in South Africa's history, was released from prison after twenty-seven years. Four years later he was elected the first president in the post-apartheid era. He worked with other leaders to establish the Truth and Reconciliation Commission, which held hearings to gather testimony from both victims and perpetrators of apartheid. These hearings were an important part of the beginning of the country's healing process.[2]

When I was there, South Africa was preparing for the twentieth anniversary of the end of apartheid. Despite the many problems facing the country (among them high poverty and crime rates), I was struck by how welcoming black South Africans were to me—a white man from the United States. They shared their culture and talked openly about the struggle to be free and the challenges they continue to face in building a multicultural country. I wondered how black South Africans could forgive what had happened to them.

During my visit I saw the following quote from the legendary Desmond Tutu, an anti-apartheid cleric and activist from South Africa. What he said about reconciliation offers an important message about accountability, forgiveness, and healing.

> Forgiving and being reconciled to our enemies or our loved ones are not about pretending that things are other than they are. It is not about patting one another on the back and turning a blind eye to the wrong. True reconciliation exposes the awfulness, the abuse, the hurt, the truth. It could even sometimes make things worse. It is a risky undertaking, but in the end it is worthwhile, because in the end only an honest confrontation with reality can bring real healing. Superficial reconciliation can bring only superficial healing.

The last line of this quote is important: *Superficial reconciliation can bring only superficial healing.* If you choose to stay in your relationship after the violence has ended, you must understand and accept that rebuilding your life together will be challenging. Your relationship is like a home severely damaged by a tornado; to repair it, you must first fix the foundation and then restore the rest of the structure. Your success will be determined in part by whether your partner wants reconciliation, whether you've truly changed, and whether you have the commitment to work through the hard issues.

Interestingly M'Liss reported that Chuck was rarely emotionally abusive. Most battered women talk about the horrible things said to them prior, during, and after a violent attack. As stated earlier this depersonalization of the victim makes committing the violence easier for the offender. But for battered women who internalize the cruel verbal attacks, forgiveness may be difficult. M'Liss may not bear those emotional scars, but she clearly bears others. Reestablishing trust isn't easy.

Starting over fresh will have its complications. Friendships and even relationships with family members may have been strained by the violence. Even if you think the abuse was kept secret, people close to you were probably aware of what was going on. Some people may respect that you are working on your relationship. Others may be judgmental, cautious, and unaccepting; they may not trust you. Although difficult, talking about your past behavior and the changes you have made may result in a degree of acceptance from your friends and family members, and perhaps some appreciation for being honest and willing to change. Talking about the past can be a humbling experience, but it may also be therapeutic and healing.

M'Liss and Chuck went public with their experience, which has forced them to be more accountable to each other. In any relationship it is easy to get into ruts and assume that everything is okay when it really isn't. When there has been domestic abuse, not every couple who decides to stay together is comfortable talking publicly about their past. Either way, make sure you check things out with each other.

If you sense you are reverting back to old patterns, take the steps to enter a domestic abuse program or discuss what's occurring with a counselor. If you're already in a domestic abuse program, talk in your group about what's happening. If you have completed a program, maybe you need a "tune-up." Attend some additional classes or groups, and make sure you're honoring your commitment. After all the progress you've made, you may be afraid to confront the reality that old behaviors can creep back into the relationship. Deal with it before it becomes a problem.

If you're going to stay together, it's important that you support and encourage your partner. When you do, you'll see dramatic changes in your relationship. M'Liss and Chuck have learned the importance of having independent lives, and they respect each other's needs. They are honestly supportive of each other's goals, a key element of their partnership. Trust must be the underpinning of any healthy relationship. For some men this will be difficult, because they still have feelings of jealousy or insecurity about their relationships. If this sounds familiar, review the material on self-talk or see a counselor. Don't slip back into the old way of thinking.

Chuck had not been violent for seventeen years, and according to M'Liss, he hadn't been abusive in any way for two decades. Ironically a few weeks prior to our interview, this changed. I could tell this was not an easy thing for either of them to reveal to me. On their way to the Domestic Abuse Project, where they discuss their experiences with men who are ordered into counseling, they got into an argument. Chuck started swearing and yelling. It brought it all back for both of them. M'Liss said she was afraid. Chuck believes he could have become violent. He didn't, but it was close. They talked through the incident at length later that evening. As Chuck and M'Liss both admit, the potential is still there even after seventeen years, despite years of counseling and sharing their story publicly.

M'Liss says that Chuck still gets an attitude. And Chuck is clear that he needs to be very aware of his emotions:

> I'd be a liar if I said I haven't come close to being violent on occasion. A couple can learn to put the brakes on things when they escalate. For me it's like driving down the freeway at sixty miles an hour and putting on the emergency brake—the wheels lock up, the brakes are smoking, and you come to a quick and complete stop.

As M'Liss says today, "I'm usually never afraid, but there are times even now when I am."

I suppose the skeptic might ask, "How can you call this a success story?" Although Chuck hasn't hit M'Liss in almost twenty years, he admits he has come close, and she admits to still being fearful at times.

First, I think the fact that they discussed this incident with me shows their accountability. They have been and continue to be very public about their experiences. Their expectations of each other require honesty, even if it reveals embarrassing setbacks. Second, the Switzers' lives, like those of other men I interviewed for this book, are in many ways under a microscope because they have chosen either to volunteer or to work in the domestic abuse field. Their credibility can be maintained only if they are honest and accountable. Third, though I don't intend to minimize the abusive behavior and its impact on M'Liss, Chuck did exercise enough self-control not to use physical violence.

If Chuck had never battered M'Liss, the incident in the car would seem relatively harmless. Couples get into arguments, say inappropriate things they don't mean, say bad things they do mean, swear, criticize, and use put-downs. In healthy relationships this happens only sporadically. Most couples have at least occasionally thrown all rationality out the window in a fit of anger. However, when battering has occurred, arguments should be viewed from a different perspective. A disagreement that results in raised voices and power struggles often brings back old feelings, memories, and fears. This incident with M'Liss illustrates that a victim probably never forgets, and perhaps this is the way it should be. Chuck and M'Liss have both told me they don't believe you ever totally get over the past.

We spent a good deal of the day talking about their experiences. Sometimes my questions brought up sensitive areas that were still a little raw, like the recent incident. Throughout the interview I was very aware of how respectful they were of each other as they told their stories and clarified things for me. In my years in this field, I have been conned by many men who batter. With the Switzers I could see their love, their commitment to each other, and their struggle to stay together and work through the tough issues.

After four hours of the interview, we were all a little tired. We walked down the block to a restaurant and had lunch and talked about relationships, travel, and politics. I'm convinced the Switzers' relationship has been helped by their talking about the past, both with each other and with others. It is therapeutic and keeps them accountable. They also acknowledge that the violent incidents of earlier days are like ghosts—experiences that will forever haunt them and that could recur if they don't both continue to work on the relationship. I got into my car with my notes and tape recorder. As I drove away, I turned and saw M'Liss and Chuck walk up the sidewalk to their house, arms around each other. I was touched—they have taken a long and somewhat improbable journey, and they have made it.

Understanding and Accepting Women's Anger

Anger is a domain still reserved for men. In professional sports it seems perfectly acceptable for one player to get mad at—and sometimes physically attack—another. The public accepts this behavior, cheering as both benches clear in a baseball game and the players duke it out. A hockey player may drop his gloves and attempt to land as many blows to an opponent's head as he can before the referees stop the fight. Professional wrestlers feign anger to inspire the roars of admiring fans eager for someone to get stomped or have a folding chair slammed over his head. Men are aggressive in the workplace, using anger to intimidate their fellow workers. This is all part of the male world of anger, violence, and power—and sadly, it is expected and accepted.

Men are often excused for displaying anger at home. Fathers have long been expected to be family disciplinarians, with anger part of the role. When my mother's discipline didn't work, she would say, in total frustration, "Wait until your father gets home!" Sometimes she would actually call him. He would leave work furious and come home to mete out the discipline. He also perfected a glare—we called it "the look." The look meant shut up or knock it off, or you'll get it big time. That's what dads did and what many still do. In a marriage, men often use their anger to intimidate or shut off discussions. Men who batter use their anger as a warning that violence is right around the corner.

This is not to say that women don't also get angry, or that mothers don't abuse their kids. They do. When angry some women scream, yell, and lash out against their partners. The difference is that a woman's anger is unlikely to intimidate her partner or shut him down, unless he's truly afraid of her.

Men in general don't like it when women get angry. To deflect women's anger, men frequently discount or trivialize it. The following exchange is an example:

Eddie: Darcy was really angry when I got home. I was late, and she wasn't able to get to her women's group. I admit I was late, but she didn't have to get so bent out of shape.

Michael: Why don't you tell us what you said and what she said?

Eddie: Well, I went downstairs, and she was folding the laundry. I tried to explain why I was late. I told her I was helping Jerome with his car so he could get to work. Legitimate, right? So she's giving me the silent treatment.

Michael: Had you tried to call her?

Eddie: No, but I didn't think I would be that late. She just totally overreacted.

Michael: So she missed her group and was angry and wouldn't talk to you. What happened after that?

Eddie: I apologized. I hate it when she gives me the silent treatment, so I ate shit. And instead of accepting my apology, she goes off on me. She says, "You think an apology makes it okay?" She starts ragging on me about being irresponsible and purposely being late so she couldn't go to her group.

Maryann: Were you intentionally late so she'd miss her group?

Eddie: I knew you were going to ask that. No. I was just late. She goes to those damn groups every week; it won't kill her to miss one. But no, it was not intentional.

Michael: What did you say or do when she confronted you?

Eddie: I guess I just tried to loosen things up a little. I said, "Darcy, you know, you look so cute when you're mad, and you are definitely mad." Then I said, "Come on, let's just drop it and go get something to eat."

Some of the group members rolled their eyes; a few chuckled.

Michael: We'll get back to you, Eddie, but I have a question for the group. What is it about a woman's anger that makes men react defensively?

Devon: I think it may have to do with our mothers. I mean, my mom would scream and kick ass once in a while, but that was my mom. Now you've got this woman who you're intimately involved with acting like your mom and that's hard to take.

Maryann: So do you mean it's okay for your mother to have authority or the upper hand because she's your mom, but with your partner it's a threat of some kind?

Devon: I think so. I mean I would kind of feel humiliated unless I stood up to that shit. I suppose it's the macho thing—about being dominated by your woman. If she starts in, you've got to get right back in her face, so she doesn't think she can boss you around.

Michael: So it's a power thing, if I'm hearing you correctly. In Eddie's example it almost seemed that if Darcy stayed angry, she would have a certain amount of power, and he didn't want that. What about the "You're so cute when you're angry" comment?

Devon: That definitely doesn't work—it just pisses them off more. But I agree with you, I do think it's a power thing. I don't know what the other guys think, but I think men learn how to use their anger to survive. I mean sometimes you gotta look angry so people don't mess with you. And with a woman, I don't know, you just don't want your wife to be angry, so you shut her up or leave.

We had a lengthy discussion about the nature of anger and why some men try to stop their partners from feeling it. There are several ways men—especially men who batter—block their partners' anger. The following are some examples from groups I have conducted.

Minimizing and Trivializing a Woman's Anger

An example of minimizing your partner's anger is trying to convince her she's overreacting:

- "Why do you get hysterical over such little things?"
- "Why are you making such a big deal out of this?"
- "I don't know what you're talking about."

We trivialize a woman's anger by being sarcastic or using put-downs:

- "Yeah, you're right, you're always right, so now you can stop being angry."
- "If you would just grow up, you wouldn't be reacting this way."
- "You sound just like your mother!"
- "I do one little thing, and now look at you."

Challenging a Woman's Anger

An example of challenging your partner's anger is comparing something she did in the past to the issue she's angry about now:

- "What about when you _____?"
- "As if you've never _____ before?
- "You don't see me getting bent out of shape when you _____, do you?"

Another way of challenging her anger is by refusing to talk things through or turning the tables on her:

- "Well, if that's the way you feel, I'm out of here."
- "I'm not listening to this shit anymore."
- "You don't care about my feelings."
- "Maybe you should go see a shrink to deal with these problems you have."
- "If you didn't hang around with _____, you wouldn't be acting like this."

Shutting Down a Woman's Anger

An example of shutting down your partner's anger is by intimidating, using threats, or being violent:

- threatening her: "Shut up, or else"
- screaming back at her or yelling in her face
- using threatening gestures or throwing something at or near her
- hitting her
- holding her by the arms or putting a hand over her mouth

If you are going stay together, you need to understand that your partner probably has significant anger—and it's likely just below the surface. Whether your violence was constant or infrequent, the memories of being battered and humiliated are often unforgettable. Little things, conversations, and anniversaries may remind her of an argument or a beating.

M'Liss told the following story:

> Chuck had beaten me up when we were traveling in northern Minnesota because I'd left a blanket where we'd camped. It was the kind of thing Chuck would get angry about. Well, years later, when Chuck had stopped abusing me, we decided to take a car trip to Canada. When we drove by the park where he had beaten me, I asked him if he remembered beating me there, because it brought back painful memories for me. He got really defensive and asked why I was always bringing up the past. It's strange because I don't bring up the past that much, but he thinks I do.

When men make the decision to change, they often think their partners should immediately accept their assurances that they'll never be abusive again. They feel hurt and angry when their partners bring up past episodes or question their sincerity. This is the reality of domestic abuse dynamics. To be blunt, if you're frustrated by your partner's mistrust and anger, you've just got to deal with it. In the past she may have been forced to temper her anger because she was afraid you would be violent. The anger she felt during those abusive days—and may still feel today—is like a volcano, dormant for years and now ready to blow. It may not explode all at once, but periodically you will feel the eruptions. If you can understand where your partner's anger is coming from, it will be easier for you to accept it, knowing that her healing will take time.

Women who stay with the partners who abused them often test to see if they really are committed to nonviolence. M'Liss told me that after Chuck completed counseling, she would actually do things to provoke him to see if he would honor his agreement to take a time-out.

EXERCISE

Please complete Exercise 1, "Understanding and Accepting Your Partner's Anger," in Chapter 7 of your workbook.

Responding to conflict in your relationship may be one of your biggest challenges. Your past approach has probably been to react defensively to disagreements. Your body tensed up, your teeth and fists seemed to automatically clench, and you felt tightness in your chest or stomach. Your brain signaled "fight," and you got ready for whatever your partner had to say. If you were having a disagreement, odds are you didn't really listen to her, except the words that made you angry. Once the conflict started you would end it on your terms—breaking something, calling her a vile name, walking out, threatening her, or using violence.

That was the old you. If you have made the commitment to stay in your relationship, hopefully a new you has emerged. You now understand that you'll always have conflicts. At the same time you have a heightened awareness of your reactions and pay close attention to the tension in your body and the old negative messages still lodged in your mind. You remember your commitment to remaining accountable for your actions. When the conflict starts you assess the situation and determine whether you can have a fair discussion without becoming abusive. You remember and follow the rules for negotiation. If you sense yourself getting agitated or if you recognize the emotional and physical cues that precede violence, you take a time-out.

It would be so easy to forget about all this. Many men have gotten into trouble by convincing themselves that the old abusive behavior is all in the past. But as the Switzers' story shows us, after seventeen years of being violence free, Chuck came close.

It will be hard at first. Your partner may be testing you, consciously or unconsciously. When her fear has subsided, a marriage counselor can teach you all kinds of useful communication techniques. As your relationship improves, you can develop healthier ways to work through problems.

Changing the Mind-Set

People don't change the way they think overnight. Education is a process, and we should all consider ourselves lifelong learners. For our inward journey we need external information, which is why I advocate counseling, education—both formal and informal—and time for reflection.

To understand algebra, you have to take math courses for some time—in my case a very long time. First you need instruction and then time to process the information and practice what you have learned before that wonderful moment when the light bulb goes on and you say to yourself, "I get it!" Men who have battered must be willing to go through a very similar educational process.

Those who made transformations in their thinking and changed their behavior took the initiative by getting help. Even though it was difficult, they went to counseling because they wanted to understand where their beliefs about men, masculinity, women, and marriage came from. They were open to being challenged. They read books like this one. Maybe they felt a little uncomfortable with some of the content, but they were receptive to considering new ideas. Most men don't want to admit that they are sexist. I know I don't. In many ways it's similar to white people not wanting to be perceived as being racist. But as a white person in this society I have privilege, and I walk through the world very differently than people of color do. Likewise, as a man, wherever I am on earth I have privileges and benefits that women don't, even though I strive not to be sexist.

Chuck Switzer told me, "I started examining the ethics of my violence. I had to confront my attitudes and beliefs about women. This issue is about sexism. I never thought that women were equal, and it was only through the confrontation of counseling that I changed that mind-set."

"For me," M'Liss said, "it was when Chuck started listening, respecting my need to be alone when he was in a bad mood, and letting me express my opinions without trying to control me—that was when I knew he was changing. When he was truly listening to me, and we could finally negotiate as equals."

Please complete Exercise 2, "Changing Your Mind-Set," in Chapter 7 of your workbook.

Getting Your Needs Met Without
Being Abusive

Boys are taught to be aggressive. To survive on the playground, in the neighborhood, or within an abusive family system, boys are constantly being tested. They tease and taunt, give and receive insults, shove and hit each other, sometimes landing the blows and sometimes enduring them. This is a boy's world. To get his needs met and to be accepted, many boys quickly learn to fight. If they don't, they risk being bullied.

Most boys adjust to and survive childhood and adolescence, even though we all lose a bit of our innocence and some of our ability to be vulnerable and sensitive. But increasingly, boys are using violence to resolve conflict in a much different way than just a generation ago. Because of easy access to guns, the fistfight is sometimes now a bullet to the head. Rejection in school from peers or from girls can result in a shooting spree. Boys who commit crimes are consistently being tried as adults and then languishing in our prisons.

When they get out of prison, most men have a difficult time reintegrating back into society because of the psychological impact of incarceration. Being relational after imprisonment is difficult. Trust and intimacy in people are diminished, and obstacles to employment and housing are a grim reality because of the felony conviction. For African American boys and young men the situation is far worse; they are incarcerated at a rate six times that of white men. Our society is failing miserably at addressing this issue, and many in the domestic abuse prevention field also fail to make the connection between boys' childhood experiences and men's later use of violence in intimate relationships.

A man who batters often perceives arguments and conflicts with his partner as a test of wills, like the childhood tests of "manhood." In our groups men frequently claim that to get their needs met, they have to be aggressive and not allow their partners to get the upper hand. Being disrespected by a woman is not to be tolerated. During an argument they might storm out of the house, swear, refuse to talk, refuse to negotiate, threaten, and sometimes become violent. However, it doesn't have to be this way. You can be assertive without being aggressive. You can get your needs met without being controlling and abusive. You can work out your problems in a respectful manner.

Being assertive involves two key elements:

1. Having the willingness to ask for what you need without being demanding, controlling, or threatening;
2. Being able to express your feelings without attacking or shaming.

In discussing the difference between aggression and assertiveness, Tom described an argument he had with his partner, Jamie:

Tom: We got into this big argument on the way home from the Christmas party. I was upset because Jamie brought up an embarrassing issue in front of the people I work with. We've been having a long-standing conflict with our neighbors over their loud parties. Anyway I got angry and I let her know. She got all upset, and there was screaming and crying all the way home.

Maryann: So you were embarrassed by something she said. You said you let her know that you were angry. What specifically did you say to let her know you were angry?

Tom: I just confronted her. I told her, "You know, Jamie, you made me look bad by bringing up the argument we're having with the Jensens." I told her our disagreement was private business. I said, "You shouldn't have brought that up. You screwed up my whole night." And then I just told her the truth. I said, "Every time we're out with people you've got to open up your big mouth." I asked whether she was trying to make me look like a fool.

Maryann: And how did Jamie respond?

Tom: She got really defensive and accused me of overreacting. And then I got even more upset and started yelling back at her. I asked her how she would feel if I brought up some embarrassing things about her in public. I named a few of them, and the next thing I knew we were off to the races. We didn't talk for two days.

Maryann: Not to take away from how you felt at the party or on the way home, but I'm just wondering if there was another way of letting Jamie know you were upset without being so attacking or blaming. I mean unless she purposely revealed something to hurt you, which it doesn't sound like she did, it would seem like a mistake. And if that's the case, do you think there was another way of communicating how you felt?

Tom: I don't know.

Maryann: What do others think? Tom was obviously upset and maybe for good reason. Are there other ways to communicate these feelings?

The group analyzed the incident and came up with a number of suggestions. Some group members thought Tom could have eliminated the comment about Jamie having a big mouth. Others thought it was unnecessary for Tom to make assumptions about why Jamie said what she did. Some questioned his need to yell. After getting plenty of feedback, we asked Tom to role-play the conversation he had with Jamie. We asked him to communicate his feelings but delete the personal attacks. Maryann suggested that Tom substitute the "you" statements with "I" statements during the role play.

After several tries, with Maryann playing the role of Jamie, we ended up with the following:

Tom: Jamie, I'd like to talk with you about something that happened at the party.

Maryann [as Jamie]: Sure.

Tom [in a calm voice]: Well, when you brought up that stuff about our neighbors, I was really upset. I thought you were disclosing private business, and I was embarrassed that people were hearing it.

Maryann [as Jamie]: Jeez, I thought what I said was harmless. But I'm sorry if I embarrassed you. It just sort of related to the issue we were talking about—you know, neighbors with barking dogs, neighbors who are inconsiderate. I didn't realize you felt this way.

Tom: I appreciate that, but I'm not really proud of this disagreement we're having with the Jensens, and I would just prefer that it not get raised in a public forum—because for me, it's embarrassing.

Maryann [as Jamie]: Okay. I won't bring it up in public again.

Tom: Thank you.

Tom was able to be assertive without being aggressive in this role play. Of course, not every conflict would necessarily turn out this way, but you *can* express your feelings without being abusive. Had Jamie become defensive, Tom could still have remained calm while also being assertive about his need for privacy.

It might be unrealistic at this stage to expect Tom to shift to this kind of exchange with Jamie. But if Jamie and Tom choose to stay together, their methods of communication will have to change so that both parties can state what they need without being controlling or abusive. Because of the history of domestic abuse in the relationship, Jamie may still be too angry at Tom to try different ways of communicating or resolving conflicts. She may not trust his motives. She may think this is just another way for Tom to control her.

If your partner doesn't want—or isn't willing—to try new communication techniques, you would probably be wise to back off. When she's ready, she'll let you know. Trust is earned and takes time. Even if your partner doesn't want to try different approaches to conflict resolution, this doesn't mean you can't change. You can eliminate aggressive and attacking responses to issues and conflicts. You can be calm in your approach yet still assertive. Right now the change process is your responsibility. If you and your partner stay together, you can eventually work out a healthy communication pattern.

You may need the help of a good marriage counselor. As stated earlier you should attend marriage counseling only after (1) the violence and abuse have ceased, (2) you have completed a domestic abuse program, and (3) your partner feels safe bringing up topics ranging from intimacy issues to your past use of violence. Try to find a counselor who is familiar with domestic abuse issues. Tell him or her about your past use of violence at the outset. Be truthful even if it's painful. A good therapist will teach you and your partner effective communication techniques. Getting feedback from someone neutral, someone you both trust, will make your journey together that much easier.

Relationships are not easy. Even the healthiest marriage has struggles and times of uncertainty. Over half the marriages in the United States end in divorce due to incompatibility, irreconcilable differences, and people simply falling out of love or wanting something different in their lives. Divorce is not failure, but it is change. For those who can and want to stay together, I truly believe you have something very special. I hope you take good care of each other and cherish your relationship.

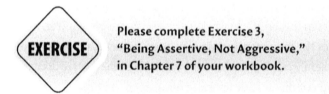

Please complete Exercise 3, "Being Assertive, Not Aggressive," in Chapter 7 of your workbook.

Taking Time-Outs

Taking a time-out means removing yourself from a potentially explosive situation. This practice may seem simplistic, and it is—but it works. However, it works only as long as you're not taking a time-out to avoid conflict or using it to further control your partner. For time-outs to be effective, you should be also be working on your beliefs about women and your role as a man in an intimate relationship. If you've read this book to this point, you might be getting tired of these continual reminders, but examining your belief system is critical to your change process. If you believe that men are entitled, that they should be calling the shots, or that on some level as a man you're better or more competent than a woman, a time-out will be counterproductive, and your partner will justifiably question your motives.

A Note to Counselors

There is an ongoing debate among practitioners who run domestic abuse groups about the efficacy of teaching skill-building practices to men who haven't changed their beliefs about women, men, and entitlement. Some programs have stopped teaching anger management techniques like time-outs altogether.

The concern raised by some in the field is that men who continue to devalue women and don't want to give up their dominant role in an intimate relationship will simply misuse skill-based techniques to further control their partners.

I share these concerns, especially for men who don't want to change. Yet for men who do want to change, time-outs, like other techniques in this book, do work. In one program I worked at, many partners of the men in my groups reported in surveys that the time-out was useful and provided a safety valve when there were disagreements and conflicts. They felt safer because of the time-out.

Like anything we teach in our groups, we can't control how time-outs get used or misused. Throughout this section I have inserted my cautions to men and women about the time-out practice.

What to Do and Where to Go

Take a time-out anytime you feel you may become abusive. Make a commitment to remove yourself from a situation that might otherwise result in your intimidating, threatening, emotionally abusing, or hitting your partner.

When people get angry, it's usually because they aren't getting what they want or because someone is doing something they don't like. Taking a time-out does not address the causes of your anger, but it does instantly provide a tool to help you avoid situations in which you might become abusive.

As discussed earlier, when you get angry or agitated, you usually have emotional and physical reactions. On an emotional level you may feel hurt, defensive, or mad. Your mind becomes engulfed with anger, and you feel an urge to vent your feelings. On a physical level you may feel tension throughout your body, your fists or teeth clenching, tightness in your stomach or neck, or a headache. These emotional and physical feelings are cues that anger and possibly violence are on the way. Pay attention to them. When you feel that you cannot express yourself in a nonabusive manner, take a time-out and leave.

You can use a time-out to get away from a potentially abusive situation, such as an argument that has escalated. Perhaps you have been thinking about present problems or past issues and feel yourself getting angry. Recognize the emotional and physical changes in yourself, listen to what your body is telling you, and get ready to take a time-out.

Here Are the Steps

First, calmly tell your partner you are taking a time-out. You may prefer to write a note or send a text. You might say, "I'm feeling angry and I need to take a time-out." By stating this clearly you let your partner know you are taking responsibility for your actions and leaving to avoid becoming abusive.

Second, let your partner know how long the time-out will last. You might say, "I'm feeling angry, and I need a time-out. I'll be back in an hour." Never stay away longer than you have indicated without calling or texting to let her know. This is so she won't be left wondering when you might return or be scared or startled when you do.

During your time-out, do not use alcohol or drugs. Do not drive. Take a walk; that's usually the best way to relax. You may also want to talk with a friend or someone from a support group, if you are in one. Whatever the conflict, use the time-out to think positively about yourself, your partner, and the relationship. Remind yourself that you are a good person, that your partner is a good person, and that, separately or together, the two of you will be able to resolve the conflict in time.

Many conflicts between partners arise over little issues that are blown out of proportion, generally because of the mood of one of the partners. When you take a time-out for what may be a minor misunderstanding, try to separate your emotion from the issue and tell yourself that your anger, too, will pass.

Sometimes, though, conflicts arise between partners because of major differences or large, unsolved issues. These might include money problems, jealousy, sex, the children, or disagreements about decisions that affect both of you. Obviously resolving these issues needs time, discussion, and negotiation. You should still take a time-out if, during discussion and disagreement, you believe you may become abusive. In this situation a walk and positive self-talk may be useful in the short term. In the long term, however, you may need to do other things to work out the problem, including setting up an environment in which negotiation can proceed fairly, without intimidation and threats and in a true spirit of give-and-take. You might also consider seeing a counselor to help you iron out the problem.

Regardless of the difficulty of the issue, take a time-out every time you recognize your cues. Let your partner know what you are doing and leave before you raise your voice or do anything else that may make her afraid.

Although I recommend taking time-outs to the men in my groups, I am also aware that some men use them to avoid working on problems. If you take a time-out every time you have a disagreement, your actions will be not only controlling but also self-defeating. Use time-outs with a constructive purpose in mind.

Time-Out Rules

1. Take a time-out when you recognize your cues and before you become emotionally or physically abusive.
2. Take a time-out when you feel that you want to become abusive or violent; do not take a time-out to avoid conflict.
3. Tell your partner you are taking a time-out.
4. Tell your partner how long you'll be gone.
5. Do not drink, use drugs, or drive.
6. Call or text a friend or group member for support.
7. Do calming exercises like walking, shooting free throws at a basketball court, or meditating.
8. Think positive thoughts. Do not dwell on the problem that caused you to become angry.
9. If you are still agitated, or if you believe you might still become abusive or violent if you go home, and you need more time than you agreed to, call or text your partner and let her know.
10. Your partner is not obliged to take a time-out; you take a time-out for yourself.
11. If your partner indicates that she is afraid of you, stay away. Find an alternative place to stay until things have calmed down.
12. When you return, do not insist that you and your partner should resolve the conflict you were having.
13. If you notice your cues again, take another time-out.
14. Whenever you follow the time-out rules, make a note of the positive way you handled the situation and its results.

An Important Note

If you are going to use time-outs in your relationship, review this section and the previous one with your partner. The time-out rules suggested above should be negotiated between you and your partner when you're both calm. You may want to practice a time-out when you are not angry so that you and your partner understand the process and each other's expectations. Your partner needs to understand the rules of the time-out so she knows what to expect.

Some programs advocate that both parties use time-outs. Usually the man has gone through a domestic abuse program and now the couple is learning techniques from a counselor. If you are at this stage of counseling, it is very important that you honor your partner's need for a time-out. Don't try to stop her if she wants to take a time-out, and don't harass her when she returns. The above rules can certainly apply to both parties.

In any relationship sometimes both people need a little time alone to sort things out when they're agitated or angry. The anger we experience may not even have anything to do with the other person. If it does, thinking it through and applying positive self-talk techniques can lessen it or at least put it into perspective. No matter how angry you feel, there is no reason to be abusive.

Please complete Exercise 4, "Taking Time-Outs," in Chapter 7 of your workbook.

8

Resolving Conflicts, Strengthening Relationships

*Seldom, or perhaps never, does a marriage develop
into an individual relationship smoothly and without crisis;
there is no coming to consciousness without pain.*

►► CARL JUNG ◄◄

People have conflicts even in the most stable relationships. How we choose to resolve our differences is frequently influenced by the behaviors modeled for us when we were growing up. For men who are violent, dealing with conflicts requires a willingness to learn new, nonabusive approaches to conflict resolution.

In this chapter you will read about developing equal relationships, either with your current partner or with a new partner. We will examine some typical areas of conflict among couples, explore how violence influences these conflicts, and consider ways to resolve disagreements in a mutually respectful manner.

Elliot's Story

Elliot explains how his attitudes about women had an impact on the way he responded to his wife, Rachel, when they had conflicts. When he came into our program, he wanted to focus only on the situations in which Rachel was aggressive. He claimed that she was frequently violent, allowing him to feel justified in his own use of violence. Elliot sees his life and his destructive relationship with Rachel differently today.

> I grew up in a rural community in Iowa. My dad was really strict, and my brothers and I tried hard not to cross him. He wasn't ever violent with my mother.
>
> I grew up believing that a woman basically had to know her place. The family was an important unit, and our values said that the man commanded the respect of his family. My childhood was pretty lousy. Dad expected everyone in the family to work hard like he did, so there wasn't much time for fun. I only went out a few times with girls in high school because my parents didn't allow dating.
>
> As soon as I graduated, I left home and went to college in Minnesota. All my pent-up frustration came out. I partied all the time. I started drinking a lot, and that's when I started fighting. I got kicked out of college, so I joined the Air Force and ended up in Vietnam.
>
> I had pretty low self-esteem. My father put me down a lot and said I was no good and would never amount to anything. I was depressed when I went into the service, and I think part of my experience in Vietnam showed that I was suicidal. Hell, I even volunteered for "door duty" on helicopters because the job was extremely dangerous. I never sought help for my depression and just used the bottle to deal with all my feelings.
>
> When I got out of the service, I started hanging around a group of people who drank and got into trouble. I was working in construction at the time. My attitudes about women weren't very good. Basically I felt women were there to be used. My thinking was that if they didn't want to play the game, then they could hit the road. There were plenty of other women. Although I was emotionally abusive, at this point I hadn't been violent with women.
>
> I married Rachel in the early 1970s. We were married for seventeen years and were in constant conflict from the very be-

ginning. I never hit her while we were dating. Both of us were drinking a lot. Both of us wanted things our own way, so our relationship was a constant power struggle.

I think I wanted to have what I knew from growing up. I wanted the kind of relationship my father had with my mother, although I didn't know it at the time. I wanted to call the shots. Rachel resisted, of course. The first time I hit her was when she accused me of looking at other women. She started screaming at me in the car and the argument spilled over into the house. She slapped me, and I hit her back. Whenever she hit me, it gave me the right to hit her back.

I have bad memories about my violence and hers, too. The way she would start things was usually by slapping me. And then I'd slap her back. I never punched her, because of our size difference. I'm sure I would've killed her. The way I would start was by picking her up and throwing her on the couch or the bed or the floor.

Sometimes when I thought I was losing a verbal battle, I would pick her up and spank her like a child. She was so much smaller than I was that I could just hold her between my arm and body and spank her.

I remember one incident when we were in Hawaii on vacation. We were arguing, and she hit me several times and then kicked me in the groin. I came up swinging and grabbed her by the hair and slapped her a few times. We fought for hours. One time we were having an argument and I was holding our son, and she tried to kick me. She was going to try to kick me again, so I started to leave and slammed the steel door. She put her arm out to stop me, and her arm got crushed. I didn't intentionally try to hurt her. I took her to the hospital, and she had some tendon damage.

I took her to the hospital another time, too, but I was so drunk I don't remember what happened. I only know that she had a head injury after I threw her. I thought the hospital officials were going to call the police because I told them what I'd done, but they didn't. When they released her, we just drove home. That was the end of it for then.

I controlled Rachel in a lot of ways. I was the breadwinner and she wasn't working, so she had to come to me for money. She would feel humiliated having to ask for it. I'm sure I withheld money as a punishment. It was easy to intimidate her. I would hold my fist up and threaten to beat her up. When she was sober she would cower, thinking I'd punch her. If she was drinking, it didn't seem to scare her. I would call her a bitch because she hated it. I'd compare her to other women as a way to put her down. I'd imply that she wasn't living up to my standards.

Our son, Robbie, saw a lot of the violence. When he was around, I would try to do or say things to blame his mother for the violence.

A couple of times I took a gun from the house and left, hoping that she'd see she'd pushed me too far. I wanted her to think I might kill myself. Well, I guess she did, because she called the police, and they took all of my guns. When I first came into the program, I couldn't seem to focus on me, it was always her. I quit the program and went into alcohol treatment. Then I came back into the program because I wanted the violence to stop and to get a handle on my life. But I realized by that time that my relationship wasn't going to work.

I'm in a new relationship now and have been married to Angie for two years. I don't have the desire to control her. I know who I am. I don't want the power I wanted with Rachel. I don't need to win when we disagree.

The most important thing that happened to me in this program was that people listened to me and didn't call me a no-good son of a bitch. It was the first time that people seemed to care. The counselors told me that I had a life to lead and that I could make changes. It was a revelation.

I try to apply some of the tools I learned in the program. I take time-outs and try to use self-talk when I feel myself going back to old patterns. I'm much more aware of my feelings. Angie and I make decisions together, although I guess I still see myself as head of the household. I think it's more of a perception than reality. I guess there's still some male stuff I need to look at—like when we get into the car, I'm always the one to drive.

I still meet with some of the guys from my group to work on things. I've come a long way, and I feel good about that.

Elliot describes his relationship with Rachel as a constant power struggle. Many forces kept them in their destructive and unhappy relationship. Elliot's belief that he is the head of the household in his new relationship shows that he still holds on to old beliefs about the roles of men and women, despite the groups and programs he has been through. However, he maintains that his life is different today and that his change is an ongoing process.

New Relationships, Old Problems

Elliot made a decision not to get involved with someone immediately after the breakup of his marriage. He wanted to work through some of his problems. Many men, however, get into a "rebound relationship"—they become involved with someone new right away. That way they don't have to fully experience the pain and grief of losing a relationship or confront the hurt they caused their previous partner.

In our groups a man in a rebound relationship will often report how everything is great with this new woman and how she doesn't have the same defects that he believes his former partner had. This is a common trick of denial. Comparing his past relationship with his present one allows him to subtly justify his past abusive behavior.

When men who batter jump into rebound relationships, they usually do not take the time to sort out the mistakes of the past. Because they aren't experiencing major conflicts in their new relationships, they don't believe they need to make changes. In the early dating stages of any relationship, we are usually on our best behavior. We want to make a good impression. We try not to reveal our flaws, and we may overlook warning signs in the person we are getting to know, because we want to give this new person a chance. Some people are starved for companionship, so they allow a relationship to move forward despite the internal voice telling them to slow down.

The problem for a man who has battered is that he often reverts to familiar ground. Once he feels that this new woman is "his," he starts seeing her as his possession and tries to control her. He might begin slowly so as not to chase her away, and she is flattered that he wants to spend so much time with her ("He must really love me"). She may be unclear about the controlling nature of his behavior ("Don't all men want to feel like they're in control? What harm could it be to play along for now?"). When his controlling behavior escalates and she resists, he uses what has worked before—threats, intimidation, and violence—to overcome her resistance.

Some men who batter look for women they see as vulnerable and then turn on the charm or pretend to be enlightened about gender issues; they really haven't done the hard work to change their beliefs and attitudes. If this seems familiar, please consider your motives and the harm you may cause both to the woman you're getting involved with and to yourself.

If your relationship has ended, take some time before you get involved with someone else to work on the issues that have led to your violence. As Anthony explains below, giving yourself time to sort things out can have positive results. You don't have to wait as long as he did for a new relationship, but the point he makes is important.

> I thought about getting involved again after Vickie and I split. I had a lot of chances, but I'd been violent with two women and didn't want to do it again. I kept going to the group. Then I went to a support group so I could keep working on my issues. It was five years before I really believed I had come to terms with all this stuff. Now I'm in a really good relationship, and I'm glad I waited.

Participating in counseling or a domestic abuse group can be helpful. You do not have to attend many sessions, and being there doesn't mean there's something psychologically wrong with you. A few sessions in which you're honest with yourself and others can be valuable.

Sorting out your prior response to conflicts and clarifying your old beliefs about women and relationships will help you know what to be aware of. If someone had filmed an argument between you and your partner and played it for you now, you could undoubtedly pick out exactly where you made mistakes and how you could have handled the situation differently. This is the kind of insight counseling and groups can give you. Here are some issues you may still need to work on:

- confronting your possessiveness and jealousy
- being abusive during an argument
- believing you're entitled because you're a man
- listening to your partner without getting defensive
- letting go of always needing to be right and having things your way
- trying to be less critical
- negotiating fairly
- finding ways of being more intimate
- practicing communicating without being controlling

The thought of living alone can be scary. However, living alone does not mean you have to be lonely. Meeting new people, connecting with old friends, and finding interesting activities can enrich your life. If your finances require it, you could choose to live with friends or find a roommate. The important thing is to *take your time.* Work on your problems, and make sure you're confident that you will remain nonabusive before entering a new relationship.

Egalitarian Relationships

In egalitarian, or equal, relationships, couples forego traditional gender expectations. Women who have been in relationships in which there were bitter and divisive struggles around gender roles and equality often want new role definitions and freer, healthier interactions with their new partners. They are quite clear about what they expect and what they are willing to accept. Similarly a new consciousness is emerging in a growing number of men. They see egalitarian relationships with women as a path to liberation rather than as a loss of control.

What do I mean by "liberation" for men? Here are some examples. Egalitarian relationships permit men to go beyond feeling *obliged* to share in child care; they're free to *want* the responsibilities of shared parenting and the rewards of being involved fathers. In egalitarian relationships, men encourage and support their partners when they are pursuing new careers or community involvement. These men are less likely to feel threatened by their partners' aspirations because they see that mutual development, growth, and support from each other enhances their partnership.

Such relationships were not common in my youth, and I suspect this was true for many of my generation—the Baby Boomers. My mother assumed the traditional female role. When she did enter the job market, her position with my father changed, because she became less dependent on him. Whether you're a Baby Boomer, Gen Xer, or Millennial, gender roles remain confusing.

Men in our groups frequently claim to have equal relationships. But as we begin to discuss roles and household responsibilities, a different picture usually emerges, as in the following exchange:

Michael: Lloyd, you say that you and Patty have an equal relationship. Tell us how that works.

Lloyd: Well, I think it's pretty equal. I do a lot of the yard work and stuff with the car, and she does most of the housework.

Michael: So you mow the yard once a week, and she does the cleaning, cooking, and child care.

Lloyd: It's not like I'm forcing her to do this stuff, but she's better at a lot of it. Look, I've tried to help out when she asks, but she's never satisfied with the way I do it. I mean she doesn't like the way I fold the towels—you know they have to be folded into three perfect sections. So she doesn't want me to do the laundry. And let's face it, most women can cook better than men, so she does that. With child care—well, she's the mother. It's not like I don't help out, but there are certain things she can do better than I and certain things I can do better than her.

Some of Lloyd's explanation may be accurate. Patty may want to assert control over the household areas she feels are her domain. When a woman doesn't have much power or many options, she will want to hold on to areas in which she has some control. In other words, she looks for a niche to call her own.

Some men in our groups admitted they do a sloppy job folding laundry, cleaning, or cooking on purpose so their partners will perceive them as incapable of doing these chores. Feigning incompetence is an old childhood strategy that worked while growing up, so why not use it now? An assortment of movies and sitcoms reinforce the stereotype of the incompetent male in the household. Living up to limited expectations allows men to avoid responsibilities.

Yet today many men realize the importance of an equal partnership. They have examined failed relationships and now see how their definitions of roles for men and women have served as obstacles. In these past relationships, conflict over unfair role definitions and work distribution took the place of friendship and intimacy.

Because egalitarian relationships can be uncharted territory, you may stumble along the path and experience confusion. Commitments to making the relationship work and to communicating needs and expectations are critical for success. We have all the tools we need to make an equal partnership work; we just need to use them.

The Equality Wheel, shown on the following page, was developed by a group of battered women and staff at the Domestic Abuse Intervention Project.

As you can see, an equal relationship has many elements. Consider this wheel from time to time. Are you relating to your partner in a manner that reflects the positive elements of the wheel? If not, review the Negotiation Guide, which appears later in this chapter, and practice some of the exercises in your workbook, especially

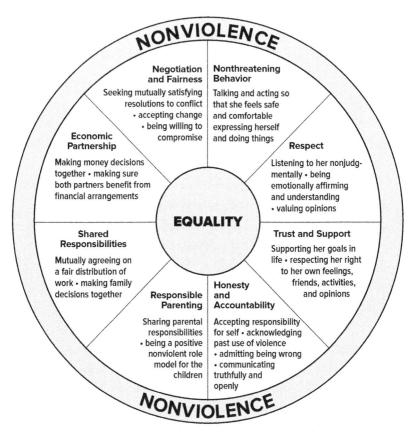

Equality Wheel

Exercise 3, "Reaching a Compromise," to get back on track. The Equality Wheel is also reproduced in Appendix A of this book.

Sharing the Load

While society has changed considerably in the last generation, the division of labor in many homes has not. The majority of families today cannot survive on one income, and both men and women must work. Yet in many households, women still do the majority of the cooking, cleaning, laundry, and child care. Arguments often occur when women express resentment about this unequal workload.

Men who think they're doing their share because they take out the trash and occasionally do the dishes are being unfair. Some men in our groups say they don't care about the cleanliness of the house or the preparation of a good meal for the family in the same way that their partners do. They are taking the easy way out. Their partners typically grow weary of the constant battle and reluctantly take on the bulk of the household responsibilities. These men often describe their partners as "nags" who are always "bitching." In one group Henry discussed an argument he'd had with his partner, Carly.

Henry: This woman is really something, man. I mean last week, almost every day she's on my ass. She says I don't help out enough. I swear, it's like living with my mother sometimes.

Michael: Does this woman have a name?

Henry: Yeah, Carly.

Michael: Men often say that if a woman is upset, she's nagging and bitching. To me those terms are used to discount women's anger.

Henry: Shit, it's getting to the point where you can't say anything anymore.

Michael: Would you ever say a man was nagging or bitching?

Henry: Let's just say she was in my face.

Michael: Okay. So she was in your face because she feels you aren't doing enough around your home. Is there any truth to what she is saying?

Henry: Ever since she went from part-time to full-time at the hotel, she expects me to do all this extra stuff at home. I work hard all day. I know she works hard, too, but cleaning rooms isn't as stressful as being a steelworker.

Michael: So even though she's working full-time, you expect her to do all the household stuff too?

Henry: You're starting to sound like her. Look, if she asks me to do something, I do it.

Michael: It's obvious you're going to continue to have conflicts around this, Henry. I mean if she has to ask you to do your part, I'm sure she'll be resentful. Is there any way you can sit down with her and figure out a plan? You know, kind of divide up the responsibilities?

After lots more discussion, Henry admitted that the position he was taking wasn't fair. He agreed to sit down with Carly and work out a plan to share the load.

When we speak about sharing the load in an egalitarian relationship, we're not talking about something like cutting an apple in half, everything fifty-fifty. Some people think equality means you do the dishes one night, and I'll do them the next night; you clean the house this week, and I'll do it next week; you take the kids to soccer this month, and I'll do it next month; we take turns paying bills and going grocery shopping. Egalitarian relationships don't have to be that rigid.

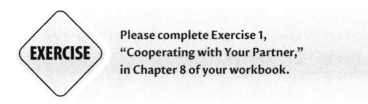

Please complete Exercise 1, "Cooperating with Your Partner," in Chapter 8 of your workbook.

Couples who become dissatisfied with their division of responsibilities but don't express it to each other can become resentful. If these feelings are not communicated, they tend to spill out during other disagreements. So it's better to deal with this issue directly, clearly, and fairly.

As you and your partner complete the exercise, you may find additional issues that need to be dealt with. One partner may also try to hold on to certain responsibilities for a reason. For example, parents often disagree about disciplining children, making them do chores, checking their homework, setting boundaries and curfews, and making other parental decisions. If one partner holds on to a greater share of responsibility for the children to influence these decisions, you need to address this as well.

Whether you and your partner have lived together for months or for years, take time every so often to make a list of your responsibilities. Talking about and changing these responsibilities can be an important and perhaps relationship-saving exercise. By looking at each other's needs and listening to each other's concerns, you pave the way for healthy negotiations about problems that have not yet surfaced. You may have to reevaluate the way you share responsibilities, but you will find the journey to true partnership that much more rewarding.

The Issue of Money

There's an old saying: "Money is the root of all evil." Money causes people to react in strange ways. Nations go to war over it, corporations use questionable practices to maximize earnings, and individuals go to jail trying to steal it. We work the majority of our lives to make enough of it to survive—and couples often disagree about how to spend it.

We live in a money-driven, market-oriented society in which we need income for the necessities of life, and most of us feel we do not have enough. The pressure to make money to survive affects everyone. So, of course, it's a source of stress in even the healthiest relationships.

Our views about money are shaped by our upbringing. If you grew up in a household with limited resources, most likely that has had an impact on how you deal with money. If you saw your parents scrimp to get by, you might be doing the same. Or you might try to do the opposite, even if you don't have the resources. If your family had money, you may have received very different messages that affect your attitudes about spending and saving.

When I grew up, my parents went from having nothing to reaching middle class, the American dream. Even though our family had greater opportunities than some families today, when we received our weekly allowance, my mother always reminded us of how hard my father worked for every dollar. When I became an adult, I adopted an attitude of "You can't take it with you," partly in response to my parents' worrying and my own feelings of guilt. Yet as much as I tried to get away from my upbringing, my parents' voices still echoed in my mind. Consequently I sometimes have been overly concerned about not having enough money or have dwelled on financial problems.

When you enter into a relationship, you and your partner have to decide together about spending and saving. If your priorities and values are different, you can have conflicts. In some traditional relationships, men believe that they should make the major decisions about family finances. (The stereotype of women having no control over their spending is still prevalent.) Even in relationships in which the woman also works outside the home, a man may assume decision-making responsibility, because he believes that men are smarter than women when it comes to handling money—and this control usually gives him more authority in the relationship.

Victims of domestic abuse often report that, besides the fear of threatened violence, what kept them locked in an abusive relationship was their lack of financial resources.

In one of our groups Frank related the following story about money:

> When we got married, we didn't really talk about money. Jackie wasn't working at the time, so I obviously was supporting the family. I would give her some cash every week to buy groceries and have a little spending money. When she went back to work and started making her own money, we had all kinds of fights, because she felt she should be able to spend her paycheck any way she wanted. She wasn't making very much, but I thought her pay and mine should be put together. I guess I was suspicious about what she was doing with the extra money, because I started accusing her of having affairs and planning to leave me. That's when the physical violence got really bad. Jackie got a protection order, and now she wants a divorce.

The experience of Frank and Jackie is not unusual. It took a long time for Frank to understand that Jackie probably felt humiliated and dependent because she had to ask for a few extra dollars to buy something for the children or herself. Though he finally acknowledged this, he refused to let go of what he believed was a fairness issue, making statements such as "Women are just out to screw men." His hurt and anger about Jackie's leaving kept him from seeing how his violence had affected her and how he had used money to control her.

When the discussion of economic control came up in our groups, men would frequently say that they "gave" their paychecks to their partners, so women really had financial control. When group members discussed fights over money, they told stories similar to Rick's:

> **Michael:** Rick, you were talking about an argument about money you had with Angie last week. You said you think she's always blaming you for the amount of debt you both carry. Do you think she's really blaming you, or is it just that she's concerned about your financial situation?
>
> **Rick:** I understand her concern, and I realize she wants to get a handle on our expenses. I mean I don't like to be in debt either. But she uses a very blaming tone when she brings up things she says we didn't need to spend money on.
>
> **Michael:** Why do you say that?
>
> **Rick:** Well, she usually mentions the things that *I've* bought or says that *my* priorities aren't right. Like she'll say we shouldn't have gotten the motor for the boat, even though she knows how much I like to fish, and that I charged a bunch of tools at Sears that we're still paying for. Yeah, I think she brings these things up in a blaming way when we get into it.
>
> **Michael:** You said earlier that you understood her concerns and that you also have concerns about your debt. Can you see any way you could resolve this?
>
> **Rick:** I don't know. It seems that whenever we talk about it, we usually end up fighting.

The issue of money in relationships is complex. When two people become a couple, do their funds become one? If one person makes more money, is that person entitled to a greater say in how it is spent? Who gets to decide?

There are no rules for dealing with money issues. Couples have to sit down and decide what feels fair to them. Each needs to consider the forces that shape the other's beliefs. The goal should be to reach a compromise. Remember that one aspect of partnership is a commitment to make tough decisions together respectfully and fairly.

Most of us have money problems at some time in our lives. For many, living from paycheck to paycheck is a reality. Others are unemployed or underemployed and have extremely limited resources. Regardless of your circumstances, working together with your partner to make ends meet will be more productive than if you're fighting with each other about finances.

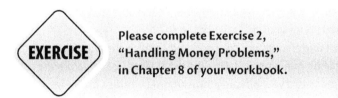

EXERCISE Please complete Exercise 2, "Handling Money Problems," in Chapter 8 of your workbook.

Expressing Feelings

I remember observing a men's group and noticing a "feelings" chart on the wall that listed about a hundred emotions. The group leaders said they used it because the men in the group had a hard time identifying what they were feeling. I thought, it's come to this—men can't even tell anybody how they feel, so we need a chart?

As men we know exactly how we feel. We may have many feelings at once, which can be confusing, but we know what we are feeling. Most of us don't like to talk about our emotions because it makes us vulnerable, and, as discussed earlier, vulnerability in men is considered a sign of weakness (by some).

The following discussion took place in one of our groups:

Dan: Barbara asks me questions sometimes about our relationship, and I just kind of freeze. My responses are usually vague. I know she wants me to say more, because she keeps asking me questions and seems frustrated. She says we don't communicate.

Michael: This seems to be a common theme. Why is it so hard for men to communicate?

Lance: I think it's upbringing. When I think of the way we played, us boys as compared to my sisters, it was totally different. My sisters would talk and talk about their friends. They would be really upset if they got into arguments. I could never understand how they put so much time and effort into sorting things out in their relationships with other girls. For us guys, hell, if you got into a fight with another guy, you just said, "Fuck him," and moved on with your life.

Michael: That's kind of sad, isn't it? Do you think that upbringing stuff has an impact on our relationships today?

Dan: It's partly upbringing. Barb always wants me to go deeper with my feelings. I don't know if I'm afraid to go deeper on an emotional level or if I'm afraid to be that vulnerable, especially with a woman.

Michael: You think you'll be hurt?

Dan: Maybe. I just wouldn't know where to start or how to do it.

Frank: I think part of it is that you don't want to hurt her. You know, I wasn't very happy in our relationship but was hanging in there for the kids and stuff. If I were really honest, I'd hurt her. I think men can express themselves but choose not to.

Michael: Does anyone else think that men choose not to share feelings?

Frank: I can't speak for all men, but I think they do. I know in past relationships I would purposely not talk to her, to keep her guessing.

Michael: Keep her guessing?
Frank: Sure. She never knew what I was thinking about her or the relationship. I always had the upper hand. Kind of a control thing.

We see that the reasons men don't express their feelings are varied. For some men it's a fear of vulnerability, for some it's confusion, and for others, like Frank, it's a way to control their partners. Many men who batter have an easy time expressing feelings after committing a violent act. Some cry and ask for forgiveness. This expression of remorse is often sincere, but at times it's simply another tactic a man uses to avoid taking responsibility for the violence or to calm his partner's anger.

Men in our society are conditioned not to express certain feelings. Most men can remember a childhood experience when they were told, "Stop crying, be a man!" The problem is that the more men repress their inner feelings, the more difficulty they have expressing themselves in intimate relationships.

In one of our groups Carlos talked about a painful childhood memory:

Carlos: I remember coming home from school one day feeling like shit because some of the kids were picking on me and I'd started to cry. I must have been about seven or eight. I mean this was big-time humiliation. I went home and my parents knew something was wrong, so I told them what happened. My dad just said I shouldn't take any crap from them, and now it's only going to get worse because I showed them I was weak. My mom wasn't much better. She said she'd call the school if it happened again.
Maryann: What did you *want* them to say?
Carlos: I just wish they'd let me know they understood.
Maryann: What would have happened if they had asked you how you felt?
Carlos: My parents weren't like that with me and my brothers. You know they had the idea that it's a rough world out there

and you gotta be tough. I think they meant well, but I'll never forget how alone I was with all that stuff.

Most men can relate similar boyhood experiences of being all alone with their feelings. In most homes with fathers, the dad takes a detached role, believing he is providing good modeling for his sons. Would it have been so difficult for Carlos' parents to ask, "How do you feel about it?" Or, "I bet you feel pretty lousy, don't you?" It would have been much better for Carlos if his parents had acknowledged his feelings or at least let him know that they understood.

Parents usually do what they think is right. They prepare boys to become men—but what are the criteria for becoming a man? "You have to be ready to compete, because it's a dog-eat-dog world out there." "You have to be ready to kill, because your country may call on you to fight in a war." "You have to be ready to win, because men are failures if they lose." "You have to be in control, because men are supposed to be powerful." These messages leave little room for emotions that aren't tied to winning, fighting, and being in control.

The problem is that for our own survival, we men often repress our feelings, but they don't go away. Men's explosive anger (an emotion generally understood and accepted) is usually primed by these other, submerged feelings. Many men use alcohol or drugs to numb other emotions, but the effect is usually temporary.

As Sylvie states, you never know what to expect with a man who holds his feelings back and then explodes:

> Living with my partner was like living under siege. He would beat me up about once a month. It was almost like things would build and build within him. He usually wouldn't tell me what was going on inside. But I could almost predict when all this rage would end up with him battering me.

What should men do with the feelings they experience? What do you do when you feel insecure, overwhelmed, scared, or unhappy? We need to find appropriate and positive ways of expressing these feeling to friends and family members and especially to our partners. Talking is a good start. It might not release all pent-up emotion, but it decreases feelings of isolation and lets others offer their support.

Repressing your feelings is unfair to your partner, because she doesn't get to know the real you. As your current relationship gets healthier, or in your new relationship, you will need to make decisions about your level of intimacy. Being in touch with your own feelings and caring about your partner's feelings are an important part of this.

You may think that not showing emotion or talking about your feelings makes you stronger or puts you in control, but in the long run it affects your mental health and increases the possibility of explosive outbursts. We all have fears, experience pain, get frustrated, and feel insecure. Denying your feelings robs you of fully experiencing all that life has to offer—the good and the bad, the joy and the pain.

One last note: Expressing feelings can sometimes be counterproductive. There's a difference between talking honestly about what is going on in your life and using your feelings to manipulate your partner. For instance talking about how you feel jealous or insecure about your partner going out with a friend *to keep her from going somewhere* is controlling. Though you should be able to talk to her about these feelings, if your intent is to make her feel guilty and not go, you are still trying to impose your will on her.

Learning to Negotiate and Compromise

How do we settle conflicts? Throughout history, world leaders, mediators, counselors, and peacemakers have grappled with difficult issues and tried to reconcile opposing views. From children on the playground to presidents of great countries, people argue, debate, and quarrel. There will always be disagreement in relationships, yet conflict doesn't have to be hurtful, and people certainly don't have to resort to abusive behavior to make their point.

A fair way to resolve conflicts in a relationship is to agree on guidelines for discussing difficult issues. For men who have been violent in the past, this is crucial. The following is a fifteen-point guide you and your partner can use to help you resolve problems fairly and respectfully.

Negotiation Guide

1. Regardless of how angry or hurt I feel, I will remain non-violent.
2. If I disagree with my partner's position, I will still be respectful.
3. I will remain seated during our discussion.
4. I will not yell, scream, or use my voice in an intimidating manner.
5. I will not threaten my partner in any way.
6. I will not use put-downs, call my partner names, or be sarcastic.
7. I will not bring up past incidents to prove a point.
8. I will avoid blaming or shaming statements.
9. I will try not to get defensive.
10. I will listen to my partner's position without interrupting.
11. I will commit to working toward a compromise.
12. I will be willing to explore my own issues and take responsibility for my mistakes.
13. I will respect my partner's wishes to end the discussion.
14. I will be honest.
15. I will talk about my feelings but will not use them as a way to manipulate my partner.

Couples have spontaneous disagreements in restaurants and movie theaters and at the homes of friends and family members. It is usually better not to try to resolve conflicts over difficult issues in public, because with others listening you can't talk frankly. On the other hand, for some couples a public setting is the best place to talk things through. One couple told me that discussing an issue at a restaurant worked for them because they didn't want to risk the embarrassment of raising their voices in public. If you are in counseling, you might want to have your discussion with your counselor present.

Before discussing the issues you disagree about, both of you should agree on a good time to work on the problem. Make sure you have enough private time without interruptions from kids, business, or phones. One of you should state your position without being interrupted, regardless of how long it takes. When that person is finished, the other starts. Remember the Negotiation Guide!

After you have both had an opportunity to talk about your position, try to see where you are in agreement. Can you find a way to compromise? Remember, if you're stuck, there's nothing wrong with getting help from a counselor.

Some disagreements can be resolved quickly; others are more complicated and may bring up painful issues. Avoiding them is not the solution. You may not resolve anything right then, but you can begin the work.

If you are still in a relationship with a woman you have abused, she may not want to work on the same issues as you do. She may not trust you very much, she may still be angry because of the abuse, and she may be confused about her feelings. The following discussion occurred in one of our groups:

> **Bob:** I don't get it. Jessie always wanted me to talk more with her. You know, talk about my feelings. Well, now when I want to, she either doesn't want to or gets pissed.
> **Michael:** What do you do?
> **Bob:** Nothing. I let it go. But I'm getting frustrated. I mean I feel like I'm making changes and I want to work on our relationship, and she's resisting.
> **Michael:** You know, Bob, you really need to give Jessie time.

After all that's gone on you can't just expect your partner to adapt to your agenda. When a woman is healing after being abused, a lot of feelings can come up for her that she hasn't been able to express, including anger at the man who hurt her. You need to give her as much time as she needs.

Arguing fairly takes two people who are committed to working things out. Bob has been learning things in the group and wants to work on the relationship. Jessie may or may not want to work things out, but either way she's clearly not ready to talk about it. The Negotiation Guide is useful only when both partners are willing and prepared to engage in a discussion.

Regardless of how your partner responds, you can still commit to using the principles of the guide. Because of your history of abuse, it's important that you set high standards for yourself. If your partner says something hurtful or inappropriate during a discussion, it isn't necessary for you to match her. Once you take that step, you're starting down the slippery slope of not caring what you say and do, and you may become abusive.

Settling differences requires three basics:

1. the desire to listen to the other person
2. the willingness to compromise
3. the strength and commitment to work things out, no matter how difficult

Sometimes we're so convinced of the correctness of our position that we build walls around ourselves. Or we may be hurt by what the other person is saying, and our response is to hurt back. Being able to truly listen to someone is a skill worth having. It takes practice and determination.

On certain issues it may be difficult to compromise. You may have to leave things alone for a while. And not everything is open to negotiation, as we see in the following group discussion:

Maryann: Art, you said last week that you had a disagreement with Ginny about her going back to school. You said you worked out a compromise. What happened?
Art: Well, basically we agreed she would wait until we were in better shape financially before she went to school.

Maryann: When will that be?

Art: As soon as I get the raise I've been promised. Maybe next year.

Maryann: And Ginny is okay with waiting? You said before that this has been a long-time issue with the two of you and that she really wanted to go back to school.

Art: I think she was disappointed, but after we discussed the pros and cons, she basically agreed with my position that we couldn't afford it right now.

Maryann: So you're saying there were no alternatives, like school loans?

Art: I don't want us going into that kind of debt. I mean she doesn't even know what kind of degree she wants. She just wants to go back to school. There's no way I want to be saddled with several thousands of dollars in school loans.

Art believed he and Ginny had worked out a compromise. He was convinced that he was being rational, but really he had just put up a roadblock that was impossible for her to go around. The following week Maryann followed up on something Art said:

Maryann: Art, you said that you're insecure about your relationship with Ginny. Why do you feel this way?

Art: I don't really know. It's like sometimes she acts kind of distant or something.

Maryann: Do you think it might have something to do with how you've treated her?

Art: Yeah, I guess it could.

Maryann: In what way?

Art: Well, I'm not sure, but you've heard some of the stuff that happened before I got sent here. I was kind of rough on her. So when she says she wants to go back to school and then get a job, I think she might not want to stay with me. I mean it's like she doesn't believe I've totally changed.

Maryann: So if she starts taking classes, she might meet someone else?

Art: The point is we've agreed that we just can't afford her going back to school right now.

The fact that Ginny accepted money problems as the reason for their decision doesn't mean she and Art had reached a fair compromise. Compromise does not mean that one party has to sacrifice what they want in order to accommodate the other person's wishes. If you follow the points in the Negotiation Guide, you should be able to resolve conflicts in a way that respects each partner and takes into account the impact on your relationship of the decisions you reach together.

Change in a relationship can be scary. Taking a different job, going back to school, joining a club, or pursuing new friendships can become problems if one partner feels threatened. For men who have been violent and are still in a relationship with the partner they abused, their feelings about such changes may be even stronger.

A man who has been abusive in a relationship is used to getting his way. As men we have all been socialized to compete and win; this impacts the way we disagree and argue, especially with women. Part of your journey must be a willingness to let go of always calling the shots and always needing to win. This is not easy. As boys we are expected to compete and succeed. Remember the coach's refrain, "Winning isn't everything, it's the only thing"? For many men, this was our experience as boys growing up in this culture. And to lose to a girl was the ultimate humiliation.

Charlie told the following story in one of our groups:

> There was this big girl in our fourth-grade class, and she would get into a lot of fights with girls and with boys, too. One day I remember getting egged on to fight her. We really went at it, and I think I fought her harder than I'd ever fought a boy. She ended up pinning me. For weeks I got shit about getting beaten up by a girl. It was the worst humiliation.

Much of this book deals with the use of violence to control intimate partners and settle conflict. When girls are growing up, they are socialized to work out problems in very different ways, and their verbal skills are usually more developed than boys' because

of this expectation. So in adult relationships, some men feel threatened when they think they're losing arguments or can't clearly say
what they're feeling and thinking. It is at this point that a man will
often resort to behavior he knows will provide leverage in resolving the disagreement. Yelling, making threats, being intimidating,
name-calling, walking out, and using violence can bring about a
quick end to an argument. But as most men who batter eventually
come to realize, this behavior has consequences. If you've made the
commitment to be nonviolent, you have to find a fair process for negotiating and resolving disputes with your present or future partner.

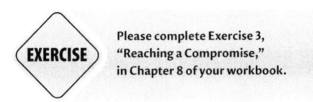

EXERCISE

Please complete Exercise 3,
"Reaching a Compromise,"
in Chapter 8 of your workbook.

Having a Fair Discussion

The Fair Discussion Guide is another tool that is primarily for you.
You can also share it with your partner. She may agree that this for-
mat could be useful to resolve problems. *If you are still in a relationship with the woman you've abused, don't pressure her to use this guide.*

Fair Discussion Guide
Before you begin:
Review these guidelines together and add any that you both decide
are important.

1. Acknowledge that a good discussion needs two people who are
   ready to talk. Don't force a discussion.
2. Reminder: You know each other's weak spots. Don't use them
   to hurt your partner.
3. Before you begin a discussion, you must first be committed to
   a fair process.

4. Define the problem—it may be different for each person. What is negotiable? How does each person perceive and define the problem? Who else will be affected and how?
5. Agree to deal with one issue at a time.
6. Agree on how long you want to discuss the issue—you don't need to resolve everything in one sitting.

Try to:
- Listen. Try to understand what the other person is saying.
- Hear things you disagree with or find painful without reacting defensively.
- Use "I" statements, like "I think" or "I feel."
- Take responsibility for your past actions.
- Be honest.
- Be willing to apologize or state that you are willing to work on an issue.
- Encourage your partner to take equal time to present her position, as well as time to change her mind.
- Work toward a mutually satisfying solution.
- Accept that some things may need to change.

Try not to:
- Interrupt when your partner is talking.
- Raise your voice (for men who have battered, you need to be especially careful with your body language, tone of voice, looks, rolling of eyes, etc.).
- Blame your partner.
- Bring up the past to make your point.
- Walk away from the discussion.
- Make threats.
- Use other people's opinions to make your point.

Before you end the discussion:
- Each person should try to summarize what was stated.
- What was agreed to?

- What have you personally committed to?
- What still needs work?
- Can you agree to short-term and long-term goals?
- What needs to be part of an immediate and then a final solution? If a compromise is needed, list several long-term solutions you both think are fair.
- How did you feel about the discussion process, and what improvements would you make in the future for it to go better?

All of this may seem difficult at first. Your habitual reaction to conflict may be to simply lash out. If someone says something you don't like or does something that makes you angry, you're ready for battle. But if you're reading this book, you know there must be a better way. The exercises and guides in this book really do work if you use them consistently—not just once in a while. At first, trying to use the rules and suggestions in the Negotiation Guide or Fair Discussion Guide may seem a little awkward. But when you resolve a conflict using these tools without being controlling or abusive, you will feel better about your partner, yourself, and your relationship.

Developing a
Personal Responsibility Plan

You've now made the commitment to be nonviolent and nonabusive, but how will you make sure that you're putting into practice what you've learned? A Personal Responsibility Plan can help you stay on track.

A Personal Responsibility Plan has three parts:

- **Commitment:** What are you willing to commit to doing differently?
- **Accountability:** How and to whom will you be accountable for past and future behavior?
- **Assessment:** How will you evaluate the progress you have made?

Commitment

If you have read this far and completed the exercises in your work-book, you have already evaluated many of the situations in which you were abusive to your partner. By now you recognize that you always had alternatives to violence. You acknowledge that you've made some bad choices and wish you could go back and change history. Obviously you can't. But what happens when similar issues and conflicts come up today, especially if you're staying with the woman you've battered? How will you deal with disagreements? How will you interact with her without being abusive and controlling? How will you manage the negative emotions that may be just below the surface? Who will you turn to when you need help staying non-violent?

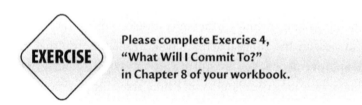

EXERCISE

Please complete Exercise 4, "What Will I Commit To?" in Chapter 8 of your workbook.

Accountability

Mahatma Gandhi said, "It is wrong and immoral to seek to escape the consequences of one's acts." If we are serious about making amends for past behavior and want to ensure that we don't repeat past mistakes, we have to do more than just apologize.

If you have battered your partner, accountability means you are answerable to her, to children who observed your violence, to people who have been affected by it—including friends, family, and counselors—and to yourself. This can be hard.

Promises that the behavior won't happen again are not enough. To be accountable the person who caused the harm must take certain steps to ensure that the behavior won't reoccur. This requires a plan and is an important process. Even if you make efforts to be accountable, your partner may still have a healthy dose of mistrust. Give her time, and make these commitments because it's the right thing to do.

Please complete Exercise 5, "Being and Staying Accountable," in Chapter 8 of your workbook.

Assessment

How will you evaluate whether your changes are making a difference? How will you know if some of your actions have had unintended consequences? You will need to get some honest feedback. But before talking to your partner or counselor, you need to have a way to measure the things that have changed and the areas that still need improvement. If you are still in a group, ask your counselor or facilitator how long you should wait before assessing your progress. Some men may want to assess their progress every three months; for others, a six-month assessment period makes more sense.

This assessment is for your benefit. If your partner doesn't want to participate, honor her request. If she does participate, you may hear things that make you feel uncomfortable. Remember your commitment. Trust the feedback you are receiving. This is a long-term process, and despite your efforts, everything you want to happen won't just magically occur.

Please complete Exercise 6, "Assessing Your Progress," in Chapter 8 of your workbook.

If you are still in your domestic abuse group, you might want to review your assessment report with your counselor or other group members. It is important to generate some ideas for how you might improve in certain areas, so feedback is valuable. If you seriously and genuinely adhere to the three components of a Personal Responsibility Plan—commitment, accountability, and assessment—you will not only realize notable changes, you will also have a sense of security that your life is heading down the right path.

9

Healing

I'd like to get away from earth awhile
And then come back to it and begin over.

►► ROBERT FROST ◄◄

In this chapter you will read about men changing: getting and staying healthy on many levels. We will also examine issues related to staying accountable in relationships, talking with your children about your violence, and keeping your commitment to living a nonabusive and nonviolent life.

Dave's Story

Dave grew up in a violent home and was abusive in most of his relationships with women. After going through substance abuse counseling, he made a commitment to get the help he needed to stop using violence. He also volunteered to participate in the Domestic Abuse Intervention Project. He went on to work with chemically dependent people and run a group for abusive men.

> The first time I saw someone getting hurt was my mom getting beaten by my dad. He punched her in the head, kicked her, and pulled her across the floor by the hair. I was five or six at the time.
>
> There was a lot of violence in our house, involving uncles, aunts, and parents. Usually it was when people were drinking. I'm sure that stuff shaped my thinking. It's strange, though,

because my brother saw it too, but he never used violence. My parents' verbal message to us was not to be violent and to treat others with respect—especially your elders. But that's not what I saw. They told us to never talk about the violence at home because it was a family matter.

My dad would whale on us kids. He worked for the railroad, and he would kick us with steel-toed boots. I remember him standing over me after he beat me and saying, "I'll kill you, you little son of a bitch." And I think the only reason he stopped was because he just got tired.

I always wanted to be accepted by my dad but never was. Whenever my mother tried to stop him from beating us, he beat her too. I remember sitting with her, and both of us were crying. I asked, "Why can't we move out?" She said, "Things will be okay," but they never were. I've always been angry about my childhood.

My partner, Lori, and I grew up in the Duluth area, but we ended up in Chicago. I was twenty-five and she was only fifteen when we moved in together. I was drinking a lot. Lori provided the things I needed—a clean house, someone to make my meals, and sex. Although we had set up house, we weren't really that committed. I didn't want to get married to her, but the relationship was convenient.

The first time I hit Lori was when we first started dating. Even though we both had other relationships, I still saw Lori as mine. When I drank, I would end up fighting with guys who were showing an interest in her.

I told Lori I didn't want her friends coming over to the apartment unless I was there. The fact that other men were interested in her became an obsession with me. Sometimes I almost goaded her into telling me about her feelings toward other men. It didn't matter what she said—it was always wrong.

It was almost a sadistic thing, like I was a military interrogator with a cigarette in his mouth. With her being only fifteen, I was able to manipulate her with my questions. I would be in a good mood and ask her questions about men, and she would think it was okay to tell me about past relationships or men that she still found attractive. Then I would slap her. She would cry, not understanding what I was doing. I would hit her and apologize and then start the whole process over again. I must have slapped her at least two dozen times one night.

The abuse got worse. I moved from slaps to punches and even hit her in the stomach when she was pregnant. My violence included pulling her hair, pushing her, and kicking her in the back when she was down. Early on I never hit her in the face, because I didn't want to look bad to family and friends.

She knew I was a perfectionist, so she always kept the house perfect, even with three kids. And while she wasn't that beautiful, she had an incredible body. Sometimes I would look at her and think this is someone I really want to be married to. Other times I would look at her and just glare.

I never trusted people, especially women. I always thought that women tried to get men to look at them or make a pass at them even if they were attached or married. I remember one time Lori was in this bowling league, and she wanted to get a new outfit. I went with her to the store and helped her pick out this really sexy top. She had such a beautiful body, and I told her how great she looked in it and that she should get it. Eight hours later I was saying, "You son of a bitch, I saw the way you were crossing your legs." Then I accused her of wearing provocative clothes even though I had picked the clothes out.

Lori never really fought back, except sometimes she would kick at me when I had her down, and sometimes she would throw things at me. When that happened I would really nail her with my fists, or I would kick her square in the ass. If she tried to run from me, I would kick her in the back.

I was always able to get Lori to forgive me. I guess I had a gift for talking, because I would say, "Things are going to be better," and be really sensitive, and then this smile would come over her face and she would say, "I know that wasn't really you."

When I look back on my violence today, I realize I really wasn't out of control. I knew where to hit her. I would try not to hit her face. A lot of times I would have Lori pinned in a corner or be on top of her with my hand around her neck, but I always knew when to stop. I would blame my violence on the alcohol. I would say things like, "You know what I'm like when I'm drunk."

Toward the end of the relationship she would say things like, "Why don't you let me go home to my parents? You can see the kids anytime." When she talked like that I would get really nervous, because even though both of us were unhappy, I didn't want to be alone. I would promise her things, like that we would get married.

The more I thought she was going to leave, the more controlling I became. I would check the phone bills to see how many calls she was making and to where. And then there was this neighbor friend of hers I was really suspicious of, because I thought she was telling Lori things. I would tell Lori I didn't want her to go over there anymore. If she was talking on the phone, I would stand in the doorway and glare at her or look at my watch and then question her after she hung up.

I'd go up to her just like my dad did to us. I could scare the hell out of her. Actually at that time everyone was afraid of me because they'd seen me going off on people, and as small as I was, I would beat the hell out of anyone. At home I would slam my fist on the table and there would be instant quiet. It gave me a certain feeling of power. I would just look at her a certain way and get what I wanted, and I liked that. I got to watch any program I wanted. Lori was always trying to keep the peace, just like my mom. She would always ask me what I wanted, and I liked that feeling.

I would call her a whore, slut, cunt, and a goddamn pig. I knew which words hurt the most. The worst was calling her a goddamn pig. I would say, "Look at you, you goddamn pig, you ugly son of a bitch, who the fuck would want you? Go look at yourself in the mirror!" She would start crying and say, "How can you say you love me and say these things to me?"

The worst incident I remember was when we were living in the Twin Cities and the family was there—her mom and stepdad and my dad. I had been in a car accident several weeks before and my leg was in a cast. She had decided that she wanted to be away from me for a while. Anyway I thought she was getting mouthy because her mom was there. When her family started to leave, I got up, grabbed Lori, and threw her down. I started whaling on her in the same way I would fight a man— ready to kill. I was on top of her, punching her everywhere about twenty times, until her dad managed to pull me off. That was probably the scariest incident.

She finally left me and moved back to northern Minnesota. I moved to California. I would call her and ask her to come back to me. One time when I called, she hung up on me. That day I flew from San Francisco to Minnesota and slapped the hell out of her. The cops came and took me away, although I was never charged with anything.

When I moved back to Minnesota I was still drinking pretty heavily. I went out with two other women for a little while. One I beat up and the other I didn't. Then I entered treatment. I met Carol after treatment, when I was getting my life together. I opened up a carpet-cleaning service, and we moved in together and things were going really well. I even told her about my past abuse.

I hit her once, and she said if I ever did it again, she would get an order for protection. She had been battered before and made it clear to me she wasn't going to put up with it again. Carol was afraid of me. I would drive the car really fast, which would scare her. She would be screaming, "Stop the car!" but I wouldn't. Carol finally got an OFP [order for protection].

I started to go to these abuse groups partly because I wanted Carol to see that I was ready to make some changes. The longer I was in the program, the more I changed. But we broke up anyway.

I knew I had to make a lot of changes. I needed to let go of my jealousy. In my relationship now, I accept that Kris has her own life and her own friends. I'm also more supportive of her and willing to listen to what she's saying, instead of just reacting.

Quitting alcohol and going through treatment forced me to look at myself. I've started to focus on my good qualities—

kindness, gentleness—things women I dated said I had, even though I never believed them.

I really feel okay with who I am. I've changed the way I think about men and women. I used to believe that women were supposed to be submissive, and I picked women who would be that way. But I'm not like that now.

I remember in group this counselor said, "If nothing changes, then nothing will change." It sounded strange, but it made sense to me, because I needed to change.

We go back into the past not to relive it but to find out about stuff that still gets in the way. I've told Kris about my past. I still take time-outs when I need to. Once you've battered, you always have to remember what you're capable of doing.

When I talk about my past, I usually say, "Once a batterer, always a batterer." And I don't mean that in a negative way, like you can't change, but it's like being an alcoholic. I still go to AA. I also use an inventory that I got in my domestic abuse class to monitor how I'm responding to Kris when we're having a conflict. I ask myself whether I listened to her side of the story without interrupting. Was I honest with her? Did I blame her? Basically am I being a respectful man? I do this because it's so easy to backslide. I still work on the things I learned years ago—taking time-outs, letting go of the need to control things, accepting who I am.

The most rewarding thing now is to talk to other guys who are abusive about what I've learned and tell them how I've changed and that they can too. It keeps me healthy. It's a long process, but you can never stop.

Dave's Story Years Later

I sat down with Dave five years after our initial interview. I wanted to find out what had happened in his life, what obstacles he'd had to overcome to remain violence free, and how he viewed his life today.

Dave worked in the chemical-dependency field and conducted classes for Native American men who had battered. He had been married for six years when I conducted this interview.

I first asked Dave whether his past use of violence had had an impact on his children.

On Talking to His Children about His Past

My kids are adults now. They've all had experiences with chemical dependency and domestic abuse. My two girls have been in abusive relationships. Even though we've talked about what it was like for them growing up in our household and how their lives have been affected by my violence, they've made some bad decisions, just like I did. My daughters have both been in treatment. I keep talking to them about substance abuse, but they aren't ready to make the changes to get sober.

But Joe, my son, he's sober now. For a while he was having problems with his girlfriend. I talked with him a lot about the choices we make and being respectful in relationships. We've talked about what he saw growing up—me hitting his mother. He understands how it might have affected him, and he can see that he's being abusive, even though he hasn't hurt his girlfriend physically. I try to use my life and the things I did wrong as a way for my kids to learn. I do what I can to help them. I wish I could erase what happened in the past, but I can't. I can only be there for them now.

On His Current Marriage

I have a great marriage today. The only problems Kris and I have disagreements about are issues with her kids. They live with us. A lot of it has to do with adjusting, and her children don't always respect my privacy. But I talk about it with Kris, and I can see that sometimes I overreact. I have a friend who's a counselor, and he gives me good feedback. It helps to talk about how I'm feeling instead of holding it in.

Kris has been in an abusive relationship before, so she's pretty aware of things. We talk a lot, checking things out. I've always been kind of jealous, and even though I've worked really hard on changing, I still get jealous with Kris. Sometimes I find myself asking her where she's going and feel like I still need reassurance from her. But I don't get jealous like I did before, because I feel so different about myself today. I'm so much more self-confident.

I'm not a young guy anymore. I'm sixty! And for Native American men, we don't live that long, especially in my family. So I decided that I want to have the best possible life. Having a healthy relationship with Kris is very important to me, so I want to make sure she's happy. Also being in recovery helps. I try and live by these words [Dave points to a framed saying on the wall in his office]:

"And acceptance is the answer to all of my problems today. When I am disturbed, it is because I find some person, place, thing, or situation, some fact of my life, unacceptable to me. I can find no serenity until I accept that person, place, thing, or situation as being exactly the way it is supposed to be at this time. Nothing, absolutely nothing, happens in God's world by mistake. Until I accepted my alcoholism, I could not stay sober. Unless I accept life completely on life's terms, I cannot be happy. I need to concentrate not so much on what needs to be changed in the world but on what needs to be changed in me and in my attitudes."

I use this saying in my work with men who batter because even though it deals with alcoholism, it applies to domestic abuse and relationships. It's hard for men to accept that they can't change their partners.

On a Close Call

There was one time when I came close to violence. We had gotten into an argument over our kids' problems. Kris put one of my kids down, and I got furious. I called her names and swore at her. On a scale of one to ten, with ten being a total rage, I was pushing a ten, but I had enough self-control not to hit her. We talked about it later, and she said I looked pretty scary. I apologized and never blamed her. But I know my capacity for violence is still there, and maybe always will be there. That was the only time I came close to being violent again.

On Making His Relationship Work

Almost every day when we get off work, Kris and I have coffee and discuss our day. We talk about money, the kids, work, our relationship—we make sure we have this special time. This is very different for me. In the past it was hard for me to communicate, especially talking about my fears and insecurities. I kept everything inside.

I try to live my life in a way that keeps me in balance. I like that Kris and I are equal, and I like the way we communicate. I try to take care of myself emotionally and spiritually. I'll go to a powwow as part of my spiritual life, and I try to keep learning things by reading. I still go to AA. I've had heart problems, so I try to keep healthy physically, although this is an area that could stand some improvement.

On Men Changing

In my work with men, whether it's in a substance abuse or domestic abuse group, I am always saying that recovery means change—and for change to happen, things must be different. Sometimes the change doesn't all come at once, but as long as there's even a little change, there's progress. To do this I had to change and keep changing. I'm happy in my life today. This discussion five years after our first interview has been hard, because my life is going so well, and I don't think about my own situation in the way I did before. But remembering the past shows me how far I've come—and I'm proud of that.

In 2007 Dave passed away after suffering heart failure. I attended his funeral and was struck by the impact he'd had on his community. I knew Dave for many years, first when he was a volunteer in my domestic abuse group. Later we developed a professional relationship when he became a chemical dependency counselor and a mentor to Native American men who were abusing their female partners. He joined the board of directors of the Domestic Abuse Intervention Project. From time to time I think about his remarkable journey. I was honored to be his friend.

Health and Balance

Healing is the process of making ourselves whole—restoring our physical, psychological, emotional, and spiritual health. Our bodies and minds are fragile. Some things are beyond our control: war, illness, poverty, persecution, victimization, accidents, and genetic makeup. We can escape or survive some of them through prevention (through the choices we make) and intervention (getting an education, medical help, therapy, advocacy). We are given a short time on this earth, and when we're given a second chance, we have to embrace the opportunity.

I first learned about the idea of living in balance and harmony from a Native American man named Marlin Mousseau. Marlin grew up on the Pine Ridge Indian Reservation in South Dakota and now works with abusive men in Wisconsin. He developed Project Medicine Wheel, designed to help abusive men in the Native American community understand their use of violence, to motivate them to live in harmony and balance, and to use traditional Indian ways of healing.[1]

Marlin states that an individual is made up of four essences: emotion, body, spirit, and mind (the intellectual side). If one of these areas is off, the person is out of balance and is not living in harmony with the world. I think men are frequently out of balance. Unfortunately we have little guidance or support for changing our unhealthy habits. The following are some thoughts on living in balance, adapted from Marlin's four essences:

The Emotional Side

Men in our groups often say they don't know how to talk on a truly emotional level. This is because like many men, they've been socialized not to talk about their feelings. Gradually they become afraid to show their true self, and their emotional side becomes disconnected from the whole. The longer men avoid expressing their feelings, the harder it becomes to change.

Occasionally I have chosen to withdraw in an intimate relationship by withholding my feelings or not talking about what's going on in my life. Sometimes I'll give just a hint of what's wrong. Every time I hold back, there's a consequence. I become more distant and the relationship suffers.

Men need to open up emotionally. We need to talk about what we're really feeling, and not just with our partners but with our friends, too—both women and men. People usually want to talk about their lives on a less superficial level, but don't think they have permission to. We feel that if we open up, our friends, family members, or partners will think there's something wrong with us, that we're too needy or self-absorbed. Talking on a deeper level takes practice, and it isn't a one-way street. You must also genuinely care about what the other person is saying, thinking, and feeling. Your concern and response will be reciprocated. You can just be there for each other without having to solve each other's problems.

The Physical Side

We would all benefit from being active, staying in shape, and putting the right nourishment into our bodies, but we often resist. Many of us are out of shape, which usually leads to physical problems as we age. Men often ignore health problems and overwork themselves, thinking they are invincible.

An exercise routine takes discipline. Exercise is not only good for the body, it is also emotionally uplifting. Yet there always seems to be something else to do or some excuse. I've often left work feeling I had absolutely no energy to exercise. All I wanted to do was go home, watch something mindless on TV, eat, and go to bed. If I force myself to go to the gym or for a run, I almost always enjoy the exercise and feel reinvigorated and glad I made the effort.

Balancing your physical side also requires monitoring what you put into your body. We hear how important it is to eat a healthy diet and eat in moderation, yet we frequently ignore the advice. Men especially think they can abuse their bodies without consequence.

Many men think that cancer or heart disease will happen to some-one else or that there's always time to change.

Go to the Internet or get a book for advice on maintaining a balanced and healthy diet. Eating more fruits and vegetables and less dairy, red meat, and sugar, reducing your intake of processed and fast foods, and eating in a balanced way will keep you healthier. You don't have to be overly rigid at every meal, but once you've eliminated certain foods from your diet, you won't miss them. Losing those extra pounds will make you feel better about yourself, too!

Some men continue to smoke despite the extensive medical evidence that tobacco use causes heart disease and cancer. They engage in unsafe sex even though they know the risks of AIDS and other diseases. They drink to excess and consume dangerous drugs regardless of the physical and psychological effects. Some men believe they are indestructible. Don't make these mistakes. Choose to care about yourself instead!

If you are not involved in an exercise routine, commit to one now. Join a Y or an exercise club and find a routine that feels good and is fun. Buy some running shoes and walk, jog, or run. Play basketball, racquetball, soccer, baseball, or tennis. Lift weights, go biking, dance, practice yoga, or join a kick-boxing class. As the saying goes, just do it! Working out at least three days a week will keep your weight down, increase cardiovascular endurance, and make you feel better.

The Spiritual Side

When I mention the spiritual level, I am not referring to attending services at a church, temple, mosque, or other place of worship, although that may be where you find spiritual connection. Being spiritual can also mean getting in touch with the world around you. This feeling of connectedness can occur through meditating, walking in a park or in the woods, or sitting by a creek. Some people pray, chant, sing, or listen to music as a way of finding a source of spiritual light.

Several years ago I went to a retreat where I learned about meditation. We were asked to focus on the impermanence of life and the limited time we spend on the earth. I remember feeling sad during this meditation, a sadness that had much to do with my own feelings at the time. I was confused about the pain in the world and wondered about the purpose of my life. I had no answer. Today when I think back on that time and the focus on impermanence, I understand the message: In the short time we are here, we need to live our lives with significance and purpose. We do not necessarily have to do something earth shattering, just live with more compassion and love.

Although it is an important lesson, I often forget it. I choose to live a spiritually unbalanced life because the world around me seems so cold, unloving, and angry. The collective pain of families and communities spills out all around me. I easily become withdrawn, and I insulate myself by becoming cynical, self-absorbed, and uncaring. When the pain I see in my work overwhelms me, I know I am spiritually out of balance, and I know it's by my choice.

When I choose to slow down, put my life in perspective, and take the steps to reconnect with what is really important, my connection to the universe around me is strengthened. I often find this renewal in the woods, near a lake or river, in the mountains, or in the sky on a starry night. We can all find our peace.

The Intellectual Side

On the intellectual level, many of us men have a difficult time being open to new ideas. We get locked into a certain way of thinking and refuse to hear opposing views. Listen, for example, to other men discussing politics or even sports. The debate becomes almost warlike, with each person determined to win. I'm not suggesting that we be afraid to debate or give up principled positions. But when we refuse to listen to other ideas, we become hardened and cynical.

You don't have to be a rocket scientist to nurture your mind. Simply be open to information and ideas. Allow yourself time to reflect. To broaden your intellectual horizons, take a class, read books or newspapers, join an organization in which ideas are shared, or volunteer in your community. A couple of the men I interviewed for this book went to college and got their degrees.

The vast array of technology at our disposal and our constant use of social media have made life more complex and less personal. It seems like everyone is glued to their electronic devices, feeling compelled to see who has communicated messages, comments, and news. Our political discourse has become increasingly toxic; people don't have to take responsibility for comments they can make anonymously. Our news media are highly partisan; programs speak to their political base without a thoughtful analysis. We can choose to be lifelong learners with curiosity and openness about new ideas, or we can settle for sound bites about our community and the events in the world.

Staying in balance is not easy. I am frequently aware of being out of balance. I remember going through a stressful time after I moved from Duluth to the Twin Cities. I left a relatively small town, friends, and familiar territory for a large metropolitan area. I was emotionally drained. I lacked motivation, and my habits changed. I stopped exercising and became depressed. I finally went to a counselor to sort things out. On an emotional level I needed to address my grieving about the move. On a physical level I needed to develop a plan to take better care of myself, which included exercise, rest, and a good diet. Slowly I worked my way through the depression.

Learn to recognize when you are out of balance, and figure out ways to make healthy changes. Embarking on lifestyle changes is hard, and the results are not instantaneous, but you *will* notice a difference. And it's worth it.

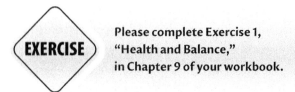

**Please complete Exercise 1,
"Health and Balance,"
in Chapter 9 of your workbook.**

Dating: How Much of the Past Do We Reveal?

Many men who have battered and are now starting a relationship with a new partner don't tell her about their past abuse. Although the reasons for this reluctance are understandable, it's important to be honest in this situation. Chances are she will eventually find out anyway. Telling her about your past is a way of being accountable. She may be surprised and alarmed by your admissions, but she may also respect your honesty. Some women will decide they don't want to be in a relationship with someone who has battered, and some women will decide to see if you've really changed. Your new partner should have the opportunity to let you know if she senses you are becoming abusive. She should have the right to insist that you make changes or seek help.

Peter described his experience:

> When I told Lydia about my past, I was scared she was going to run. She seemed a little shocked at first, but I think she really trusted my commitment to nonviolence. Once I made the decision to tell her, I knew I had to be totally honest about everything. Afterward I felt incredibly free—as if a ball and chain had been removed from my leg.

Being honest about the past can be hard and sometimes humbling, but it's a way to measure your commitment to honesty and accountability. Many men who have told their stories in this book have indicated that staying violence free is a lifelong commitment. They must be continually aware of how they interact with women to avoid backsliding into past abusive behavior.

The following discussion about honesty in a new relationship took place in one of our men's groups:

Daniel: I don't see why I need to tell Tanya about my past relationship with Jill. It's over. I want to get on with my life.

Maryann: What do the rest of you think?

Matthew: I told my Abby about my battering. In fact, I tell her what I learn in these groups. She was a little surprised when I told her, but I'm glad I did. I don't want to repeat what I did to Molly. I mean I really want this relationship to work. I'm committed to being honest about everything with her, and her knowing about my past will help keep me honest.

If you are in a new relationship, you and your partner will be exploring each other in many ways. When you tell her about your past abuse, she may not tell you all she's thinking or feeling, and it may take time for her to sort through her reactions. It wouldn't be unusual for her to be concerned or even test your commitment to nonviolence. Your awareness of her need for caution can help establish trust in the relationship.

If you are living a violence-free life with a woman, check in with her from time to time about how you have handled certain situations, especially conflicts. For instance after a discussion you might ask if she felt afraid at any point. Ask if your body language or voice was intimidating, so you can correct that behavior the next time you disagree. During one of our discussions, Don said:

It's important for me to know if Connie is at all scared of me or if she feels I'm getting close to past behaviors. She's told me on certain occasions that she's withdrawn or backed off because she could tell I was getting irritated. It didn't feel good to hear that, but I need to know about it if I'm going to keep changing.

Talking to Your Children about Your Violence

Children often assume the blame for things that go wrong in their families. I remember my parents having a big argument late one evening. I strained my ears to hear if it had anything to do with us kids.

My immediate thought was that I had done something wrong. My next thoughts focused on whether my parents might get a divorce. I kept thinking how I might intervene. At six I felt responsible for making things right between them.

In families in which there has been violence, children feel enormous responsibility and therefore guilt. And it is in these families that parents are unavailable, leaving children nowhere to turn and no one to talk to.

Some research indicates that in families in which there has been domestic abuse toward a spouse, the risk that the children have been abused is higher than usual. If you have been abusive to your children or think your discipline is becoming abusive, seek help from a mental health center in your community.[2]

Some of the men I interviewed for this book indicated that they talked with their children about their violence. Their motivation was to apologize and offer assurances that it wasn't going to happen anymore.

Look for an appropriate time to talk to your children, but never force them into talking. They may not be ready, and the experiences they have had with you and your violence may be too fresh and painful. They may not feel safe with you, and pressuring them to talk could cause further harm.

If you talk to your children, be honest. Explain that what occurred in the past was your responsibility. Reassure them that they were not to blame. Let them know that you are taking steps to change and that your past abusive behavior was wrong. Admitting your violence to your children will not be easy, but they will respect your honesty even if they can't tell you so.

When you make the decision to talk with your children, never talk about your abusive behavior in a way that implies your partner or ex-partner is equally responsible. In no way should you blame her. Too many parents have done grave damage by trying to get their children to take sides with them against the other parent.

Remember that your children may not be ready to have this discussion. Smaller children especially may feel uncomfortable. Do not pressure them. It is far more important that they see the way you're acting now. Also, be sure not to promise that your violence will never happen again, especially if you're in the beginning stages of your change process.

Mental Health

By reading this book you can see that you're not alone. Life is hard, and we all have challenges. Sometimes it seems like we just can't see the light at the end of the tunnel. I know the despair that many men have felt. Dave, whose story you read at the beginning of this chapter, hit bottom many times because of his alcoholism and his violence. Yet he knew there was more to his life than self-destructive behavior. He knew he had the capacity to love, and he wanted to be loved back. He made the commitment to change regardless of the hard road ahead.

Many men in my groups have co-occurring conditions, meaning that they have more than one serious problem at the same time: substance abuse, depression, and domestic abuse, for example. You might not be able to deal with these problems by yourself. While I know people who have quit drinking or drugs on their own, most people need help, whether it's going to AA, getting chemical dependency treatment, or working with a mental health counselor who is experienced with addiction. Don't go it alone if you need help.

Men often have a difficult time coping with the loss of a relationship, getting arrested, being on probation, feeling guilty for their behavior, or having no idea what to do next in their lives. Losing your job or having money problems can make things even worse. We all get depressed from time to time; we feel a sense of hopelessness or shame over something we have done. We may experience a loss of pleasure in activities that used to bring us happiness. Thankfully for many of us these moods are short-lived. However, if you feel like your life is spiraling downward, if your mood is affecting your relationships, work, school, and outlook on life, or if you are preoccupied with negative thoughts for more than a couple of weeks, seek help from a mental health professional in your community.

Many men try to blow off these moods and medicate themselves with alcohol or drugs. Unfortunately they think that asking for help from a counselor is a sign of weakness. It isn't—and it could save your life.

At various times in my life, I've felt like I'm in a rut. I tell myself that my state of mind doesn't seem rational and that I shouldn't be depressed. I'm going to work, exercising, and having a social life, yet sometimes I still feel like a black cloud is hanging over my head. It might be a major decision that I need to make, seeing the pain in the world around me, grieving the death of a loved one, or a cluster of feelings. When I feel these moods are affecting my mental health, I'll see a therapist. I feel no embarrassment about making the decision to get help. It is an opportunity for me to talk to an objective listener. He doesn't need to say too much. For me a few visits will do the trick, but I know that some people need to go to therapy for longer periods. Some people need to be on antidepressants. The important thing is to reach out for help when you need it. Your mental health is important!

Changing your outlook on life takes some initiative, but when you're down, you owe it to yourself to find new approaches to getting back on track.

Staying on Course: A Lifelong Commitment

Earl, a man in one of my groups, talked about the challenge of staying on course.

> I had promised my wife, Kathy, that I would never hit her again. I really made an effort to apply the things I'd learned in my group and the self-control techniques I'd worked on. I was determined not to repeat my past behavior. We were having an

argument about something, and I leaned across the table and yelled, "Now you listen!" She was really startled, and I was kind of shocked that I did it. I felt the same rush I used to feel when I battered her, and I was aware of her fear. I saw how easy it would be for me to slip back into old behaviors.

As Earl discovered, drifting back into familiar patterns of reacting to conflict, anger, and agitation with abuse is a real danger for men who have used violence in the past. The power of an abusive act brings an immediate response. The conflict ends, and it ends on your terms.

Most of the men I interviewed for this book told me they work continually to avoid backsliding. Whenever they feel hurt, jealous, or angry, their first impulse is to react in a way that will get them what they want. Being intimidating was so much a part of how they handled conflict in the past that it remains almost an automatic reaction. Yelling or grabbing their partners would make them afraid and put them on the defensive.

To avoid this all-too-familiar path, men who lead violence-free lives practice some of the ideas in this book and do the exercises in the workbook. They maintain self-control. This is not like the thinking in AA, where "slips" are expected. If you have used violence against your partner, there can be no "slips" in the future. At the Domestic Abuse Intervention Project, if a group member is violent, we report him to the courts. Most, but not all, domestic abuse programs have this policy to ensure accountability, even if it means that some group members won't reveal their violence while participating in the groups. Do you need to be perfect? No. You only need to remain nonviolent and monitor yourself to determine if you are using abusive behaviors.

Acknowledging positive and healthy responses to problems and conflict resolution is important, too. Be sure to make note of your achievements. This journey that you're on is hard, and you should be proud of the changes you are making.

Your commitment to change cannot be temporary; it must become part of who you are. At first you may not get much support from friends, family, or coworkers. But you'll know your new path is the right one to be walking down. You'll feel better about yourself.

Try to be a true friend to other men. When you see or sense that a friend or family member is being abusive to his partner, make it your business to intervene. Choose an appropriate time to talk to him, and strongly encourage him to get help. Use your own experience as a guide; tell your story and tell him what you know. He may reject your attempts, but you might also plant a seed. You can be understanding but honest.

As you change, your relationships will improve and you will feel differently about yourself. When you make this lifelong commitment, you are making a personal statement about who you are and your capacity to change. Will you make mistakes? Sure you will—we all do. But your willingness to learn and grow from them is an essential part of your journey.

Please complete Exercise 2, "What Have I Learned?" and Exercise 3, "Building a Support System," in Chapter 9 of your workbook.

10

Prevention: Getting Men and Boys Engaged with Ending Gender Violence

Manliness consists not in bluff, bravado, or loneliness. It consists in daring to do the right thing and facing consequences whether it is in matters social, political, or other. It consists in deeds not words.

▶▶ MAHATMA GANDHI ◀◀

Steve's Story

Steve talks about how he justified his violent behavior and how he got support from other men when he was being abusive. Although he embraced feminism, at the time he didn't see his own behavior as wrong. Steve's beliefs changed, as did his behavior toward his intimate partners. He became accountable and went public about his battering. He is determined to engage other men who have gone down the same path he did.

> I grew up in a middle-class family in a small town. My dad was a plumber and my mom was a homemaker. I was overweight as a kid, and so I didn't have a lot of experience with girls.
>
> I abused my very first girlfriend, Darci. She wanted to break up with me, and I was really angry. I called her up and started swearing. Her dad was listening on the other line, and because of my behavior, she got grounded. I heard through the grapevine that Darci was pissed at me because of it, and she

was going to tell me off and slap me at this dance. I remember talking to my friends about how I was going to hit her back, and they told me not to take any shit from a girl. Well, sure enough Darci came up to me and slapped me. I punched her so hard that she went flying. I felt really exhilarated. My buddies came up and slapped me on the back. I got total reinforcement from them.

Even though I felt powerful when I hit her, I also felt bad about it. I didn't really want to hurt her, but I felt this huge pressure to protect my honor as a man, especially with my friends. I just couldn't let a girl hit me without hitting back.

Then I met Sharon, and we dated for a long time before deciding to get married. We had a kid soon after that. My violence started with me breaking things, smashing chairs, putting my fist through walls, screaming. I could get her to stop arguing by screaming at her. I guess she thought I'd hit her, so she would just shut up.

I didn't have to be accountable to anyone. No one seemed to criticize this kind of behavior unless you hurt someone really bad. Even though we had a child together, I didn't feel very responsible.

I came home one night, and Sharon confronted me about not letting her know where I was. I told her I'd been out with my friends, and she said something like I was a stupid, irresponsible fool. I told her not to call me that, and she did it again. She kept calling me stupid, and I told her if she said it again she was going to get it. She was lying on the bed on her stomach and kept repeating that I was stupid. I punched her in the middle of her back as hard as I could. She doubled up and screamed with this incredible pain. I remember her picking up the baby and sitting in a chair, sobbing. She couldn't stop.

We were married for seven years, then one day she came home with a police officer and took her stuff. We got divorced after that.

I started dating Rhonda. We lived in a small town near Minneapolis. I started being violent right away. She said something that embarrassed me at a party. When we were driving home,

I told her I didn't like what she said. She said I was overreacting, so I backhanded her across the face. She cried all the way home. We got to my apartment and by then she was saying it was all her fault. I wasn't budging. I wouldn't accept her apologies, and even though I wasn't angry anymore, I was getting off on her groveling and the pure power of the situation.

I would be violent every couple of months. One time I came to her apartment and she was typing something for class. I wanted to talk, but she told me she needed to finish. I started making fun of her for going to school and demanded that she talk to me. When she got mad and told me to leave, I became enraged at the rejection. I pushed her over a chair and threw her around the kitchen, slapping and punching her and throwing things. A guy from the downstairs apartment came up to see what was going on, and he and I started fighting. I finally left.

Things got more intense when she wanted to get out of the relationship. One night we were at a bar, and she talked about breaking up with me. In the middle of the argument, I grabbed her, threw her down on the floor, and started choking her. I didn't stop until people in the bar dragged me off. After that incident Rhonda slept with a baseball bat under her bed, she was so scared of me.

Our relationship was on-again, off-again for fourteen years. It didn't seem unhealthy to me at the time, and I'm sure Rhonda didn't think so either. Our fights seemed dramatic, but I certainly didn't see myself as a batterer. Outwardly I was a total intellectual. I believed in equality and feminism and was into the art scene. Looking back I can see I had this outward image, but really I felt that women were to be used, mostly for sex and emotional support.

I always thought the abusive stuff was just sort of a glitch in the relationship. Things would be going along fine, and then we'd have an episode. I felt justified when I was abusive, because she made me angry. I'd minimize what I did, and when she would confront me, I'd say, "You're crazy."

I'd punch out windows, slam doors, drive fast in the car to scare her, and pound my fist on the table. I'd get this rush, and it gave me an incredible sense of power. I felt important. I thought my response was appropriate to the situation.

Rhonda was so outgoing, and I was really jealous. I would do what I could to isolate her and keep her from talking to other guys. I'd do this big guilt and pity thing and say things like, "You don't give a shit about me."

You get a lot of support from other men when you're abusive. I remember one time I put my fist through a window and had my hand all bandaged up. I went down to the bar, and my friends asked me what happened. I said I'd been fighting with Rhonda again. No one ever confronted me on my abusive behavior. No one said I was wrong. Instead they said, "Yeah, those fuckin' women," and, "Why do you put up with her?"

But then I started getting confronted by some of my women friends who were into music and politics—and men, too—on my attitudes about women and on my battering. I had to look at myself, and it wasn't pretty. That led to a personal decision to change. I realized it was hard to defend what I was doing even though I had rationalized it in my head.

I didn't want to batter again, and I didn't want any woman I loved to be afraid of me. It took a while, but I hooked up with some other men who wanted to address men's violence in our community. We met once or twice a month and discussed the origins of our violence. We talked about how we grew up, the expectations of being a man, what our culture taught us about masculinity, and how we thought we were superior to women.

It wasn't easy to admit some of my behavior to the other men. The more we met and talked, the more I learned about myself and the more determined I was to change. I started speaking out publicly about my violence. I think to be public is a real motivator for change, whether it's getting confronted by people or getting arrested. It's very humbling.

Even after I committed to not being violent with Rhonda, she was still afraid of me. I knew if I got angry or depressed, she couldn't be sure what would come next. I had to learn to express my anger in different ways. I was responsible for her fear because of my past use of violence, so I figured I was responsible for helping her feel more secure. If we got into a disagreement, I told her upfront I wasn't going to be violent. I reassured her and tried to create a safe space.

My relationship with Rhonda ended anyway. I'm convinced that my battering was a key reason. Even though I was committed to being nonviolent, there was a certain level of trust that we could never restore, and we lost emotional spontaneity because of it.

This national TV show was doing a program on domestic abuse. I was asked to be on the show because Rhonda and I had told our stories publicly in Minnesota. When I explained that my violence was an attempt to control and punish Rhonda, people in the audience asked, "What did she do to provoke you?" The whole thing about provocation can be so tempting—it's a way to blame her for what you do. But my violence was a personal choice.

In my current relationship I have more of a dialogue going on in my head. I'm aware of what I'm doing and what I'm saying; it's kind of a self-monitoring process. I listen more. I talk honestly about what's going on in my life. I realize now that when I was abusive I was getting my way, but I was also losing out. My partners didn't trust me. They had to be concerned about my moods. They were fearful when I got angry. It's difficult to be intimate when someone is afraid of you.

Men don't understand what kind of fear many women live with—the fear of rape and being beaten, of even being afraid in intimate relationships. It seems to me that we men have to take responsibility and confront our violence.

It has been important to me to tell Linda, who's my present partner, that I battered. I think she has a right to know who she's dealing with. It's part of being accountable.

I like working with men and sharing my experiences with them. I feel rewarded when men talk straight about these issues and really make some commitments to change. It gives me hope that if men keep talking to other men, we can begin to change the attitudes that lead to violence against women. This work forces me to continue to examine my own life as a man.

Support for Changing Men

Some men might claim that the analysis and self-reflection this book asks of the reader brings only shame and guilt about being a man. But the opposite is true. Awareness of sexism and the willingness to make changes are liberating. How you define your own masculinity is up to you, but being a man doesn't mean you have to be sexist or support sexism. Men who are comfortable with their masculinity don't feel the need to defend sexist beliefs and locker-room attitudes.

Develop a deeper awareness by talking to people, both men and women, about the issues discussed in this book. In most communities men are getting together, even though it might be in small numbers, to talk about masculinity, men's violence, and prevention. Some men join organizations that focus on preventing gender violence. Others work with civil rights and human rights organizations, because the issues associated with violence against any group of people are very similar. Some men work with domestic abuse programs, facilitate groups, or volunteer at shelters and schools that are addressing community violence. Stay involved—it will remind you of where you've been and how far you've come on your journey.

If you have battered but have not been ordered into a domestic abuse program, or if you're worried that you have violent tendencies, volunteer to attend a program in your community. Go for the information, and be sure to get the help you need before your abusive behavior escalates. I know many men who have built solid friendships through these programs. Like the relationships recovering alcoholics often build, friendships developed in a domestic abuse program can help men who batter. Together these men can grapple with personal issues and support each other in their commitment to remain nonviolent.

Your decision to change your life may require you to give up certain friendships or activities, just as an alcoholic gives up situations where there's the temptation to drink. Going to a bar, party, or social function where other men are telling sexist jokes or devaluing women soon becomes objectionable to men who are trying to change their lives. You may want to challenge these men in a respectful manner, tell them you don't appreciate their sexist comments, and try to have a meaningful discussion about why the jokes are offensive. Or you may just decide you prefer to be around men who don't see humor in sexism.

Several years ago I was at a YMCA, sitting in the sauna with six or seven men, and one of them began telling sexist jokes to the amusement of the others. When I said I thought his jokes were sexist, the sauna became quiet and uncomfortable. One man told me to "chill out," and said, "They're only jokes." Someone else said, "It's not like there are any women here." I left wondering if I had overreacted. Then I thought, would I have been silent if someone had made a racist or anti-Semitic joke? What was the difference? And what difference did it make that no women were there?

Because I know how destructive sexism is to women, I try not to remain silent. This doesn't mean I confront everyone who does or says something sexist. Sometimes it simply isn't worth it. Challenging someone can make the situation worse. But when I can, I try to educate in my own way without making anyone feel ashamed, since that makes people defensive, and they close their minds to new ideas. The rule I try to follow is this: Keep your sense of humor and don't be condescending.

Hopefully, like many of the men in this book, you will seek out friendships that are not superficial. Talking about cars or sports is fine, but there is more to life than overdrive transmissions or yesterday's box scores. The more you learn about the destructiveness of sexism, and the more deeply you become committed to making change in yourself and your community, the more you will want relationships with men and women who support each other's growth and change.

New Definitions of Masculinity

Masculinity is defined by our culture, whether we like it or not. The messages and expectations we are exposed to shape who we are. For many men, caring for others or showing sensitivity to a friend is difficult. Ralph shared this example:

> After that last group, when we talked about what it meant to be a man, I thought a lot about all the comments that were made. Then last weekend I went down to the bar to watch the Vikings game. I watched the men around me. They all seemed lonely, sitting there with their booze and football talk. I sat down with a few buddies and had a beer. We talked about the game and hunting. I tried to get them talking about some more personal things, but all that came out was Ben's divorce and how he thought he was getting screwed. Then we talked about who might make it into the play-offs.

This sort of superficial conversation is typical of the patterns of "male bonding" men learn from childhood on. "Sensitive" boys are ridiculed by their peers if they don't conform. This taunting emphasizes stereotypical male interests and keeps us from developing all aspects of ourselves and forming deep relationships.

Look at this definition of "manly" from the *American Heritage Dictionary*:

> 1. *Manly* pertains broadly to admirable qualities of men. *Manly* suggests braveness, resoluteness, or forcefulness.

If braveness, resoluteness, and forcefulness are the characteristics of being manly, then being compassionate, gentle, and nurturing isn't what a man should be. It is because of narrow stereotypes like these that men in growing numbers are seeking a healthier definition of masculinity, an emerging understanding that a man who has courage and is resolute can also be compassionate, gentle, and nurturing. There is room in a fully developed human being for both sets of qualities.

Allowing yourself to be sensitive and nurturing does not diminish your masculinity; it makes you more human and more compassionate. You become a better father, a closer partner, and a stronger friend. In fact, in many ways allowing yourself to feel helps you gain greater courage, strength, and fortitude.

The idea of changing can be frightening. It's a lot easier to stay the way we are. So many men in my groups are living lives that lack fulfillment, hurting others and themselves, and modeling a destructive path for their children. It doesn't have to be that way.

In my interview with Cassie, she said, "I think on some level Antonio really wanted to change. He would tell me he planned to get help, but he wouldn't follow through. Things would go along pretty well, and then something at work would happen, and he'd take it out on me. He didn't see any other way of living, because he never got any help."

Some men are threatened by talk of redefining masculinity. They're concerned about what they may have to change or give up. We discussed this issue in one of our groups.

> **Neil:** I don't know if I believe men need to change. I agree that we don't need to be so violent, but basically I like being a man.
> **Michael:** I don't think it's an issue of whether you like being a man or not. But I think there are ways we get socialized that have a negative impact on how we live our lives. I mean why are we here?
> **Tom:** We're here because the court said we had to be here.
> **Gordy:** I know what he's saying, and I pretty much agree. We grow up in a culture in which men are supposed to be a certain way. And violence is a big part of growing up male. I think controlling women is part of it, too.
> **Michael:** If what Gordy said is true, are there ways we can redefine masculinity, keeping the positive stuff and throwing out the negative?
> **Gordy:** I think so. You know I think back on my childhood and I feel bad. My father never said he loved us kids, even though I

know he did. He purposely was distant and never gave us approval. I think he was just incapable of telling us.

Michael: That's sad.

Neil: Yeah, but fathers have to project that image of strength. I mean I have a hard time saying that stuff to my kids. Just because I don't say it doesn't mean I don't have those feelings.

Michael: I think this shows something about how our culture defines masculinity. It also speaks to what we are losing as men and as husbands and fathers.

We should be proud to be men. Throughout history men have fought against oppression and injustice. Mahatma Gandhi, Tenzin Gyatso (the fourteenth Dalai Lama), Cesar Chavez, Martin Luther King Jr., Nelson Mandela, Elie Wiesel, and many others have resisted violent struggle or changed their views on violence as a means to settle conflict—the opposite of what might be considered a "typical male" response. At the turn of the twentieth century, men like Fredrick Douglass aligned with women during the suffragists' movement in the United States; this effort culminated in the passage of the Nineteenth Amendment, giving women the right to vote. Many men who fought in the Vietnam War came back and joined other war resisters to bring an end to that war. Men and women protested and struggled peacefully against insurmountable odds during the civil rights movement in the 1960s, which led to sweeping changes combating discrimination.

Today many men are working to confront violence in their own communities. With the rash of school killings committed by boys and rampant inner-city gang violence usually perpetrated by males, men are working to sensitize society (and especially other men) to the impact of violence. Dave Grossman, in his book *On Killing,* discusses the ways the military desensitizes men to killing through systematically training soldiers to dehumanize the enemy. He further questions what makes today's children bring guns to schools and use them when their parents did not. He hypothesizes that in our modern American society, a systematic process is defeating the age-old psychological inhibition against violent, harmful activity toward one's own species.[1]

James Garbarino points out in *Lost Boys* that easy access to guns and a willingness to use them to settle conflicts is extremely disturbing. Garbarino describes what happens when boys are taught not to exhibit fear or vulnerability and how accumulated inner damage all too often results in aggressive behavior. He especially notes that the school environment and peer groups play powerful roles in influencing a boy's behavior.[2]

School shootings and gang violence also point to the male characteristics and male socialization that have been discussed in earlier chapters. The failure of boys and men to live up to the unrealistic expectations of being male in our society leads to feelings of powerlessness, isolation, and rejection. Young male assailants who have been bullied, rejected by several girls, or just angry at the world have decided to take their rage out on others, often killing fellow students at high schools and universities.

When girls and women are hurt or rejected, they handle their emotions very differently than men do. We don't often see a women picking up a gun and killing her family members, then turning the weapon on herself. Nor do we often see a woman committing carnage at her place of employment because she lost her job. We don't see many girls taking out their aggression on students and teachers and committing premeditated murder. While female violence, including female gang violence, is increasing, the number of murders committed by girls and young women is extremely small compared to the everyday killing by boys and young men of other males, sometimes for the most minor indiscretions.

As men and as fathers we owe it to society to change this disturbing reality. In growing numbers men and women are making contributions in addressing gender violence. Most readers of this book have a lot to offer, because you've been there. You know the cost of violence.

Men can define masculinity for themselves, and these new definitions can include many important qualities. Within men is the ability, and often the desire, to be sensitive and caring. We can be loving husbands and fathers. Courage doesn't solely have to be about taking dangerous risks or being tough; it can be about having the guts to be different. Both our strengths and our caring inner selves can emerge when we reject the old masculine characteristics: control, anger, and entitlement.

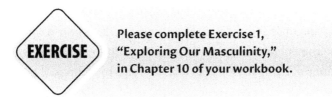

Please complete Exercise 1,
"Exploring Our Masculinity,"
in Chapter 10 of your workbook.

Examining Our Sense of Entitlement

Changing the culture is not an easy task, or we would have done it by now. Until we recognize that in many ways all men benefit from the status quo, we won't mobilize the critical mass necessary to challenge it. We've been focusing so much of our attention on intervention that we are just beginning to talk about prevention. We need to begin by having meaningful dialogue in community after community about how we can all participate in changing the beliefs and attitudes that contribute to men's violence against women.

Changing the culture means that men model egalitarian relationships with women so their children see respectful relationships. It means that institutions such as our schools, athletic programs, and community organizations insist on environments in which objectifying and abusing women isn't okay. It means men challenging sexism, speaking up, and refusing to participate in behavior that fosters violence against women. It means men beginning to engage other men and boys through programs that address gender violence. If a program doesn't exist in your community, you can be the leader and start one.

When I see the way that far too many men behave at bars, parties, sporting events, and social gatherings, and the way we are portrayed in commercials, I'm shocked that more men aren't embarrassed. We have this image of men (in some cases, justified) in a perpetual state of male adolescence. We should be appalled. Through our behavior, or our silence, we perpetuate a belief that sexism and the exploitation of women are harmless. They aren't. Many men reject the way our culture exploits women and have respectful and equal relationships with their partners. But too often we are silent when we are surrounded by a socially constructed message about men and masculinity that appears to be the norm. It doesn't have to be this way.

Men who are dedicated to social change should not rely solely on women for support and encouragement. They should make the changes for themselves and for the greater good. They should take responsibility and help to undo a system of violence and entitlement that generations of men have constructed. Your rewards will be healthier relationships, children who value equality, and the knowledge that you are part of a movement that someday will bring about a more peaceful world.

Male entitlement is both blatant and subtle. The more obvious forms of male entitlement include expectations that men make more money, are more likely to be promoted, and should be the CEOs of companies and major corporations. Even today women are expected to do more of the housework and child care. A more subtle example of male entitlement is the space some men take up in public places—for instance spreading their legs or sprawling out on the bus, at a meeting, or at home. Most men don't worry about their safety when they walk to their cars, to the bus, to the subway, or in their own neighborhoods, while most women have their danger antennas up, especially when a man or men whom they don't recognize are present.

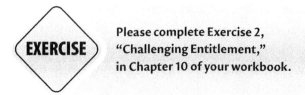

EXERCISE Please complete Exercise 2, "Challenging Entitlement," in Chapter 10 of your workbook.

Men Going Public

Many men have gone public with the fact that they were abusive to their intimate partners. They decide to do so for a variety of reasons. For some men, telling others about their abuse is a way of staying accountable. For others, the motivation is to help other men by sharing their experiences and their process of change. And for still others, going public is a way to participate in changing society by confronting the attitudes and beliefs that foster violence.

A man who was in one of my groups now speaks at police training sessions on domestic abuse intervention, where he explains his many years of battering. After listening to him, the police officers have a clearer understanding of the dynamics of battering, the danger of these cases, and the ways men who batter can manipulate law enforcement. As a result of this training, officers can more effectively intervene in domestic abuse cases.

We can address violence against women in our communities in many ways. Men can take a more active and visible role in confronting sexual and domestic assaults. We can join neighborhood crime watches, participate in antirape marches, and organize community meetings. We can initiate dialogue in our schools, churches, local governments, unions, professional associations, and community clubs. We can write letters to newspapers, post online, and talk to our friends; publicly confront judges who refuse to take domestic abuse cases seriously; and lobby our mayors, state legislators, and Congress for tougher laws to protect women and children who are being abused.

We can teach our sons and daughters that attitudes and behaviors that in any way degrade girls and women are wrong. We can talk clearly and with conviction to our children. We can help shape their thinking about men, women, equality, and violence. We need to remind them that if they witness inappropriate behavior at a party, on the bus, in the school yard, at the park, or on social media, they do not need to participate.

Men can and should take the initiative to confront violence in their homes and communities, because most violence is perpetrated by men. Women don't usually kill people; they commit less than 15 percent of the homicides in the United States. When women do kill, it is often in their own defense, notes Angela Browne, author of *When Battered Women Kill.*[3] Gang violence, fights, domestic and sexual assaults, and sex trafficking are primarily male phenomena. It is our responsibility to put an end to them.

Women have struggled for years to end rape and domestic violence. They have organized movements, fought for resources, lobbied for legislation, and spoken out about the magnitude of these problems. Men who ally with these movements should support women's leadership. If you plan or seek funding for a program or an event, talk and work with women's groups in your community.

I'm convinced we can make a difference. I believe we will see more and more men speaking out and confronting sexism and men's violence. We can make a difference today, so that future generations will not have to experience the violence and abuse that occur in our communities.

Prevention: The Next Frontier

Intervention is critical. We need to hold offenders accountable for their violence. But intervention by law enforcement and the criminal justice system generally comes *after* the violent act. Intervention comes *after* the physical and emotional pain a victim experiences at the hands of her boyfriend or husband. Intervention comes *after* the terror and humiliation of a rape perpetrated by a stranger or, more likely, an acquaintance. Intervention comes *after* a trafficker's victims are freed from forced prostitution. The fundamental question is whether we can stop or significantly reduce men's violence against women through prevention.

Examining how society has responded to other social problems can be instructive as we think about preventing men's violence against women. Most successful social-change movements have followed a three-part approach:

- **Changing laws:** This occurs when special interest groups and advocates of a specific social change successfully pressure government to create laws.

- **Changing community/organizational practices:** This occurs when those same interest groups pressure community institutions to adopt policies, procedures, and practices to enforce the new laws.

- **Changing culture and social norms:** This occurs when the culture expresses approval or disapproval of certain social behaviors and people choose to conform to what is considered to be acceptable rather than risk being ostracized.

Consider the progress that has been made to reduce tobacco use in the United States. When I was a boy in the 1960s, smoking was pervasive. If you smoked, you were considered sophisticated, urbane, and stylish. The tobacco industry poured millions of dollars into advertising to show just how classy you could be by smoking their particular brand. Everyone on TV and in the movies smoked. Even doctors endorsed cigarette brands in ads in magazines like *Life, Look,* and *Time* and in commercials on our black-and-white TVs. People smoked everywhere—in movie theaters, airplanes, buses, trains, workplaces, and even hospitals! Every house had ashtrays out, even if the residents didn't smoke. No one gave a second thought to lighting up anywhere at any time.

Today smoking is stigmatized. We know the health hazards to smokers and, through secondhand smoke, to nonsmokers. Health organizations have successfully lobbied governments at the local and national levels to pass laws prohibiting smoking in most public places. Community organizations promote quitting smoking (or not starting) as healthy behavior. Social norms have changed, and smokers are often scorned. The rate of smoking in the United States has sharply declined.

Smoking is only one example.

- Think about how society views littering today. Pitching garbage out of the car window was once common. Although it is still done, it's socially unacceptable and illegal.

- Using a seatbelt was once considered an inconvenience, but not doing so is now a primary offense in most states, with a resulting dramatic decrease in automobile deaths.

- Many Americans have significant weight problems, but many others are adopting healthy eating habits and exercising.

- We used to lock up people with mental illnesses in "insane asylums" that were essentially human warehouses. Today, although mental health programs are still seriously underfunded, we have deinstitutionalized the system and are trying to find more humane approaches to treating and housing people with serious mental illness.

- The death penalty has long been considered "just what is deserved" for the perpetrators of particularly terrible crimes; today an increasing number of states are rethinking their death penalty statutes not only because of questions of morality but because of evidence that innocent people are being executed.

We may never wipe out conduct that is negative, harmful, or criminal, but we can work to reduce it. Let's look at how this social-change model applies to the problem of men's violence against women.

Changing laws: In the 1970s the women's movement and then the battered women's movement pressured policymakers to pass laws that hold offenders accountable and protect victims.

Changing community/organizational practices: When these laws were enacted in the 1980s, advocates worked with law enforcement, the criminal and civil justice systems, and human service providers to change their policies and practices to enhance the safety of victims through their interventions.

Changing cultural and social norms: Although domestic violence is not considered the private matter it once was and tolerance for battering has diminished, significant cultural change has been harder to achieve. Boys and men are still bombarded with messages about what it means to be a man and what as men we're entitled to. Some of those messages are that men are superior to women, that it's okay for men to objectify women, that men can buy women for their sexual satisfaction, and that men can abuse their intimate partners to put them in their place.

This is where we as men need to get to work. This is where prevention begins.

I interviewed Jackson Katz, author of *The Macho Paradox,* for the documentary *With Impunity: Men and Gender Violence.* He observed the following:

> One of the things we know from social-norms theory is that when men think that they're the only one in a room with other men who feels uncomfortable with the sexist behavior of another man, they're much less likely to say something than if they know that other guys in the room share their sentiments. But if nobody says anything, then how do you know that other people share your sentiments? I'm convinced that a lot of men remain silent in the face of some men's abuse—not because they agree with the abuse and not because they approve of it, but because they have decided that it's not worth saying anything because they don't want to lose standing. The policing

mechanisms that we engage in as men consciously and unconsciously keep men in this narrow box.[4]

Changing Laws and Organizational Practices

Many countries have changed their laws to criminalize domestic abuse, rape, and trafficking, with varying degrees of success. In some countries laws have not been implemented, and agencies in the criminal justice system adhere to practices that maintain longstanding structures of male domination. For example, in Morocco, until 2014 a man would be exonerated if he would agree to marry the woman he raped. This law was repealed in 2014, but the country's current rape laws are ineffective because of the sexist attitudes among personnel in the law enforcement and the criminal justice systems ("If a woman is raped, she must have been complicit"). While the laws in Morocco and other countries are changing due to pressure from human rights organizations, legal barriers, a lack of resources, and cultural practices make it difficult if not impossible for battered women to escape from abusive husbands.[5]

In countries with rigid patriarchal cultures, women are less likely to be free from violence and oppression. Does this mean the West is more advanced? Some of the differences are nuanced. In the United States and other Western countries, even with changes in the law, crimes against women such as rape, domestic abuse, and trafficking go unreported for the same reasons they aren't reported in countries like Morocco, India, Bangladesh, South Africa, Bosnia, and the Congo: Women don't think they will be believed.

Organizational interventions *have* made a difference, depending on the strength of the laws and the commitment of the criminal justice system to enforcing them. Domestic violence has declined in the United States, presumably because changes in the law, interventions, penalties for offenses, and additional ways to ensure victims' safety have made a difference.

Change can't come solely from laws and the organizations that have the responsibility to enforce them; that is, the law enforcement and criminal justice systems. The broader community must be fully engaged. What could be accomplished if the following community organizations were to commit to addressing gender violence?

- faith organizations
- athletic groups
- neighborhood groups
- colleges and universities
- businesses
- criminal justice agencies
- fraternal organizations
- media
- medical community
- community centers
- child protection services
- mental health agencies
- elementary, middle, and high schools
- violence-prevention organizations

Prevention: What Men Can Do

Social change can occur when the institutions in our communities become part of the solution. Men need to start stepping up, talking to other men and boys about the destructiveness of gender-based violence, and identifying the benefits of egalitarian relationships, equality, respect, and love in our families, relationships, and communities.

Prevention means more than simple slogans like, "Real Men Don't Buy Girls," "My Strength Isn't for Hurting," or "How Would You Feel if Someone Abused Your Mother, Sister, or Daughter?" While well-meaning, these sayings contain an indirect message to men and women that all men "can" rape and beat women but shouldn't. They also communicate a long-held myth that a man's role is to be the "protector" of women, thereby perpetuating men's privileged position in society. Prevention strategies involve engaging men and boys in honest dialogue about sexism and entitlement and challenging community institutions to reject gender violence.

Primary prevention in the gender violence field is in its infancy. Primary prevention is usually defined as a public health approach to change social norms that lead to unhealthy or antisocial behavior.[6] Borrowing from other primary prevention initiatives, the goal is that through community interventions, men and boys will recognize the harm caused by gender violence and will seek healthy, nonviolent, and nonexploitive relationships with women.

Here are some initiatives that have demonstrated positive results, as well as a list of national and international organizations that are working on primary prevention strategies:

BEST Party Model

The BEST Party Model is a step-by-step guide for college students on how to throw parties that are safe, respectful, and fun for women. It provides an opportunity to change the social environments that contribute to sexual and domestic violence at colleges and universities. The model has also been a tool for students, staff, and faculty to shape campus spaces such as residence halls, locker rooms, student lounges, and classrooms, with the goal of creating an overall campus environment that equally empowers male and female students, faculty, and staff.
www.menaspeacemakers.org

A Call to Men

A Call to Men is a national organization providing training and education for men, boys, and communities. It partners with schools, universities, corporations, governmental units, and social service agencies to end all forms of violence and discrimination against women and girls. It also promotes healthy and respectful models of manhood and has consulted with the National Football League, the United States military, and the media on ways institutions can prevent gender-based violence.

www.acalltomen.org

Education for Critical Thinking (ECT)

Education for Critical Thinking explores meaningful ways to challenge community institutions to do more to end gender-based violence, including domestic violence, rape, trafficking, and violent pornography. It produced the documentary *With Impunity: Men and Gender Violence* and provides training nationally and internationally.

www.educationforcriticalthinking.org

Futures Without Violence

Futures Without Violence provides technical assistance to organizations around the country that are engaging men to prevent violence against women and girls. It has also organized the Coaches Leadership Program, which equips coaches to talk with athletes about respect for women and girls and remind them that violence doesn't equal strength.

www.futureswithoutviolence.org

Men Can Stop Rape

Men Can Stop Rape is an international organization that mobilizes men to use their strength to create cultures free of violence, especially men's violence against women. It has developed education programs, public-awareness messaging, and training. Its approach is grounded in the social-ecological model for primary prevention.

www.mencanstoprape.org

The MENding Project

The MENding Project asks traditionally male-run or male-oriented businesses to provide free or reduced-cost goods and services for victims/survivors of sexual and domestic violence and trafficking. The MENding Project provides educational materials for business owners to help them answer questions about their participation in

the program, including window and countertop display cards that promote the message of men's collective responsibility to end sexual and domestic violence in the community.
www.themendingproject.org

MenEngage Global Alliance

MenEngage is an alliance of nongovernmental organizations that seek to engage men and boys in effective ways to reduce gender inequalities and promote the health and well-being of women, men, and children. This international project has developed a "tool kit" for good practices to carry out advocacy campaigns and act as a collective voice to promote a global movement of men and boys engaged in and working for gender equality.
www.engagement.net

Men Stopping Violence

Men Stopping Violence is a national training institute that provides communities, organizations, and individuals with the knowledge required to mobilize men to prevent violence against women and girls. It offers an innovative community-restoration program for men who have completed their domestic abuse program and are interested in giving back to the community.
www.menstoppingviolence.org

Mentors in Violence Prevention

Mentors in Violence Prevention provides education and training on the prevention of gender violence, bullying, and school violence. Its training is focused on the "bystander model," which empowers students to take an active role in promoting a positive school climate.
www.mvpstrategies.net

MensWork

MensWork is a grassroots organization that develops and supports male leadership to prevent bullying, sexual harassment, rape, dating

violence, domestic violence, and sexual exploitation by engaging men and boys through an array of programs and community events.
www.mensworkinc.com

PreventConnect

PreventConnect is a national project of the California Coalition Against Sexual Assault. Building on the strengths of the rape crisis and domestic violence movements, its goal is to advance primary prevention of sexual assault and relationship violence, using various forms of online media to connect people and ideas to stop the violence before it starts.
www.preventconnect.org

Prevention Through Athletics

The Minnesota Men's Action Network has collaborated with high-school sports leagues to design an online course for coaches to help them embed gender equity and sexual and domestic violence prevention into team culture.
www.menaspeacemakers.org/programs/mnman

Promundo

Promundo is a Brazil-based organization that promotes caring, nonviolent, and equitable masculinities and gender relations in Brazil and internationally by conducting research, developing transformative interventions and policies, and carrying out advocacy to achieve gender equality and social justice. It engages teachers, health sector workers, businesses, and community organizations.
www.promundo.org

Sonke Gender Justice Network

The Sonke Gender Justice Network is a South African–based NGO (nongovernmental organization) that works across Africa to strengthen government and civil society organizations and to support men and boys in taking action to promote gender equality, prevent domestic and sexual violence, and reduce the spread of AIDS.
www.genderjustice.org

White Ribbon Campaign

The White Ribbon Campaign is a global organization that examines the root causes of gender violence, creating a cultural shift that challenges negative, outdated concepts of manhood that lead to violence against women. It positively engages men, young men, and boys through education, outreach, technical assistance, and partnerships. **www.whiteribbon.ca**

XY

XY is a website focused on men, masculinities, and gender politics. It's a space for the exploration of topics related to gender and sexuality, and the daily issues of men's and women's lives, and for practical discussions of personal and social change. **www.xyonline.net**

These are just a few of the national and international organizations that are doing important prevention work. Their websites can give you ideas on how you can make a difference in your own community. You don't have to be a big nonprofit or NGO to make things happen locally. Programs in your own community, state/province, or schools may already be doing this work. Talk with like-minded men and women, and start organizing!

Leadership

Who are leaders in the effort to end gender-based violence? They are women and men in key positions in our communities who are taking a stance, exhibiting courage, and using their influence to create organizational and cultural change. They are people with power in their community, village, state, or nation who are both speaking out *and* taking action.

Ann Jones, author of *Next Time She'll Be Dead,* talks about such leadership in her work in Africa:

Women all over the world are working to try to change things. When I was working in Africa with women in villages... in post-conflict situations, women were working to rebuild their communities. They were working to end domestic and sexual violence in ways that had not been done before. In some villages the male leadership and the women's own husbands became so proud of what they were doing that they began to look at the women differently because they were doing something that was effective. I had given them cameras to take pictures of their village and identify the problems.

The chief of one village said, "We want these women to continue doing this work." And in some communities where the women pointed out the violence, the chief would say, "Stop the violence. I don't want this in our community." In another village the chief invited the women to join his advisory council. So overnight, women who had never had any role in public life before became advisors to the chief. Not only did they stamp out violence of all kinds in their community, but now the chief has been instrumental in working with the women to get them a radio station to broadcast their message all over the country.

So the great lesson I learned is that while women are working all over the world to end gender violence and to make peaceable lives for their communities, they can do it more successfully when they have men with some power behind them. But men don't come forward in notable numbers anywhere in the world.[7]

This story illustrates the importance of men getting involved to end gender-based violence. Gender violence isn't just a women's issue. Although men should be taking leadership from women on intervention and prevention strategies, we should also be coming forward on our own initiative and asking, "What can I do? How can I help? How can we work together to end gender-based violence?" Whether it is village chiefs in Africa or community leaders in the United States, men and women in leadership positions can make profound changes.

The county attorney in my community has been a leader in a

countywide effort to reduce sex trafficking, starting with a policy decision not to prosecute children who were being prostituted. The private and public sectors in my state have both been working with hospitality associations on ways to help staff recognize the signs of sex trafficking—for example, paying for a room in cash or not having luggage. Law enforcement officers, prosecutors, and advocates explained the dynamics of sex trafficking at trainings to help staff intervene and notify authorities. Truckers' associations have trained truck drivers to recognize runaways—the children who are most vulnerable to sex traffickers. Minnesota has passed legislation providing millions of dollars to build a safety net for child victims of sex trafficking. Part of the legislative package allocated funding to train prosecutors and police officers statewide on how to intervene in these cases. The other component was an appropriation for housing, legal assistance, and services for child victims who are being prostituted. Other states have also implemented innovative legislation to address gender violence.

The faith community can do much more to address gender violence. We are a world of multiple faiths. While religion has historically upheld patriarchy, clergy and congregations in the religious community are starting to address the conflicts between doctrine and the essence of their faith. Oliver Williams, executive director of the Institute on Domestic Violence in the African American Community, discussed in an interview the organizations' efforts to make changes in the faith community:

> We've gone to many African American communities across the United States. We've been working with mega-churches and in rural communities getting buy-in from ministers. In one very rural community, the church is now doing major work to develop a rape crisis line, and they have established relationships with battered women's organizations. In all of these different types of environments, we're trying to get ministers to take on this issue. In immigrant communities, we're working with imams. We are getting clergy to talk about domestic violence,

because the church should be about healthy families, and if you're trying to promote well-being in the family, you can't ignore violence against women.[8]

Changing the Culture

People all too often talk about how some cultures accept male dominance in the family as a justification for domestic and sexual violence. This is a convenient explanation that allows men who oppress women to validate their actions. The Power and Control Wheel (see page 91 and Appendix A) has been translated into twenty-four languages and is displayed in shelters and social service centers around the world—and around the world battered women recognize the tactics listed on the wheel as those used against them. It's as if their male partners are interchangeable. We have heard this repeatedly from international visitors at the Domestic Abuse Intervention Project, where the wheel was created. Regardless of race, ethnicity, or culture, men around the world justify their controlling and abusive behavior using the same reasons.

Beliefs change. Music, television, theater, literature, advertising, and the internet shape the way people think about issues, gender, and relationships. Not everyone accepts the messages of the day, but popular culture is a formidable force that influences mainstream society. I interviewed Beth Richie, author of *Battered Black Women: A Challenge for the Black Community*. She talks about how popular culture impacts women, especially African American women.

> If we're serious about ending violence against women, in particular younger African American women, we have to find ways to critique the dimensions of popular culture that objectify them, that degrade them, that surround them and formulate other people's images of them. We have to look at music, movies, magazines, and the new genre of popular novels that are produced very quickly. It's not particularly good writing, and it's full of negative stereotypical images of Black women that lots of people are reading. It's almost everywhere we look.

There are very strong negative stereotypes influencing how we think about contemporary Black women coupled with the way we have looked at Black women historically, and they reinforce each other quite profoundly.[9]

We have just begun to scratch the surface of examining how our culture supports the behavior of men who rape, batter, and objectify women. Boys and men are deeply influenced by cultural norms conveying the message that violence is an appropriate response to resolving conflict, whether in our neighborhoods or schools, or in relationships with intimate partners.

Boys begin glamorizing war when they are very young, first playing with toy guns, then watching war and science fiction movies in which the enemy or alien invaders are destroyed with state-of-the-art technology, then playing video games in which players can kill the adversary at will. The debate about whether this violent imagery desensitizes a person to violence is ongoing.

In many countries the armed services are now integrated, and women are participating in conflicts around the world. But historically it is difficult to ignore the significance of gender in war. Ann Jones, author of *War Is Not Over When It's Over,* makes a point:

> I often say that war is a guy thing. Guys are the ones who start the war. Guys are principally the ones who are engaged in fighting the war, even though they rely upon women to support them in a great many ways. And then guys are the ones who get together and say, okay, now we're tired of fighting. We're going to make a deal and split up the prize here or the power or the resources.[10]

EXERCISE

Please complete Exercise 3, "Why Are We Silent?" Exercise 4, "Social Change Activities," and Exercise 5, "Creating Change in Your Community," in Chapter 10 of your workbook.

Counselors Working
with Men Who Batter

Almost anything you do will be insignificant,
but it is very important that you do it.

▸▸ MAHATMA GANDHI ◂◂

Emma's Story

Counselors who conduct domestic abuse groups are not immune
from being misled by participants. Emma talks here about surviving
her relationship with a man who came very close to killing her. She
and her husband lived in rural Ireland. She said that in public, he
could be incredibly charming, and some of the people who know
him have a hard time believing her account.

John was your typical tall, dark, and handsome lad, and I was
easily physically attracted to him. At that time most of the boys
I dated were around my own age, but John was a bit older, which
was something special to an impressionable young woman like
me. I had just turned seventeen, and he was twenty-one. He
was working, and at the time he seemed like a "good catch."
After our first year together, there were signs that he was
abusive. John had a reputation as a "hard man" and had been
in many bar fights. I didn't notice his cruel, mean, dangerous

streak, but I suppose when you're in something like this, you only see what you want to see. After the first physical incident, I had a gash on my shoulder, which John had kindly given me, and I knew that the people we hung around with believed he had done it.

Every week there would be either mental, emotional, or sexual abuse—the physical violence would occur at least every two weeks. I don't know if we ever had good times once the abuse started. In the early days I do remember looking forward to seeing him on the weekends, but I don't know if that was because I was getting away from my mother, who was very domineering.

He abused me when he wasn't drinking, but when he was drunk it was more severe, physically and emotionally. I remember how he would come home after a night out and would start shouting and fighting with me. What really hurt was that he would get a mirror and hold it up close to my face and force me to look, and he'd say, "This is the ugly thing that I have to come home to." He would then proceed to go through all my facial features. I would have to listen to him and agree with him. I'd say, "Yes, I'm ugly and I will try harder."

I would try to do different things, try and be more attractive to him, but, of course, it never mattered. If we were going out for the night, I would get ready and go up to him, and he would say things like, "You're not going out looking like that, are you?" Or "That thing looks hideous on you." Or "Have you nothing better to wear?" This wore me down until I couldn't choose my own clothes anymore. I would leave that up to him; I didn't trust my own choices. After leaving him it took me quite a while to be able to look at myself in the mirror. He had actually brainwashed me into thinking I *was* ugly and unworthy.

We had a puppy that wouldn't do as John wanted, and he shot him through the head with a crossbow. The pup didn't die right then, and so John pulled the arrow out of his head and fired again. Another time one of our dogs chased some sheep we had, which made John angry. He tied the poor dog to a post and ran electricity from the car battery to his testicles to teach him a lesson. These were animals that we loved, or should I say, I loved. We'd had them since they were pups. When we had children, John killed the remainder of the dogs. He felt that they might be a danger to the kids, and so he shot them all through the head with his gun.

I believe that if I had stayed with him, I would be dead now. His temper, his cruelty, his controlling behavior, how he isolated me from my friends and family—I had no friends when I left, but luckily I had a good family. I think I could have easily been a statistic had I not left when I did.

John never took responsibly for his actions. He told me that he had never raised a hand to a girl until I came along, and so his actions must be my fault. When he broke my ankle, he refused to accept responsibility for doing it. My mother worked at the hospital, and John said, "I'm sure your mother got one of her doctor friends to put that cast on just to make me look bad." I was on crutches for six weeks, and he never expressed any remorse. The night he broke my ankle, he made me apologize to him for making him do it. I did. It was the only way I could calm the situation down.

Another time he burned my car so I would appreciate all he did for me and so I wouldn't take him for granted. Again he never apologized. I was terrified of this man. I believed his threats. I believed him when he said that he would hunt me down wherever I tried to hide. I believed him when he said he would kill my family, my kids, and me if I ever left. I was used to living with these fears. "Better the devil you know than the devil you don't know." When I would leave John, I would telephone my mother or John's mother before coming back home to see what kind of mood he was in. I had lived my life by John's moods for so long that I found it really difficult to get through each day without knowing whether he was angry or upset.

Throughout our marriage he had total control over me. He decided what music we would listen to, what television program we'd watch, what clothes I wore, and where and when we'd go out. At the time I wanted to be the woman who would stick by him no matter what, who would not leave him, and

I was. He had told me all of the bad experiences he'd had with women in the past, and I really believed I could be a different kind of woman for him.

I never involved law enforcement. We lived in an isolated area, so if an incident was taking place, I would have had to walk for a mile to get to a pay phone. I wouldn't leave the girls with him, so I just had to deal with his beatings. He had guns, which he wasn't afraid to use, and there were many nights that he would fire shots to scare me. This was terrifying. He would lock me out of the house in the middle of the night, but I would never leave to get help, because I couldn't stand the thought of leaving the children with him.

My eldest daughter had nightmares when we first left. She dreamt that he was coming to take us home again. The girls had seen John firing guns at me. They also were present the night when he threatened to burst my head open with a lump hammer.

I believe my children are better off without him as their father. I'm sure witnessing the violence, the threats, and seeing me in constant fear must have had an impact on them, but fortunately they are fairly well adjusted. When I finally left, they didn't see him again for about four years. I like to think that I left before they were too damaged and that they have forgotten a lot of what they may have seen or heard.

When I left John and went to the refuge [shelter], I was asked by the refuge advocate if I was ever raped, and I answered no. But it is only recently that I am acknowledging that I was raped repeatedly during those times. I thought if I didn't verbally say no to him that I was consenting to sex, but "no" wasn't an option. If I didn't want to be sexual, then I risked another beating. Even though having sex with him repelled me, I would have to show enthusiasm toward the sexual act.

John always wanted sex after abusing me, especially if he had drink in him. When he was drunk, he would have a difficult time keeping an erection (it's called the "brewer's droop" here in Ireland). When this happened, he would blame me, so it would be up to me to make him "come," and he wouldn't go to bed until he had an orgasm. I never had a choice around sex; he got it on demand, and he liked to demand it.

To be honest there were two times when I fought back. He once told me, "You should fight back. It makes me mad when you're so submissive." So one time during an argument, I slapped him across the face, and he beat me much more severely, so I never hit him again.

After years of being beaten, raped, and terrorized, I remember feeling that there was nothing left of me. My spirit was nearly broken. I felt that I was down a black hole with no way out.

I never considered taking my own life, because I would never leave the children with him. But I used to pray to God to let John die in a car crash or some other form of death, but it never happened.

The reality was that I was so afraid of John that I never ever raised my voice to him, never answered him back, and tried to do what he wanted so he wouldn't get agitated. The day I actually left, I didn't have a plan—it was a spur-of-the-moment decision. Usually John wouldn't let me go to my mother's house. He would lock the door and hide the key. But this was a special day for me, because we had relatives visiting from Canada. We were quite a large family, and everyone was going to be there for Sunday dinner. John was in one of his moods that day, and he was building into a rage. It had a taken me a week to ask him permission to go to this event, and so I was expecting him to do something to prevent me from attending.

He started complaining about me gallivanting around the country while he had to stay home with nowhere to go. I said that he was welcome to go with me, but he was only insulted by the invitation. How could he spend a Sunday afternoon with the likes of my family? Did I really think he was that pathetic? He started complaining that he had no money to do anything (meaning to go for a drink).

He started arguing with me. He overturned the kitchen table and was breaking things. I went down to the living room where the children were, and my eldest was crying because of the screaming and the broken items. I tried to quiet her. He followed me into the living room, and when he saw her crying, he went into a rage and started shouting, "You stop that crying!" She began to hiccup and was unable to stop. I managed to draw him away from her and got him back into the kitchen. He continued ranting and raving. He grabbed the kids and made us all get into the car. He drove into town, which was about thirteen miles. He was driving like a lunatic at speeds of 110 miles an hour. The children were scared; they were only two, five, and eight at the time. We got to my bank in town, and he made me take money out of my account so he could go drinking. Eventually we made it back home, although we were all terrified.

John came down and said that I could go up to my mother's, but I had to be back by 6:30. He gave me the keys to the car, and as I was walking out of the house he made a comment about the handbag I had with me (he would regularly check my handbag). He said that I looked like a bag lady, so I left the bag in the house with him, even though it contained my ATM card. We left that day with only the clothes on our backs—nothing else.

We arrived at my mother's, and, of course, most of my family had finished their meal and had returned to their own homes. My cousins from Canada were there. My mother and my sister knew some of what was going on. I was in bits when I walked in the kitchen. My sister took me back outside and asked me what was wrong. I burst into tears and told her of the day's events and how scared I was to go back to John when I knew that he was going drinking that night.

I told them that I couldn't live like this anymore and couldn't take another beating. My sister got me the number of Women's Aid, and they gave me the number of two women's refuges. Luckily one had a space for my kids and me. I still have contact with the refuge. I often go to see them. I will never be ashamed of having lived in a women's refuge, because they saved my life.

When I was with John, I used to think that if I could just get away from him, life would be perfect and things would be great. It turned out to be the opposite. I was so scared that he would find me that I would scan streets before walking down them to make sure he wasn't there. In my mind's eye he would be waiting for me with the gun, ready to shoot me.

John didn't know where I was and couldn't find me. I was staying in refuge housing. One day about four months after I had left him, an advocate told me that a bag had been left hanging on the handle of the door with my girls' names on it. Inside the bag were three bottles of pop, three bars of chocolate, and three bags of chips. This scared the hell out of me, and I went to the police. He never did show up. I always felt that John was capable of killing me, and when access to the kids became an issue, I was afraid that he would kill them to get to me, but luckily he is not in our lives and life is much better and worth living.

When I was married to John, I only listened to music that he liked, so after I finally got free, the music I chose to listen to was music I'd liked before I met John. I had to rediscover what I liked to watch on TV, not what I *had* to watch. I had to discover what my likes and dislikes were, and I am still doing that.

I haven't had a relationship with a man since John. I would love to experience sex with someone special, as I'm sure it must be great. I think sometimes that it will never come my way, and it does make me really sad at times. I like to think that I am healed, but I know I am fooling myself. I would say that I don't have a mistrust of men, but I don't trust my judgment. I know there are good men out there, but I feel that in a room of fifty men, the one I would choose would be the only one capable of violence. That really scares me, and so I am scared of falling in love in case the same thing happens again.

As Emma said in telling this story, John could be incredibly charming. Throughout my years of facilitating domestic groups, I have had many likable and articulate participants who have done horrific things to their partners. Without accurate information from the partner, victim advocates, or the criminal justice system, it's easy for practitioners to get conned.

Emma never called the police, so if John had volunteered to see a counselor or even attended a domestic abuse program, we most likely wouldn't have known just how dangerous he really was unless he was totally honest about his past behavior. Having victim advocates in our programs who contact victims before, during, and after the program gives practitioners a way to monitor both a participant's progress and, more important, the danger he poses to his partner. Our responsibility goes beyond therapy, counseling, or educating clients or group participants. Our first priority is keeping the victim safe.

Expectations of Counseling

In the late 1970s and early 1980s, all fifty states enacted pro-arrest statutes for domestic abuse cases. These statutes required law enforcement officers to arrest a suspect if they had probable cause to believe that the individual had committed a crime. Before these laws, officers rarely made arrests in domestic abuse cases unless the assault was severe or occurred in their presence. When these laws passed, the number of arrests skyrocketed. Many people in the battered women's movement originally questioned the value of the court ordering domestic abusers into counseling, asserting that offenders needed more severe consequences. The courts, already concerned about crowded jails, typically stayed jail sentences with probation conditions that required offenders to attend counseling or education classes. Failure to complete the program, or reoffending while in the program, was grounds for revocation of probation, and the jail sentence was to be executed.

In some jurisdictions a coordinated response by law enforcement, the courts, and batterer intervention programs has provided an effective community deterrence. However, in far too many communities, domestic abuse cases are still relegated to the back burner. A violation of a civil court order or failure to attend counseling unfortunately results in a slap on the wrist. When this occurs, victims are at greater risk, because the offender thinks he can continue to batter with impunity.

I interviewed Edward Gondolf, PhD, a highly respected practitioner and researcher on domestic abuse and treatment for offenders. The interviews appear in two films produced by Domestic
Abuse Intervention Programs in 2007. Gondolf maintains that supervision and sanctions by the court, along with encouragement
from counselors and other participants in batterer groups, can have
a profound effect on the change process.

> What we call "coerced treatment" is actually quite effective,
> as is evidenced by the success of drug courts. The threat of
> sanctions works and motivates offenders to complete treat-
> ment and abide by other court orders. I found that some men
> stopped their abusive behavior simply because it was in their
> self-interest—the consequences weren't worth it. Other men
> really did learn things in the groups and became more self-
> aware. People change in varied and complex ways.[1]

The very nature of counseling implies that something is going to
change, and we presume that an offender will alter his behavior as a
result of it. But many offenders don't want to change, see little wrong
with what they've done, and would batter again if a similar situation
occurred. We simply can't predict who will choose to become and
remain nonviolent. Should we give every man who walks into our
groups an opportunity to change? Absolutely. And if an offender
doesn't alter his behavior and continues to assault and terrorize his
partner, the state must intervene and impose more severe sanctions
to stop the violence.

We just don't know which participants will change. I remember
one man who rarely said anything in group, and when he did it was
almost always negative. I thought he was just putting in his time.
Some time later, his partner called to report how much things had
changed in their marriage and how they both attributed his altered
behavior to his participation in the group. I've learned that it's impossible to predict outcomes.

A victim may naturally feel frustrated if her partner is simply going through the motions to satisfy the courts, if he doesn't want to change, or if he becomes more abusive during the counseling process. Effective domestic abuse programs provide advocacy to the men's partners so they know what is being covered in the groups. Women can talk with a victim advocate or with other women in similar situations about the progress—or the lack of progress—their partners are making. As a result some women lower their expectations that their abusive partners will change, and they choose to reevaluate their relationships.

Evaluating the success and analyzing the outcomes of counseling programs is not an exact science and is never easy. Do we base success solely on recidivism—arrest, protection orders taken out, self-reporting—or do we evaluate the partner's perception of changed behavior? Should we accept evaluations of programs that claim high rates of success after assessing the offenders' behavior after only one year, or do we need to examine the sustainability of treatment over a period of years?

We should be realistic about counseling. When an individual man completes his required number of group sessions, we can never be sure he won't be back. We must accept the fact that many men who complete our programs will batter their partners again or assault new women. Over the years men have come back into group with new stories and sometimes new rationalizations. Some are truly ashamed; others are simply resigned to the reality that they got arrested and are now being mandated to a domestic abuse program.

A man who batters begins to change when he has sufficient incentive to do so. These incentives include being arrested, having a protection order filed against him, or losing his relationship. Sometimes a man must repeatedly suffer unpleasant consequences and loss before he is willing to take a long, hard look at himself. But when he makes the commitment to change, resistance to new ideas begins to dissolve and honest self-reflection can begin. He then must explore some difficult issues:

- his attitudes about what he thinks he entitled to as a man
- his beliefs about men being superior to women
- his expectations of women and marriage
- his reasons for wanting to control his intimate partner
- his alternatives for resolving conflicts in his relationships without being abusive or violent
- his willingness to take steps toward living a healthy and fulfilling life

If he allows himself to experience the vulnerability of being human, a man who batters may come to realize that his abusive behavior is ultimately self-defeating, and he will do almost anything to change. Not every man is willing to have his life and everything he believes in twisted inside out—it's hard and often painful. Some men who batter make changes on their own; however, most need the information, challenges, and support provided by batterer groups.

Counseling Frameworks: Theory and Practice

The philosophy and practices of domestic abuse programs are a continuing source of contention. It's tempting to argue, "Whatever works," but the issue is more complex than that, especially if we believe that victim safety is central to our work.

Most domestic abuse offender programs approach their work from one of four frameworks that are based on sometimes conflicting theories about what causes men to batter in the first place and what interventions and treatment models create change. (The four frameworks are described later in this section.) Generally programs share a common goal—to stop the violence—but differ significantly in their approach. Claims of high "success" rates should be viewed with a hefty dose of skepticism. As the men in this book have stated, transformation takes years, and for most of them the process is still ongoing.

Edward Gondolf, whose multisite research on domestic violence recidivism is well known, has conducted a study that backs up this observation. He has found that accurately evaluating program effectiveness requires collecting data over a comparatively long period:

> An experimental design is what we do in clinical trials where one group is randomly assigned to "get the pill" and is ordered into programs and the other half is not. In those studies, we don't see a real effect—in other words, the recidivism rates are similar. However, those studies have a lot of shortcomings and are often unreliable, because the research focuses only on offenders who complete the programs, when many participants actually drop out.
>
> When we look at outcomes in a more sophisticated way, we see very different results. For instance, when we completed our four-site quasi-experimental research, we interviewed hundreds of male participants and their female partners every three months over a four-year period. We had about a 70 percent response rate. About half of the men in these programs reassaulted their partners within the first fifteen months. However, if you look at the trends over a longer period of time, you see significant behavioral changes and a clear de-escalation in violence.
>
> When we examined recidivism over a four-year period, 85 percent of the men court-ordered to these four programs that used a cognitive-behavioral model had not re-assaulted. The vast majority of these men had stopped using violence. We can see the success when women whose partners were in the programs reported that they felt very safe after the four-year period. Two-thirds of the partners who stayed in the relationship reported that their lives were much better off after their partners completed a counseling program.[2]

The debate over the effectiveness of counseling models has been going on for decades and will most certainly continue. Following is an overview of some of the theories that guide the practices of counseling programs, batterer intervention programs, and the counselors and facilitators who work with men who batter. It is not intended as a critique of the new models that have surfaced over the years but as a grouping of approaches into four broad frameworks.

Psychological Framework

We Americans have an appetite for viewing social problems in psychological terms. To help understand and explain criminal behavior in all its various forms, we have created a symbiotic relationship between the criminal justice system and the mental health community. The courts assume that the antisocial behavior they see every day must have a psychological basis. They often turn to psychologists, psychiatrists, therapists, and social workers in the mental health field to work with offenders who are incarcerated or under some form of court supervision. In domestic abuse cases, the courts are increasingly sending offenders to mental health centers for evaluation and/or treatment.

Although mental health practitioners today have a deeper understanding of domestic violence than their predecessors did a generation ago, they still too frequently do a disservice to both the victim and the offender. Well-meaning mental health practitioners, in part due to their educational and professional orientation, have labeled battered women as masochistic, codependent, passive-aggressive, having poor self-images, or exhibiting learned helplessness. A battered woman must explain why she got involved in an abusive relationship and why she stayed, and she must defend her coping and survival skills. Rather than exploring the historical precedents for gender-based violence in our culture, many mental health practitioners assume that the victims' choices reflect their psychological problems. This is not to say that some battered women can't benefit from mental health counseling. To start with, healing from the trauma of being battered is painful and complex.

Similarly many mental health practitioners believe domestic abuse offenders batter because they have psychological problems.

They diagnose men who batter with a variety of disorders, among them antisocial, borderline, narcissistic, avoidant, dependent, compulsive, obsessive, paranoid, and attachment disorders. They label men who batter as having poor impulse control, low frustration tolerance, and a fear of intimacy. Most therapists and psychologists who accept third-party insurance payments must provide a diagnosis consistent with the American Psychological Association's *Diagnostic and Statistical Manual of Mental Disorders* (DSM-V) to have the treatment covered. Once the diagnosis is made, treatment is based on certain assumptions. If the diagnosis is an attachment disorder, the practitioner may help the offender examine childhood relationships with his parents, exploring how those experiences now impact his fear of intimacy, his inability to trust, and his anxiety over losing his intimate partner. If the diagnosis is a reaction to childhood trauma, then the practitioner may work with the client to help him understand the roots of his shame and explore the pain and anger created by those family experiences (e.g., physical or sexual abuse, observing domestic violence, or growing up with parents who had substance abuse problems).

The assumption is that if the offender weren't insecure or shamed, if he had worked through his childhood trauma experiences, then he wouldn't batter. However, plenty of seemingly secure men with strong self-concepts see nothing wrong with beating their intimate partners. In 1987 actor Sean Connery told interviewer Barbara Walters on national TV that you slap women only "if you've tried everything else, and—women are pretty good at this—they can't leave it alone. They want to have the last word, and you give them the last word, but they're not happy with the last word. They want to say it again, and get into a really provocative situation. Then I think it's absolutely right." The late Aristotle Onassis, a wealthy tycoon, was stopped by the police after assaulting a woman in his car. He told the police he had stopped beating her because he was tired.

More recently actor Charlie Sheen, who was arrested for domestic assault on two occasions, maintained that every woman who made allegations that he was an abuser was lying, calling them "sad trolls." Singer Chris Brown pleaded guilty to a felony assault against his girlfriend, singer Rihanna. In the police report Rihanna stated that Brown punched her numerous times, put her in a headlock that restricted her breathing, and threatened to "beat the shit" out of her. He said later, "I was trying to prove myself as a man."

These men don't seem overly insecure—and they are not anomalies. They just happen to be celebrities.

This assumption also doesn't explain why most women who have significant childhood trauma experiences (experiencing incest or abuse at the hands of a parent, witnessing domestic abuse) don't batter and rape their intimate partners. While some women use violence and are controlling in their intimate relationship, most do not batter (use physical and sexual violence, intimidation, threats, and coercion to dominate their husbands or boyfriends).

Focusing on the individual psychological problems of an offender at the expense of challenging his beliefs and attitudes about women and male entitlement will not produce significant changes in behavior. This is not to say that some men who batter don't have mental health problems that need to be addressed. The question is whether the court should order the "therapy du jour" for a man who has beaten his wife.

This description of the psychological framework and discussion of the mental health community is not intended as a general criticism of an admirable field. Many mental health practitioners are well-informed about domestic abuse issues. Unfortunately others still have little contact with battered women's advocates, they are insufficiently trained in the dynamics of battering, they provide marriage counseling at inappropriate times, and their agencies have weak policies regarding offenders who use violence while in the program.

It is true that some offenders have co-occurring conditions, such as depression, substance abuse problems, and personality disorders. The question is whether these mental health problems caused their violence; most men who suffer from them don't batter their intimate partners. This is not to say that some offenders ordered into domestic abuse programs with co-occurring conditions wouldn't benefit from additional counseling. Screening and assessments can help programs determine those offenders who because of the severity of their mental health problems are inappropriate for groups.

Relationship-Conflict Framework

Some practitioners trained in family-system approaches believe that both parties in a relationship contribute to domestic abuse. While careful never to say the victim is responsible for getting beaten by her partner, they often imply that her behavior provides an impetus for his reaction. The practitioner then assumes the couple is engaging in mutual combat, or that the wife provokes her husband by below-the-belt arguments, aggravating and escalating the confrontation. Practitioners will sometimes describe this scenario as a "dance" between the partners and deem the violence an interpersonal transaction.

If the goal is to repair the relationship through marriage counseling, the therapist will try to help the couple resolve conflicts in a nonabusive manner, work with them to explore ways to redistribute power in the relationship, and teach healthy conflict resolution and communication techniques. These goals are certainly valid when the threat of violence isn't present. However, the challenge is determining when it's safe to provide marriage counseling to a couple. Victims have reported being beaten in the parking lot of a therapist's office immediately after a counseling session. From a practical standpoint, how can a therapist help a couple redistribute power when one person isn't ready to relinquish control? How can one party talk honestly about issues in the relationship when she's afraid of retribution?

Some people say marriage counseling is never appropriate in domestic abuse cases. This position is also misguided—some couples do stay together. Practitioners should follow clear guidelines, and agencies ought to adopt rigorous policies to protect victims. Marriage counseling should be provided only under the following circumstances:

- The offender has successfully completed a reputable domestic abuse program that challenges the belief system that men are entitled to be in control in intimate relationships.
- A practitioner who has worked with the offender is convinced that he has ended his battering—violence, coercion, threats, intimidation, and psychological abuse.
- The battered woman has worked with a victim advocate and has developed a safety plan to get help if her partner becomes abusive.
- The battered woman feels safe.
- The practitioner has discussed the risks associated with marriage counseling privately with the woman and feels relatively sure abusive acts will not take place as the result of their sessions.

Many offenders who are ordered into our programs become upset when we won't make a marriage counseling referral for them. They protest and argue, "How can we work on our problems if we aren't in counseling together?" Offering marriage counseling at an early stage of intervention implies that the couple is having marital problems, and it gives the offender a rationalization for his behavior. He may use the counseling sessions against her. He might say, "Remember we are both in this together," "You know that it takes two to tango," "If you would just stop doing that, I wouldn't have to hit you," "Remember what the counselor said about the way you handled that situation."

When a battered woman tells her story in marriage counseling, she might say she feels some responsibility for the violence:

"I shouldn't have said that," "I should have waited to talk to him about it," "I could see he was in a bad mood," "I shouldn't have gotten in his face." Her interpretations of events may provide the offender enough space to escape responsibility for his actions. The practitioner may then unintentionally collude with him, offering an implied acceptance that his behavior was an understandable reaction to her actions, despite qualifying statements that the violence was nevertheless wrong.

In some cases the defense attorney, the offender, or the couple themselves tell the court that they are already in marriage counseling and request that they be allowed to continue. Unless educated on domestic abuse dynamics, judges and probation officers often believe the offender's motivation is sincere, and they fail to recognize the dangers of court-mandated marriage counseling in lieu of other sanctions. In one of my interviews with Edward Gondolf, he stated:

> We're seeing an increased attention to couples counseling because a lot of clinical psychologists are trained to look at these cases from a family-systems model. Yes, there may be family-system dynamics, but that doesn't explain what causes one person to cross the line and assault someone. Research shows that those offenders who attend couples counseling don't do any better than the men who go to a traditional batterer intervention program.[3]

Anger-Management Framework

In the anger-management framework, the practitioner views the client as having poor impulse control or as having patterns of reacting to conflict or stress with aggression. The inherent assumption is that the offender's stress and anger builds until an incident triggers a violent outburst.

Practitioners who subscribe to this theory believe anger-management techniques can be taught to the offender so he won't batter. The focus is on teaching him to be aware of physical and emotional cues when he's upset or angry. Physical signs might be tightened fists, clenched teeth, or rapid breathing; emotional signs might be stress, anxiety, or feeling hurt or disrespected. Offenders are taught de-escalation techniques. The time-out—during which the offender removes himself from a conflict if he feels he might become abusive—is perhaps the most effective strategy. Other techniques include meditation, deep breathing, and self-talk.

Anger-management techniques within a holistic intervention approach can be effective, and most domestic abuse programs teach them. I support some of these skill-building techniques with the following caveats. Anger management alone usually won't stop a man who batters from using violence; it may provide an intermittent respite when religiously practiced, but fundamental behavioral change will occur only when the offender begins to change his beliefs and attitudes about men, women, and entitlement. Time-outs, if used effectively, will calm a tense situation, but they won't resolve the issue. A man who batters is likely to admit that eventually, when a disagreement won't go away, he will resolve the conflict by making a threat, using forms of intimidation, or being violent. Maybe not in every instance, or over every conflict, but his need to control a situation and settle things on his terms frequently wins out, and he resorts to abusive behavior he knows will be effective.

While perhaps not intended, the anger-management framework is supported by another theory: that of the cycle of violence. In 1979 Dr. Lenore Walker, an important voice in the domestic abuse field, outlined the cycle of violence as a typical scenario in abusive relationships. She describes a tension-building phase, during which minor escalating incidents, including verbal abuse, occur. The offender's stress escalates to the point at which an acute incident occurs and, unable to control himself, he beats the victim. In the next step of the cycle, the couple moves into a honeymoon phase, during which they experience emotional closeness, the offender is remorseful, he is given another chance, and all is forgiven. Then the cycle starts all over again.[4]

This well-known theory accurately explains the dynamics of *some* couples in abusive relationships, at least early on. Some battered women say they knew things were never going to change when their partners stopped apologizing. But for Holly, and for many other abused women, the cycle of violence doesn't describe their reality:

> My husband and I were at a bar, where he was playing pool. He had gotten upset with me because I wanted to go home and he didn't. The next thing I knew, he told me to go outside with him, which I did. When we got there, he grabbed hold of me and punched me in the face with all of his might and said, "There you go, bitch, now go home!" I was really shaken. I picked myself up, dusted myself off, and went home. The next day I had this huge fat lip. When my husband came downstairs, I expected an apology or some kind of recognition of what he'd done—you know, like, "I'm sorry, I was drunk" or "I don't know what got into me." But when he saw me he never said a word; he never even acknowledged what he had done.

The cycle of violence theory doesn't apply in cases like Holly's, and neither does the anger-management framework. Holly's husband was angry, but his violence wasn't about losing control. He was agitated and wanted her out of his hair. His behavior was methodical; using his fist, he was saying, "I will go home when I want, and I don't want any hassle from you. Case closed."

The tension-building phase described by this theory implies that, unless interrupted, the stressors active in the offender will inevitably produce a violent outburst. But if this were always true, how do we explain the many irrational violent attacks by an offender for very trivial issues? How do we account for the offender who wakes his wife up in the middle of the night to beat her for no discernable reason? While anger is a powerful emotion, and usually precedes a violent attack, it does not *cause* the violence. Perhaps more important, the theory doesn't explain why the offender's partner is the target of his violence, when he might actually be angry about something or someone totally unrelated to her. The theory also doesn't explain why an offender doesn't assault his boss, coworkers, friends, or a stranger on the street when he's angry.

The Domestic Abuse Intervention Project initially conducted anger-management classes for court-mandated offenders. Because we adhered to this framework, men would explain their reasons for attending in terms of anger: "I'm here because I can't control my anger." "I've got a short fuse and got into trouble with my girlfriend, so the judge told me to come to this group." "When I get provoked, I lose it and get violent." "I've got an anger problem, so I'm court-ordered to this program." "My probation officer thinks I need to get hold of my anger." But the anger-management framework gives men who batter the wrong message: These explanations don't address the intentionality and purpose behind violent and abusive behavior.

Perhaps more problematic, this framework puts the burden on the victim to change her behavior so she doesn't "provoke" her husband. She is taught to recognize when her partner's anger is beginning to escalate and to do things to lighten the tension—an awesome responsibility to put on a victim. After all of these years, I'm still amazed at how many shelters, battered women's programs, and police officers still use the cycle of violence theory to explain battering.

Anger management should be part—but only part—of a treatment plan for offenders. For a man to stop battering, he must go much deeper into his understanding of his sense of entitlement and why he wants a woman in his life.

The Cognitive-Behavioral Framework
I was traveling in British Columbia some years back. I had been scheduled to conduct trainings in several cities, so I decided to rent a car and enjoy the scenery as a break between events. As I traveled down a highway, I came upon a construction site and was directed

to stop my car. A road construction worker told me it would take about a half hour before the road would reopen. Since I wasn't in a big hurry and the landscape was beautiful, I parked the car and walked over to the river adjacent to the road.

Soon a truck pulled up behind my car and the driver got out. He heard the same explanation about the road and decided to come visit me by the river. He was a big guy—about six feet four inches and weighing around 270 pounds. I'm five feet seven inches and weigh about 170 pounds. He wore a Harley vest over a bare chest, exposing several tattoos, and I was wearing a suit jacket. I thought so much for my peaceful time by the river. As he approached, for some reason I spit on the ground. It was one of those guttural kinds of spitting—a reflexive male-bonding thing I learned in my adolescence.

We started to make small talk. I asked him about his job as a trucker and the current state of affairs in Canada. He filled me in on both subjects. Then he asked me what I was doing in British Columbia. I thought for a minute—do I really want to tell this guy what I do for a living and then have to talk about domestic abuse?

"I'm sort of a social worker," I said, then tried to change the subject. "How 'bout those Maple Leafs?"

He answered, "They'll stink again. A social worker, eh? What kind of family troubles do you work on?"

I figured he wasn't going to drop the matter, so I told him. "I work with men who beat their wives."

"Men who beat their wives," he said with some surprise and amusement.

"Yup," I said.

There was a slight pause in the conversation; then he looked me square in the eyes and said, "You wanna know why women get beat?"

He seemed so confident.

"Why?" I asked.

He said, "I'll tell you why women get beat. They get beat 'cause they don't listen."

And then he spit. And then I spit and pondered for a moment. I thought, should I confront this guy? There's no way he can out-argue me on this subject. After all I read, lecture, train, and write about domestic abuse. I eat and drink this stuff. Then again if I did confront him, I could be putting my life in jeopardy by having a philosophical debate with a guy who had "One Way—My Way" carved into one arm and "Instant Asshole—Just Add Alcohol" on the other. I thought about what he said about women not listening, and I realized that, in an odd sort of way, he was right. His explanation distilled the thinking of most men who batter into one observation. When I think about the hundreds of men I've worked with over the years, except for incidents of true self-defense, men batter (1) to get their partners to stop doing something, (2) to stop their partners from saying things or to end an argument, or (3) to punish their partners for something they've done. It really is that simple.

We said our good-byes when the road was reopened—just two guys on the highway.

I tell this story because every time we try to come up with psychological theories or explanations for why a man who batters is violent, we shortchange victims and offenders alike by providing a rationalization. We treat and work around the edges, missing the "because they don't listen" explanation at the heart of every story. This statement, which asserts the right to control what one's partner does, suggests the reason why cognitive-behavioral treatment is an effective approach: It challenges the thoughts and beliefs that rationalize battering. When "women don't listen" becomes "we listen to each other," balance in a relationship can be established or restored.

Cognitive-behavioral treatment (CBT) focuses on helping people with behavioral problems explore the relationship between their thoughts, feelings, and behaviors by examining how they create patterns that lead to actions and conduct destructive to themselves and others. CBT is used by corrections and community-counseling programs to deal with an array of problems, among them substance abuse, sexual misconduct, domestic abuse, and personality disorders.

Under the broad CBT umbrella is a group approach, a curriculum titled *Creating a Process of Change for Men Who Batter,* which was created in Duluth.[5] Embedded in the Duluth curriculum is the premise that men's violence against women is learned behavior. Men who batter abuse their intimate partners because on some level they are convinced they are entitled to call the shots in the relationship. They get to end a dispute when they want it ended. There are variations on this thinking, but belief in male superiority is a central theme for many men, especially for men who batter.

Using the Duluth curriculum, counselors and facilitators help offenders analyze key elements of their violent and abusive behavior. The elements are:

1. naming his abusive actions
2. identifying the intention for his use of that behavior
3. examining the underlying beliefs that he used to justify his actions
4. identifying the feelings that motivated him to act and then connecting those feelings to his beliefs
5. becoming aware of the ways he minimizes, denies, and blames his partner for his behavior
6. examining the effects of his actions on the woman he abused, on their children, and on himself
7. acknowledging how his past use of violence impacts his partner's responses to him
8. recognizing that there are always alternatives to using violence

Facilitators and counselors then engage participants in a dialogical process to help them think critically about their actions and beliefs and to seek nonviolent and noncontrolling alternatives to dealing with conflict. The Duluth curriculum gives participants insights into what an equal relationship with an intimate partner looks like—one involving respect, fairness, trust, support, honesty, and shared responsibility. There is more information on the Duluth curriculum in Appendix B.

Of course, not all men who have used abusive behaviors in their intimate relationships believe males are superior to females. Some men find themselves in power struggles with their partners. A small percentage could even be described as battered men, and protection and advocacy for these men should be no different from that provided for battered women. Occasionally couples engage in true mutual violence; in these situations both parties need not only counseling but also legal sanctions to protect each of them from future acts of violence by the other.

Batterer intervention and domestic abuse programs that have a feminist (sometimes called profeminist) analysis maintain that men's violence against women is a social problem with deep historical roots. Such programs usually use a cognitive-behavioral or psycho-educational approach in their work.

Challenging beliefs and attitudes and helping men who batter think more critically about their behavior is central to this approach. The groups are designed to help them construct a different kind of relationship, one based on egalitarianism and respect. The focus is not only on eliminating physical and sexual violence but also on reducing and eliminating the many other abusive behaviors that constitute battering.

Some of these programs combine various therapies within the CBT framework, and most of them work closely with or are connected to battered women's programs. EMERGE in Boston, RAVEN in St. Louis, the Domestic Abuse Project in Minneapolis, the Domestic Abuse Intervention Project in Duluth, AMEND in Denver, ManAlive in Marin County, and Men Against Violence in Atlanta were some of the early programs based on a profeminist analysis. Today there are an estimated twelve hundred to three thousand such programs nationally.

Edward Gondolf asserts that the CBT approach can decrease or eliminate the need for psychological treatment approaches in offender programs:

> Some practitioners can use their clinical skills with men in groups who need more attention, but you always run the risk of diffusing the ultimate goals of the group when practitioners are focusing on personality disorders. When you use a cognitive-behavioral approach, you don't necessarily need to develop a therapeutic relationship with the men in the groups. First, we usually don't have the time, and second, cognitive-behavioral treatment helps men recognize their thought processes, which is what we should be focusing on in groups.
>
> Men in our programs frequently have multiple problems. Where the psychology field is divided is on the relationship between the personality disorders/mental health problems and the abusive behavior. With a cognitive-behavioral approach, you are attempting to interrupt the violence and abusive behavior and then treat the other problems later. It's similar to chemical dependency treatment—you first want to get the person sober, then you can deal with issues of depression and other problems.
>
> If we look at the psychological profiles of offenders, I think that cognitive-behavior approaches are more successful with men who batter. Their distinguishing profile is that they have tendencies of narcissism, and a highly structured cognitive-behavioral model is most effective with this population.[6]

Backlash

A small number of practitioners and researchers have recently been challenging the assumptions and guiding principles of the battered women's movement and profeminist domestic abuse programs. Critics have assailed mandatory arrest as being counterproductive. Community and state standards to ensure offender accountability have been weakened. In some communities offenders are simply referred to a treatment provider recommended by the court or chosen by the offender. One-day treatment programs are sometimes offered as an alternative to traditional programs lasting six months or longer. In some jurisdictions an online anger-management class satisfies the court.

Some practitioners are retreating from any feminist analysis and now use gender-neutral language when describing battering. To appease funders and critics they may avoid discussing the long history of men's violence against women as a form of oppression. Some practitioners claim that women are as violent as men, and despite the risks involved there is a renewed emphasis on promoting couples counseling.

The Duluth curriculum has also been a target of this backlash. Much of the criticism is based on flawed research, and some of the challenges come from researchers and practitioners who are repackaging old psychological theories about domestic abuse. Many critics erroneously consider the Duluth curriculum to be the same thing as the Duluth Model; the curriculum is only one piece of the Duluth Model, an overall community intervention approach that, when implemented properly, unquestionably enhances the safety of victims.[7]

In his book *The Future of Batterer Programs*, Edward Gondolf sums up the problem:

> At the heart of the contention over batterer programs is the divide between the gender-based, cognitive-behavioral approaches that dominate conventional programs and the more psychodynamic approaches that claim to be more therapeutic and ultimately more effective. A careful review of the evidence, however, shows that many of the claims about the alternative approaches have weaker research and even contradictory findings behind them. And there is substantial generic evidence that cognitive-behavioral approaches are well suited for the men in batterer programs and are just as effective as other approaches, if not more so.
>
> The critical characterization of gender-based cognitive-behavioral programs, such as the Duluth program, has also been shown to be a distorted stereotype. Many of these bat-

terer programs are incorporating therapeutic techniques to better engage unresponsive men. What does emerge from the research is evidence of a subgroup of men who have psychological problems that contribute to program dropout rates and make the men resistant to change. More supervision and additional treatments may be warranted for them.[8]

How Well Does Counseling Work?

Edward Gondolf also writes about some of the problems with research comparing domestic abuse interventions:

> The current evidence-based practice is vital to sort out inefficient and ineffective interventions across the criminal justice system.... But the misuse of evidence can be disruptive and detrimental to program development. Overemphasis on tentative findings, highly selective use of studies, and quoting one or two studies to make a point can be misleading.... Evidence-based practices in some ways are constricting programs with their dogma of experiments and bottom line messages about what works. You have research and practitioner factions with their own agendas that are promoting and using this research. They are using more of a medical model to determine effectiveness. This doesn't work in this field very well.[9]

Clearly the domestic abuse field has challenges ahead, and it will evolve to meet them. As in substance abuse treatment, new approaches will be tried, research will be conducted, and programs will modify their practices. Whatever the future brings, I remain optimistic that the hardworking practitioners and advocates who are striving to end men's violence against women will continue their efforts with passion and determination.

As Ellen Pence said, "Whatever the counseling approach, whatever the debate on 'what works'—it'll all be a mere footnote in history. What *will* be remembered is that in the 1970s and 1980s, we made wife-beating a crime, and women are safer today because of it."[10]

Tips for
Counselors and Facilitators

Practitioners bring their own style and approach to facilitating domestic abuse groups. Our training, education, and even our personal experiences shape how we interact with the men in our groups. The following are a few hints that have worked for me.

Challenge the Group and Challenge Yourself

The issue of gender violence reaches the inner core of any man or woman doing this work. It is impossible to divorce your own feelings, beliefs, and experiences from your work with men who batter. We've all been socialized by the cultures in which we live, and we've all had conflicts in our relationships. When facilitating a group, avoid the us-and-them attitude; the men in your group will sense it and will shut down. Talk instead about your own experiences and struggles with sexist beliefs and how you have worked and continue to work on your issues.

Believe in the Capacity of Men to Change

Try to be affirming in your group. Let men know when you think they're working hard on an issue, and acknowledge their successes. Don't give up on resistant men. Some men who batter keep the rough facade to cover the pain and fear they often feel but don't talk about.

Stay Connected with Battered Women's Programs

Practitioners are often isolated from battered women and their advocates. Sometimes I'm invited to sit in on a women's group or listen to a group of battered women tell their stories at a workshop. I always accept, in part because when we are facilitating groups the stories we hear are those of the men. Listening to battered women is a reality check for me.

In one group a man named Darrell told me how great things were going in his relationship and how he was using the tools we were teaching to better communicate in a noncontrolling manner with his wife, Carol. Later that week I was sitting in on a woman's support group when a woman named Carol began telling a story very similar to the one Darrell had told earlier in the week. The good communication Darrell was so proud of turned out to be very serious threats to take the children and leave the state unless Carol gave up the idea of going back to school.

Be Compassionate Without Colluding

Part of your role is to facilitate an environment and group process in which group participants can think critically and reflect on who they are as men and how they got to the point where they battered their intimate partner. In dialogue you are genuinely curious about what an individual man in your group thinks. You ask probing questions and challenge ideas that are presented, while speaking your own truth and without being dogmatic or shaming.

Model Respectful Relationships

Ideally groups are cofacilitated by a man and a woman. Spend some time together prior to the group reviewing the material you will be presenting, and be clear about your respective roles. For instance you might alternate duties every other week, with one of you recording feedback and comments on the board while the other pays more attention to how the participants are responding, asks questions of individual men, and keeps the group process focused.

Be open to critical feedback from your cofacilitator or from staff members monitoring the group. Male and female facilitators should model respectful interaction. I've observed some groups in which the man failed to challenge group members, leaving the woman in that unenviable role. Balance and support are key ingredients to successful cofacilitation. When the session is over, discuss what worked and what didn't.

Keep the Group Focused

It is easy to get sidetracked when you're facilitating a group. Often a group member will go off on a tangent in an attempt to defend his position, especially when it comes to rationalizing his behavior. When dialogue breaks down and the group gets diverted, bring it back into focus by pointing out that participants are making choices when they are violent and controlling. Emphasize that there are always alternatives to being abusive. If someone is dominating the discussion, respectfully interrupt and bring others into the dialogue by asking another group member what he thinks about the issue being discussed.

Opening the Group

Most groups have what is commonly called a "check-in" during which group members explain why they were ordered into the program. Some check-ins require the participants to report what happened to them during the past week and to talk about issues affecting their lives. Some groups have participants talk about the violent incident that got them ordered into the program or their most violent incident. At the DAIP we decided to abandon check-ins because they were too time consuming, group members were using the check-in to avoid the material being covered, and some groups had started to sound like AA meetings. I observed one group in which the check-in took an hour and fifteen minutes; consequently the counselors had only a half-hour to cover the material. Two other options may be useful:

1. Eliminate the check-in altogether. Just begin the group with the material you are going to cover.
2. Observe a three- or four-minute period of silence or meditation before beginning. Some counselors in Duluth have found that this time allows the men to relax, reduce their apprehension, and get rid of their negative self-talk. After the meditation the group leaders immediately get into their material for the day.

Related Groups and Programs

A support group can be an important component of your program. Men who are serious about making changes need a place where they can continue to talk about gender and violence issues and get support from other men. Unfortunately offering a support group may be difficult due to limited resources, and few court-ordered offenders take advantage of this service when it exists.

Parenting Classes/Child Visitation Centers

In Duluth, parenting classes have been required by the court if there is evidence a man is inappropriately disciplining his children. One of the goals of the Duluth Child Safety Center—the Visitation Center—is to reduce the trauma to children when a judge has ordered an offender to be excluded from the household or has set a visitation schedule. The Visitation Center is a place where children can be safely picked up and dropped off without the couple having contact. It also provides a neutral location where supervised visitations can take place in a fun and safe environment for the children.

Culturally Specific Groups

It is always a good idea to discuss implementation of your program with diverse groups in your community. For instance the Native American community is the largest minority group in Duluth. Court-mandated Native American men who batter can choose to go a Native group or a mixed group. The Duluth curriculum was adapted for these groups to incorporate traditional Native American values about healing and living in balance. In other cities with large Latino, African American, and Asian populations, culturally specific groups are often offered.

Gay Men's Groups

It is estimated that of the 9.5 million gay men in the United States, about 500,000 are victims of domestic abuse. Counseling services for gay offenders and victims exist predominantly in larger cities, but increased awareness of the extent of the problem has resulted in program development in the LGBTQ communities around the country.[11]

Most state statutes don't differentiate between same-sex violence and heterosexual domestic abuse, and mental health agencies have been slow to offer groups for gay perpetrators and victims. It is inadvisable to court-order a gay man into a traditional (straight) offender group in which he would in all probability have to be "closeted" due to the reaction of other men. Consult with members of the LGBTQ community about how to start a group and how to get the word out to various interveners in the community.

Risk and Danger in Domestic Abuse Cases

Once social change begins, it cannot be reversed.
You cannot uneducate the person who has learned to read.
You cannot humiliate the person who feels pride.
You cannot oppress the people who are not afraid anymore.

▸▸ CESAR CHAVEZ ◂◂

When Desperation Turns to Tragedy

Desperation is an emotional state of despair in which a person feels a situation is hopeless, making them more liable to make rash, impulsive, or inappropriate decisions. Despair may give rise to obsession: a compulsive preoccupation with an idea or with unwanted and overwhelming feelings. The loss of a relationship (or the threat of losing it) can produce obsession. Both men and women obsess over the loss of intimate partners and behave poorly. For most people an obsession is short lived, but too often when people feel desperate, their behavior results in tragedy.

Men and women behave differently when a relationship ends. Men are far more likely to stalk, use violence, or kill their partners or ex-partners. Females are twice as likely as males to be killed by intimate partners. In 2007 women made up 70 percent of victims killed by an intimate partner, a proportion that has changed very little since 1993.[1] Half of the women killed by an intimate partner had experienced violence within thirty days of the homicide. Although leaving an abusive partner can end the violence, attempting to leave a relationship was also the precipitating factor in 45 percent of the murders of a woman by an abusive man.[2]

In the mid-2000s a brutal homicide occurred in a bedroom community in St. Paul, the city where I live. There was something about this case that cried out for more explanation. After the murder, the Elk Lake County Attorney stated to the press, "If someone really wants to kill [someone else], there's nothing you can do to stop them." While there is some truth to the statement, in this case that explanation rang hollow for me, and it certainly did for the victim's family.

On a windy fall evening in the small town of Franklin, Minnesota, Elizabeth Benson and her partner, Jake Allen, were brutally shot to death by William Perry. Elizabeth had done everything a domestic abuse victim should do when she recognized the signs that her estranged boyfriend was dangerous. Most important she trusted her instincts—she knew he was dangerous. It's hard not to conclude that the criminal justice system failed them.

Elizabeth's sister Patty came to see me. I was a member of the Minnesota House of Representatives and had a history of working on domestic abuse issues. Patty was angry at the criminal justice system and wanted to know what we could do differently so that people like Elizabeth are protected from an intimate partner who shows signs of being dangerous. Her acute sense of injustice and pain at the loss of her sister was wrenching.

During a lengthy discussion we examined the areas where the system had broken down. While it would be easy to blame the judge, the prosecuting attorney, the local police, and the sheriff's deputies, after looking at the case more carefully it became clear that there were systemic problems that caused interveners to respond the way they did. Whereas the judge, county attorney, and law enforcement officers had more or less followed their policies, they failed to detect the danger Elizabeth was in from Perry. They had handled many "domestics" in the past, so they thought they were doing the right thing.

Single-handedly Patty catapulted the heinous murder of her sister into the spotlight. She wanted to ensure that justice was attained for her sister and other victims of domestic violence. The heartbreaking story received significant attention after a national television show devoted an hour to the case.

Elizabeth's Story

Elizabeth's first marriage ended tragically. Her husband, with whom she had four children, was driving home with their daughter Tara when he lost control of his car, hit a tree head-on, and was killed. Elizabeth became a widow.

About a year after her husband's death, Elizabeth began wondering if she should start dating again. She missed the companionship of an intimate relationship. The death of her husband was an emotional blow, and the thought of starting over with someone new was not something she took lightly. Still she knew that she needed to get on with her life.

She started attending social events that her employer sponsored on the weekends. She met William Perry at a company volleyball game. He was attracted to her and would leave unsigned notes on her desk at work. They became friendly. William asked Elizabeth out and she accepted. Elizabeth was also attracted to William. She would tell Patty that they had fun together and that he would help with the kids, make dinner, and go with her to the kids' sporting events. With four children, Elizabeth appreciated the help. Disturbingly William would send not-so-subtle messages to Elizabeth that most men wouldn't hook up with a woman who had four children. She believed him and became emotionally dependent on him.

Elizabeth thought William was controlling, but early on he wasn't physically abusive to her or the children. After two years of dating, things started to change. The relationship became rocky. Although he was not violent at this time, trust issues surfaced, and Elizabeth questioned whether the relationship would work. She broke up with him several times, but they would always reconcile. She complained most about his dishonesty. According to Patty, William had a secret life that Elizabeth didn't know about for a long time. He was paying "high-dollar call girls" for "services." He would go off to Las Vegas and not tell anyone. It was this mysterious private life—his lying and dishonesty—that finally got Elizabeth thinking that the relationship wasn't going to work.

The more Elizabeth showed independence, the more upset he would get. After two years she finally broke off her relationship with him, but that didn't end things. William would show up at the kids' games. Part of Elizabeth thought that he really did care for her children. Another part of her thought that he was using them to get at her. He would often stay in his car and watch the game from the parking lot, or sometimes just sit in the stands and watch, but he wouldn't sit with her. Eventually William asked Elizabeth if he could watch the game with her, and she relented. She got hooked into seeing the qualities that had originally attracted her to him.

Patty was troubled because Elizabeth was still seeing William. Elizabeth would say, "You know, there are times when I really like him, and I like that he still pays attention to the kids." She was clear that she had no intention of getting back together with him, but she wanted to remain friends.

When Elizabeth ended her relationship with William, she reconnected with an old friend from high school, Jake Allen. They started dating. This was the beginning of the end. Jake knew about Elizabeth's fear of William, so he helped her install a security system in her home. On a Saturday night Elizabeth went to a bonfire party and stayed overnight with friends. The kids were safely at her parent's cabin. When Elizabeth came home the next morning, she found beer cans in the mailbox. It became clear that William had taken the house keys from her daughter's backpack; Tara had told her mom the day before that she must have lost them. Elizabeth called her neighbor, who confirmed that William had been at her house; she had seen his car. Elizabeth also called the police. They had arrived to talk to her when William called. An officer got on the phone and warned him not to come to Elizabeth's house again or he would be charged with trespassing.

When the police left, Elizabeth again called her neighbor. She was extremely upset that William had entered her house, and she asked the neighbor to please call 911 if she ever saw him at the house again. At that point William pulled into the driveway. He entered the house with two butcher knives, threatening to kill her. This all happened while Elizabeth was on the phone with her neighbor. The neighbor could hear William saying, "You've done this to me, now the only way for us to be together is for me to kill you and myself." The neighbor called 911.

Elizabeth was petrified. William had a crazed look and seemed determined to kill her. She frantically ran behind the dining room table and picked up chairs to block his attempts to stab her. He kept saying, "I'm going to kill you." By this time police sirens were blaring in the background. She pleaded for her life. Elizabeth's face, arms, and back were severely bruised from William's grabbing her, but he never slashed or stabbed her with the knives. She bolted out the front door, and William followed.

Hearing the sirens getting closer, William took off in his car. Before he left, he made a threatening comment to her about the kids. Now her immediate concern shifted from protecting herself to the safety of her family. If William was willing to kill her and kill himself, would he harm her children? She called her parents and warned them to get the kids out of the cabin.

The officer who investigated this initial assault later told the neighbor that he had a bad feeling about leaving the scene. It's not unusual for police officers to have a sixth sense about a suspect, which is why risk assessments at many levels of intervention are so important. That afternoon the Elk Lake County deputies arrested William at his home in Wisconsin. He was charged with second-degree assault, terroristic threats, and burglary. He was arraigned the following Monday.

Elizabeth pleaded with the judge not to set bail or at least to set it higher. She said, "I have no doubt that this man will return to my home and kill me." She thought that the county attorney was minimizing the incident and that William should have been charged with attempted murder. She called the county attorney's office to ask why they had never picked up the knife-scarred chairs at her house for evidence. A week later an investigator finally arrived to take pictures of the chairs, but the photos were never presented in court.

William's bail was set at seventy-five thousand dollars. The judge made a no-contact order a condition of the release. William was put on administrative leave from his job because he was in possession of acetone. The county attorney later said, "It was one of those he-said, she-said cases." The judge said, "The conditions imposed were standard for the charge."

Elizabeth had the locks on the doors changed. Despite the no-contact order, William had his friends call Elizabeth and ask her to drop the charges. She didn't realize that this was a violation of the no-contact order, so she didn't call the police. Then William sent her a disturbing e-mail, and she immediately called the police. According to Patty, the officer "blew her off" and ignored the complaint, because the e-mail had come from William's father's e-mail account. She was furious at the officer, who told her, "The e-mail is just his way of trying to get back together with you." She argued with him, saying, "No, he wants to kill me!"

Elizabeth then called the sheriff's deputy and tried to discuss the e-mail. One of the deputies told her, "You don't have to worry about William. I talked to him, and he's not going to come after you. He feels really bad for what happened." Incredulous, Patty told me that the police department had the e-mail. They could have arrested him but didn't.

Elizabeth had alerted the principal at the children's school about what had happened and had explained her fears. She made copies of the no-contact order and wanted all the teachers and staff to have copies of it. She believed that William would take the kids, and Tara had been told that if he ever came to the school, she was to report it. When William violated the order again and showed up at Tara's volleyball game, the principal called Elizabeth and the police. They had William on the security camera at the school, and Elizabeth was told that an arrest warrant would be issued.

Although a warrant for William's arrest was issued, the police never sent a copy to the neighboring county in Wisconsin, where he lived. (After the killing, the department justified this inaction by claiming that they couldn't send the warrant because it had been issued in Minnesota.) Elizabeth was terrified.

William left a voicemail with a friend in which he matter-of-factly stated that he was going to kill Elizabeth. He said, "She ruined me, she left me, and she deserves to die." He also said he was going to kill himself.

William rented a car and early the next morning drove to Elizabeth's house, cut the phone lines, and used a crowbar to break the patio window. He then quietly walked up the stairs. The security alarm never went off. He entered the bedroom where Elizabeth and Jake were sleeping and shot Jake three times, killing him. He shot Elizabeth once in the stomach. As she lay dying, he reloaded the gun, shot her two more times, and slashed her arms with a box cutter. He then shot himself.

Tara, who was sleeping in the same bedroom because of her own fears of William, managed to escape when the bullets started flying. The other children hid in a closet. When Tara left the house, the security alarm went off. The police didn't enter the house for ninety minutes. They talked to Tara and knew what had happened, but they still didn't enter the house. After the incident they said it took a while to get the department SWAT team together.

When they finally entered the house, they found Elizabeth's frightened boys in the closet. They saw the bloody carnage in Elizabeth and Jake's bedroom. Elizabeth and Jake lay dead, and William sat wounded in the corner. He still had his gun. The police fired three shots at him; one bullet hit his thumb. They arrested him and took him to the hospital.

At the trial the judge pushed for a plea agreement, which upset Elizabeth's family. Elizabeth and Patty's father, a quiet seventy-five-year-old man, said, "Absolutely not. Let it go to trial. I don't want him to ever get out of jail." The trial proceeded, and William was found guilty of first-degree murder.

I asked Patty who she is angry with. She said, "I'm angry at William Perry, the alarm system company, the police, the prosecutor, and the judge. They all should have seen the red flags. My sister's killer lost his job, he made threats to kill her, he attempted to kill her, he had access to guns, and he violated court orders. The prosecutor minimized her case, saying, 'This is just another domestic.'" Patty was also angry that there wasn't more training for police departments on when and where a civil protection order can be enforced.

William Perry was sentenced to life in prison. Elizabeth's four children are living with Patty and are adjusting as well as they can. This family has survived a horrible tragedy and is determined that justice be done. They are strong advocates for making significant changes so that law enforcement, the criminal justice system, and communities believe and protect women in situations similar to Elizabeth's.

Homicide Prevention: Assessing for Risk

This section is written primarily for counselors, advocates, and interveners in the criminal justice system who have contact with men who batter or with their victims.

For over twenty-five years, researchers, advocates, and practitioners in the domestic violence field have worked to document the elements of lethality and dangerousness faced by domestic abuse victims/survivors. In the 1980s battered women's shelters experimented with the use of risk assessment forms. They listed risk factors based on common assumptions in the literature and also on the experiences of battered women and advocates.

Counseling programs sought to assess the dangerousness of offenders through a series of questions. At intake, practitioners would look at the man's history of violence, pattern of abuse, use of threats and coercion, methods of intimidation, sexual abuse, degree to which he isolated his victim, access to weapons, drug and alcohol abuse, psychological evaluations, and other red flags (e.g., stalking behavior or obsession with the loss of his partner). Police reports and court orders also became part of the file.

It has become evident that intake forms alone are an inexact measurement of an offender's danger to his victim, so many practitioners have been reluctant to contact the court or the victim without additional evidence—for example, when an offender actually makes threats in a counseling session or his partner reports them to the program. Without such information there is concern that a practitioner might assess the situation incorrectly and unnecessarily alarm the victim. Conversely there is a fear that assessments conducted during intakes rely too heavily on limited sources (e.g., the offender's criminal history or his answers to questions) and that dangerous offenders aren't being detected.

The advocates at the Domestic Abuse Intervention Project in Duluth have been vital resources for staff in the men's program. We've had many discussions with them about men we had concerns about—something someone said in group might set off an alarm. With victim safety a central feature of our program, the advocate finds the appropriate time (when the male partner isn't home) to contact the victim and check on her well-being.

Assessing for danger is becoming increasingly common as we learn more about risk factors. The Blueprint for Safety, implemented in St. Paul in 2010, is an interagency approach with a collective goal of maximizing victim safety. Ellen Pence and her colleagues at Praxis International, along with criminal justice practitioners in St. Paul and Ramsey County, developed the Blueprint for Safety. One of the ideas behind it is that danger assessments would begin at the 911 call and continue through the police officer's investigation, to the charging decisions made by the prosecutor, and be part of the recommendations made by the probation officer to the judge. This is accomplished through a series of protocols for city and county law enforcement agencies, city and county attorneys, 911 communication centers, victim witness programs, probation departments, and judges. Each protocol contains specific risk questions and instructions on documenting responses and assessing for danger. This requires coordinating the activities of community agencies and sharing information about cases, including risk information, at every stage of the intervention. (For more information about the Blueprint for Safety visit www.praxisinternational.org.)

In 2013, recognizing the growing importance of assessing for danger, the National Institute of Justice (NIJ) began providing funding to jurisdictions that are trying new ways of reducing domestic violence homicides. Demonstration initiatives have been funded by the NIJ to help build the capacity of state, local, and tribal jurisdictions to improve services for high-risk victims while better monitoring high-risk offenders to reduce the incidence of domestic violence homicides. Like other demonstration projects, the research is often mixed and open to interpretation, but NIJ is to be commended for recognizing that we need to do more preventive work with victims and offenders alike.

In conducting research for this book, I had conversations with advocates, counselors, and researchers to better understand the dangers inherent in domestic abuse cases and how interveners at every level can do a better job of assessing for risk. I also interviewed Barbara Hart, JD; Jacquelyn Campbell, PhD; David Adams, EdD; and Edward Gondolf, PhD. All four of these individuals have been leaders in this field, and their contributions toward helping us understand the dangerousness of some offenders is invaluable. Their impact—creating guides, assessment tools, and profiles of dangerous offenders—has, I believe, saved lives. In interviews I asked each of them to reflect on their work, what we have accomplished, and what we still need to do.

Barbara Hart: What Law Enforcement and Victims Should Know

One of the early guides, which has been used primarily by law enforcement, was designed by Barbara J. Hart, JD, Director of Strategic Justice Initiatives in the Justice Policy Program of the Cutler Institute on Health and Social Policy at the Muskie School of Public Service. Barbara's leadership and advocacy have had a significant impact on developing sound policy across disciplines in our field.

Barbara Hart and a police officer were conducting a workshop on domestic violence. During the officer's presentation, he mentioned a disturbing case that he was working on. He talked about five incident reports involving a specific woman; her assailant had committed serious acts of violence against her, stalked her in two states, and threatened her. He told the participants that he was struggling to figure out how he might help her. A small group at the workshop discussed some strategies to assist this woman, who was clearly at risk.

For Hart this was a case in which law enforcement recognized the danger posed by an offender. She realized that laws and legal strategies offered inadequate protection to battered women with potentially lethal partners. She also realized that there was a need to design an assessment guide that law enforcement, advocates, and battered women could use to better understand risk. The list of indicators in the guide would alert them to elevated levels of danger.

Although the guide has not been validated through research, the tool, with Hart's explanations, continues to help interveners and victims alike. The following is the assessment guide that Barbara Hart designed for law enforcement.

> Some men who batter are life endangering. While it is true that all men who batter are dangerous, some are more likely to kill than others, and some are more likely to kill at specific times. Regardless of whether there is a civil protection order in effect, officers should evaluate whether an offender is likely to kill his partner or other family members and/or police personnel at the scene and take appropriate action.
>
> Assessment is tricky and never fool-proof. It is important to conduct an assessment at every call, no matter how many times an officer has responded to the same household. The dispatcher and responding officer can utilize the indicators described below in making an assessment of the batterer's potential to kill. Considering these factors may or may not reveal potential for homicidal assault, but the likelihood is higher if these factors are present. The greater the number of indicators that a man who batters demonstrates or the greater the intensity of indicators, the greater the likelihood of a life-threatening attack.
>
> Use all of the information you have about the suspect—current as well as past incident information. A thorough investigation at the scene will provide much of the information necessary to make this assessment.
>
> 1. Threats of homicide or suicide. A man who batters and has threatened to kill himself, his partner, the children, or her relatives must be considered extremely dangerous.
> 2. Fantasies of homicide or suicide. The more a man who batters has developed a fantasy about whom, how, when, and/or where to kill, the more dangerous he may be. A man who batters who has previously acted out part of a homicide or suicide fantasy may be invested in killing as a viable "solution" to his problems. As in suicide assessment, the more detailed the plan and the more available the method, the greater the risk.

3. Weapons. If a man who batters possesses weapons and has used them or has threatened to use them in the past in his assaults on the battered woman, the children, or himself, his access to firearms increases his potential for lethal assault. The use of guns is a strong predictor of homicide.

4. "Ownership" of the battered partner. If a man who batters says things like, "Death before divorce!" or "You belong to me and will never belong to another," he may be stating his fundamental belief that the woman has no right to life separate from him. If a man who batters believes he is absolutely entitled to his female partner, her services, her obedience, and her loyalty, no matter what, he is likely to be life endangering.

5. Centrality of the partner. If a man who batters idolizes his female partner, depends heavily on her to organize and sustain his life, or has isolated himself from all other community, he may retaliate against her if she decides to end the relationship. He rationalizes that her "betrayal" justifies his lethal retaliation.

6. Separation violence. If a man who batters believes he is about to lose his partner, he might (if he can't envision life without her, or if the separation causes him great despair or rage) choose to kill.

7. Depression. If a man who batters has been acutely depressed and sees little hope for moving beyond the depression, he may be a candidate for homicide and suicide. Research shows that many men who batter who are hospitalized for depression have homicidal fantasies directed at family members.

8. Access to the battered woman and/or to family members. If a man who batters can't find his partner, he can't kill her. If he does not have access to the children, he cannot use them as a means of access to the battered woman. Careful safety planning and police assistance are required for those times when contact is required, e.g., court appearances and custody exchanges.

9. Repeated outreach to law enforcement. Partner or spousal homicide almost always occurs in a context of historical

violence. Prior calls to the police indicate elevated risk of life-threatening conduct. The more calls, the greater the potential danger.

10. Escalation of risk. A less obvious indicator of increasing danger may be the sharp escalation of personal risk undertaken by a man who batters; when he begins to act without regard to the legal or social consequences that previously constrained his violence, chances of lethal assault increase significantly.

11. Hostage-taking. A hostage-taker is at high risk of inflicting homicide. Between 75 percent and 90 percent of all hostage-takings in the United States are related to domestic violence situations.

If a police officer or other professional concludes that an offender is likely to kill or commit life-endangering violence, extraordinary measures should be taken to protect the victim and her children. This may include notifying the victim and law enforcement of risk, as well as seeking a mental health commitment, where appropriate. The victim should be advised that the presence of these indicators may mean that the offender is contemplating homicide and that she should immediately take action to protect herself and should contact the local battered woman's program to further assess lethality and develop safety plans.[3]

A Note to Counselors
Working with Battered Women

For a woman who has been abused by an intimate partner, risk assessments can be useful diagnostic tools to examine the risk markers that are most likely to put her in danger. Ultimately she is the one who knows her partner or ex-partner. The assessment she completes today may produce very different results from those of an assessment she completes three months from now, depending on the situation, such as the decisions she's made, the decisions her partner or ex-partner has made, and other changes in her life.

You can help her navigate this process by helping her evaluate her own safety. Barbara Hart has created the following guide to help women with this process:

Risk assessment and safety planning are ongoing processes. Without continuing reflection on risks and consequent safety planning, battered women may not make the most effective decisions about strategies to avoid or minimize coercive violence and about participation in the legal system.

Thoughtful analysis of the particular risks posed at any moment in time is essential for generating valid conclusions about the array and significance of domestic violence risks. Battered women are best equipped to assess imminent, short-, and long-term risks. Risk assessment should not exclusively utilize formulas or rely upon prescribed lists of questions. Standardized assessment tools not only do not fit all battered women, they often create the impression of certainty and yet produce significant inaccuracies.

Battered women are uniquely situated to assess risk(s) and devise safety strategies. They are best informed about individual acts and patterns of abuse by batterers, as well as the intent of batterers as they employ coercive controls and violence. While law enforcement, counselors, and other professionals have the capacity to draw simple, straightforward conclusions about batterer behavior and the risks it portends, battered women can better evaluate the nuances, context, history, complexity, patterns, threats, and desperation of batterer behavior, the changes in batterer life circumstances, and changes in batterer conduct leading to heightened criminal or social sanctions. Greater intelligence about risks can enhance the validity of conclusions about recurring coercive controls, violence, injury, or death by battering partners.

A battered woman might consider taking the following actions for risk assessment and safety planning:

> Reflect on all the locations in which she and her children live their lives. The list will be different for each battered woman. It may include home, work, school, church, public

transportation and/or cars, library, athletic activities and events, healthcare, shopping, government offices, court-house, and residences of friends and neighbors. The list is likely to be much longer.

> Recollect the strategies she has utilized to minimize or avoid abuse.
> Recall whether allies intervened to assist her and whether those allies acted in ways that were helpful or not.
> Assess her need to develop new allies or interveners in high-risk locations.
> Identify resources required to implement her safety planning.
> Rehearse safety or risk-reduction strategies.
> Evaluate each safety strategy employed individually and as part of the array of strategies utilized to promote risk reduction and safety.

Risk assessment and safety planning must be continuous and comprehensive to be effective. While the actions described above may seem daunting, both risk assessment and safety planning can readily be incorporated into the daily lives of battered women. Thoughtful, respectful assistance from allies, including advocates, attorneys, criminal justice system personnel, healthcare providers, and clinicians, in risk assessment and safety planning will save the lives and promote the well-being of adult and child victims of domestic violence. It is important that all stakeholders demystify these simple processes and support battered women as they seek to better assess risk and both craft and implement plans to enhance safety and well-being.[4]

Jacquelyn Campbell:
Creating a Danger Assessment Tool

Jacquelyn Campbell, PhD, RN, is a professor at the Johns Hopkins University School of Nursing. She has published more than two hundred articles and seven books. Her pioneering work in developing, testing, and updating her Danger Assessment has challenged our thinking on the risks faced by domestic abuse victims/survivors.

Campbell's Danger Assessment has been considered the gold standard for accuracy in evaluating levels of risk. When I talked with Jacquelyn Campbell about her work in creating her original Danger Assessment, I wanted to find out whether these tools could indeed be used to measure and predict who was at risk of being killed by an intimate partner. I wanted to know how practical these tools were and who might use them—for example, advocates, medical personnel, practitioners in the mental health and criminal justice systems, counselors at offender treatment programs, and, of course, victims themselves.

Campbell designed her first Danger Assessment for use by health care workers and battered women's advocates. She revised the tool after the National Femicide Study was completed. Research for the report, conducted in eleven cities, provided the most extensive information to date about women who were killed by their intimate partners.[5] The National Femicide Report provided extremely useful data that gave additional validation to Campbell's revision of her Danger Assessment. The tool provides a weighted score that lets a victim know the range of danger she's in. The danger levels are "variable," "increased," "severe," and "extreme."

In our interview, Campbell talked about some of the unexpected findings of her research:

> There were many surprises with the new data that refuted some of my earlier assumptions about risk. For instance extreme controlling behavior was a high-risk factor, but not as high as I had previously thought. The threat of suicide, while again of concern, was not as significant a factor as I had originally assumed. Any one of the following ten risk factors increases the risk to a woman by 5 percent, although a combination of any of them significantly increases the risk, which makes assigning a score possible. The top ten factors are these:
>   > owns a gun
>   > is unemployed
>   > threatens to kill the victim

> threatens with a weapon
> has been left by his partner after living with her during the past year
> has a stepchild in the home (her biological child, not his)
> forces sex
> has choked or attempted to strangle the victim
> threatens to harm the children
> increases the severity and/or frequency of abuse

The updated Danger Assessment contains two parts: a calendar to document acts and a twenty-item scoring instrument. The calendar helps to assess severity and frequency of battering and ranks the incidents. (More information can be found at www.dangerassessment.org.)

Campbell's data show that potentially lethal men who batter are significantly more likely to threaten to kill than are other men who batter. Of the offenders who have actually killed or almost killed their intimate partners, 57 percent had made overt threats, compared to 14 percent of other batterers who did so. This means that threats are significantly predictive and should be taken seriously by counselors, advocates, law enforcement, family members, and, of course, women at risk.

Another finding was that, by and large, domestic assault killers don't have more significant alcohol or drug problems than other abusive men do. Although the data did show that some of the killers were drunk or high on drugs when they committed their crimes, they did not always have addictions.

The new data and research indicate that men who threatened to commit suicide did not pose as high a risk as originally thought. The batterers who do kill themselves are usually not considered severe batterers by the system and frequently haven't been arrested, although they have committed often severe acts of domestic abuse.

Campbell discussed the critical need for training mental health practitioners in domestic abuse:

There is a large group of men who batter with mental health problems who seek help in the mental health care system by seeing a therapist, a psychiatrist, or a psychologist, or who go to their own doctor because they are depressed. There is a huge problem in that so many mental health practitioners are not thoroughly trained on domestic violence and the dynamics of battering, and have limited knowledge in assessing for risk and danger. I rarely see psychiatrists and psychologists at the many domestic violence trainings that I have conducted. Yet these are the very practitioners that a man who batters or a victim will often seek out for help with emotional or psychological problems. Instead of meaningful danger assessments, treatment, and referrals, drug prescriptions are dispensed and opportunities to assess for risk and other interventions are lost.

I testified as an expert witness in a wrongful death suit. A psychiatrist had examined a man who was suicidal and had fantasies about killing his wife. The psychiatrist released him from the hospital, and the man later killed both his wife and himself. The psychiatrist's defense was that he had not received any training on domestic violence and assessing for dangerousness in any of his classes at the university he'd attended. I believe licensing agencies should require a certain amount of training on domestic violence and dangerousness/risk assessment.

Through proxy interviews (interviews conducted with people in place of a subject who is unavailable) I found that very few of the women who had been killed or nearly killed had sought help from shelters, advocates, or battered women's programs. They were more likely to have sought help from their doctor, therapist, or others in the health care system. It is unknown whether these women divulged the level of abuse or their fears to medical and mental health practitioners.

Counseling programs that work with men who batter could reach out more to the men's partners. These programs could significantly improve the partners' safety by conducting risk assessments of offenders and sharing the results with the criminal justice system, especially if there are reassaults. A battered

woman whose partner is in a court-mandated counseling program should also have access to the results so she can evaluate
potential danger.

The safety of a victim who provides information for the
Danger Assessment (or any other assessment of risk posed by
an offender) could be further jeopardized. The offender might
discover that she has provided information that has resulted in
higher bail or a longer sentence and find a way to retaliate. If
the victim understands the risks of providing information but
believes more controls are necessary for her own protection,
her voice should be heard, and it should count.

This situation illustrates the need for victim advocates and court
personnel in the criminal justice system to be thoroughly trained
in risk and danger assessment tools. It also illustrates the need for
thoughtful discussions between advocacy programs and the criminal justice system before policy changes are made to avoid unintended consequences of using assessment tools.

The Blueprint for Safety, discussed earlier, identifies the court's
two primary goals in setting the conditions under which the defendant will be released prior to trial: (1) to ensure that the defendant
will make future court appearances, and (2) to protect the community, the alleged victim, and any other person. Because in domestic
abuse cases a victim may be especially vulnerable to coercion and
intimidation, the goal of protecting her requires specific attention to
the risk that the defendant may cause her further harm.

Whether or not a risk assessment is used, the court should consider the pattern of intimidation, coercion, and violence used against
the victim; the history of violence; and the danger posed by the
defendant and others in the incident based on risk questions in law
enforcement reports and other points of intervention. With input
from the victim, this may result in more or fewer controls placed on
the defendant.

The information from law enforcement who've been to the
scene of the incident is critical and is often the first step in assessing

danger. In many jurisdictions law enforcement has abandoned the checklist on their investigative reports in favor of three fundamental questions:

1. Do you think he/she will seriously injure or kill you or your children? **What makes you think so? What makes you think not?**

2. How frequently and seriously does he/she threaten, intimidate, or assault you? **Is he/she changing? Getting worse? Getting better?**

3. **Describe the time when you were most frightened or injured by him/her?**

The questions in bold reflect the core of the risk assessment. The officer is no longer looking for merely a yes/no response but probing into the perceptions of the victim at the scene of the incident, when emotions and fears are most pronounced.[6]

Campbell continues:

> It would be helpful for judges to have more training on domestic abuse and risk assessment, or at the very least have some kind of bench book that can be utilized when reviewing police reports, probation recommendations, and testimony from the parties. I'm concerned that most probation departments use ineffective risk assessment tools that may address basic criminal history issues but fail to examine the context of domestic violence and risk through the same lens as someone trained in domestic violence dynamics and risk to battered women. Again this is partly a training issue, but it's also an organizational deficiency.
>
> While a relatively low 9 percent of the offenders who killed their intimate partners had been investigated for child abuse, I see the number as a cause for alarm and believe there are policy implications for the child protective services (CPS). CPS workers need more domestic abuse training and understanding of the risks to a battered woman from an abusive partner.
>
> On the other hand I have serious concerns about mandatory reporting by medical personnel of all domestic violence cases

to CPS unless a child is being physically harmed. Mandatory reporting would have a chilling effect on victims talking to their doctor, emergency room nurses, and other practitioners. The Danger Assessment tool could be used when ordering supervised child visitation and could be used at child safety centers or visitation centers [centers in which visitation takes place under court-ordered conditions]. Again, those administering the tool need thorough training, and programs need a protocol designed to ensure safety of the victim and her children.

The science is getting better at understanding danger assessment, and I agree with others in the field that the more information a battered woman has about the risk and danger she faces, the more opportunities and options she has to seek help, flee an abuser, and make use of safety planning.

According to proxies only half of the women who were killed by an intimate partner thought their husbands and boyfriends would kill them. This is an important statistic, because it implies that many battered women don't know how much risk they may actually be in, which heightens the need to expand the use of risk or danger assessments to advocates, medical personnel, and mental health practitioners who come in contact with victims and offenders. This information lets victims know the reality of their situation—whether they are living with a man who might kill or are in more danger because they have fled an abusive partner. It is important that interveners listen to a victim's perception of how dangerous her situation is.

I would caution against agencies and practitioners using the Danger Assessment or any other risk assessment tools without undergoing thorough training, developing policies and protocols, and understanding the importance of creating safety plans with women whose partners might score high on the assessment. I'm also opposed to allowing the assessment tool to be used by attorneys in divorce cases, because I fear the potential for manipulation unless there is a documented and irrefutable history of domestic violence.

When I conducted proxy interviews with family and friends of victims, I found that family members wished they had had more information on the risk their loved one faced. Anything that helps women make the best decisions about her safety, all the better. I'm personally very gratified at the increased use of the Danger Assessment tool and what we learned over the years in designing the tool. If it saves one woman's life, all of my work has been worth it. Hopefully people will keep working on it and making it better.

David Adams:
Distinguishing Factors in Domestic Homicides

David Adams was one of ten men who organized EMERGE, which was among the first programs in the United States to begin working with men who batter. The organizers of EMERGE were all part of various social change movements. Many were partners of women starting shelters at the time in Massachusetts.

Adams became motivated to do research on men who kill after there was a spike in domestic homicides in Massachusetts. Then-Governor William Weld actually declared a state of emergency for women in the state. Adams and the late Susan Schechter, author of the pioneering book *Women and Male Violence,* began to examine what distinguishing factors were evident in domestic homicides. They researched and interviewed men convicted of killing their intimate partners, as well as relatives of the women who'd been killed. In our interview, he described their investigation:

> We got access to the criminal records of many of the men convicted of killing their partners and were able to get into the prisons to conduct interviews. This was very time consuming, because each interview took about five hours and often required returning to the prison to complete them. I conducted the majority of the prison interviews.
>
> I interviewed thirty-one men convicted of killing their intimate partners, twenty victims of attempted homicide, and nineteen additional victims. I wanted to get life histories of these men, to get a sense of their relationships with their

intimate partners and what had motivated their violent behavior. First, I asked them to describe their perceptions of why they started battering. I wanted to know if the violence was motivated by a need to control or if there was another reason for such extreme and lethal behavior. I explored their adult histories—whether they were employed, the status of their health, their use of substances, and significant events in their lives. Then I asked them about their childhoods. We wanted to know about their trauma events—whether they were physically or sexually abused as children and whether they were exposed to domestic violence.

We found that these are the best predictors for risk of homicide:
> past threats to kill
> past threats of suicide [Campbell's research differs here]
> access to guns
> history of serious domestic violence
> stalking
> substance abuse
> estrangement

I had been interviewing men in Minnesota prisons who had killed their intimate partners when Adams was working on his book *Why Do They Kill?* In different states both of us conducted our interviews in stark prison meeting rooms with tape recorders. We both thought we'd find that at the very least some of the men who'd killed their intimate partners would take more responsibility for their actions. After all, one would think, if you were convicted of murder and you may never get out of prison, you might be more reflective about what had happened. Some of the men weren't even remorseful but rather were angry that they'd gotten caught. We were surprised how most of these offenders continued to demonize their victims.

Adams states that justification is part of their psychology—that men who batter are highly narcissistic and often continue to blame their victims for their predicaments, even after they've murdered them. In other words, what many of these men were saying was that if their partners hadn't behaved the way they did, the women would be alive today and they, the men, wouldn't be sitting in prison. Men who batter often project their own characteristics on others, and so they view their partners as the controlling ones—the partners are the ones responsible for provoking a violent and even deadly response.

> Killers in general claim to disassociate, which is a convenient way of not having to deal with what they have done. I assume there is also a hesitancy to be forthright or reveal more than what they already had, because some were still hoping that they might appeal their convictions and get out of prison. A third of the killers I interviewed for my book *Why Do They Kill?* were convicted of first-degree murder, one-third of second-degree murder, and one-third of manslaughter.
>
> What was missing from these tragic stories and the research I conducted in the prisons were the victims' accounts of what happened. We began interviewing victims of attempted homicides to better explain what it was like living with a potential killer. When victims of domestic violence are able to step back and examine their relationships through a clearer lens, they often remember signs that they should have paid attention to: controlling behaviors, threats, jealousy, possessiveness that they didn't fully understand at the time, and sexual abuse that many had buried deep in their subconscious. Some women described the toxic mix of guns in the house, drug or alcohol abuse, and antisocial behavior that they now know was indicative of someone capable of murder.

David Adams found that easy access to guns can create dangerous situations:

> Guns are a major factor in domestic homicides. I thought I'd find more premeditation in the killers I interviewed. What my research found instead was that the men who killed their intimate partners were substance abusers with guns or jealous drunks with guns—these were far more lethal combinations.

In states with permissive gun laws, there are higher rates of domestic homicides, and the mere presence of a gun in the home makes the situation more dangerous.

I believe that law enforcement and the courts need to do a better job of enforcing the Lautenberg Amendment, which prohibits offenders convicted of a domestic assault or those with a civil order for protection from possessing a gun. We need to make it harder for people to get handguns, and I believe that those who sell guns should do a better job of screening for domestic violence. I'm convinced that some of the domestic homicides we researched would not have been committed if guns hadn't been easily accessible.

The United States has the weakest gun laws of all the industrialized countries. Because of inaction on meaningful gun laws at the federal level, states have begun to address the issue themselves, especially in light of the research on the lethal intersection between gun access and domestic homicides. States with weak gun violence–prevention laws and high rates of gun ownership have the highest overall gun death rates through homicides and suicides.[7] Some states require convicted domestic abuse offenders to surrender their firearms to law enforcement or third parties. In states that have universal background checks (including gun shows, private sales, and firearms purchased over the internet), more domestic abusers are being stopped from purchasing or carrying firearms. Other states provide records of prohibited abusers to the National Instant Criminal Background Check System (NICS). And still others give law enforcement more discretion in denying permits to purchase or carry.

As part of the Violence Against Women Act, federal law disqualifies convicted domestic abuse offenders from possessing firearms. Unfortunately the law is silent on requiring domestic abusers to surrender their firearms after a domestic abuse conviction or if the offender is subject to domestic violence restraining orders.

Given that gun possession is such a high risk factor for domestic homicides, our state and federal gun laws need to be strengthened. While I support legislative changes that prohibit offenders from possessing firearms, we should also be conducting research on the outcomes of these laws. Battered women's advocates have raised concerns that some victims will be reluctant to call the police if they know that offenders will have to surrender their firearms. Will the intimate partners of law enforcement officers and military personnel (whose employment is predicated on having a firearm) report domestic abuse if they know their partner's career will be in jeopardy? Advocates in rural areas of the country, where hunting and gun possession are more engrained in the culture, have raised similar concerns.

Adams stated that based on his interviews, he concluded there were five types of killers:

> Possessively jealous types (65–90 percent) are far more dangerous when their relationships end. These men act in a premeditated manner and will kill with or without guns. Triggers for this group are estrangement, divorce, and infidelity or suspected infidelity.
>
> Substance abusers (50–65 percent) can be either functioning or nonfunctioning, and their relationships often revolve around drugs and alcohol. Consistent with past research, substance abusers use more severe violence when they are high or drunk. Common triggers for this group are conflicts over drug use and finances, infidelity or imagined infidelity, pending criminal charges, complaints by the victim, petty arguments, and general deterioration. Most of the substance abusers are also possessively jealous and their frequent alcohol use fuels their jealousy.
>
> Depressed and suicidal abusers (20–40 percent) are typically older, emotionally unstable, highly depressed, and isolated; many also have substance abuse problems. Common triggers are estrangement, loss of a job, loss of children, and a belief that there is nothing to live for if the relationship ends. Most of these men are also possessively jealous and extremely emotionally dependent on their partners.

Materially motivated types (20–25 percent) are obsessed with making money and having possessions. Some of them fit the antisocial personality profile and exhibit less jealousy than do other offenders who kill. Common triggers for this group are financial loss or pending loss, criminal charges, and perceptions that their partners are "bothering" them.

Career criminals (15–20 percent) have problems with authority, often have antisocial personalities, are exploitive in their relationships with women, and tend to support themselves through crime. Common triggers for this group are financial loss, the victim fighting back or being defiant, arrest, incarceration, and feeling "pressure" from the partner to change.

There is significant overlap within these categories. For instance 43 percent of the killers fit two of the types (the most common combination was possessively jealous and substance abusers) and 20 percent of them fit into three types. Most of the substance abusers and the depressed suicidal men also fit the possessively jealous profile.

I recommend ongoing danger assessments as a continuous process of risk management. Practitioners must recognize that the safest course for a victim may not be the use of the criminal justice system. This means we should have greater expectations for others in the community who may come in contact with the victim or perpetrator (employers, clergy members, therapists, medical personnel, friends, and family members) to intervene. They need to be educated about the "red flags." This will require an acknowledgement that other institutions in the community have a responsibility to train staff on domestic violence, risk, and danger.

Edward Gondolf: Ongoing Risk Assessment

Like David Adams, Edward Gondolf, whom I quoted extensively in the previous chapter, contends that risk assessment must be an ongoing process. In his book *The Future of Batterer Programs* he writes:

Merely triaging batterers based on a cutoff score, or sending them to longer or shorter programs, could be a misuse of risk assessment, and a misleading one at that. Several researchers argue for making risk assessment more of a process that incorporates the perceptions and experiences of victims. Those considerations have, in fact, been shown not only to improve prediction but also to increase prevention of new offenses.

Risk is more of a process; it ebbs and flows based on various situations and dynamics. Risk can change when someone drops out of the program, whether the program has ongoing contact with the partner, whether the offender starts using drugs and alcohol—there are multiple events that can change the initial assessment.

The tough question facing batterer programs, and the criminal justice field in general, is how to identify the especially dangerous men. Several validated risk assessment instruments have been developed to help do this—based on either checklists of actuarial factors or topical ratings for structured professional judgment.... All of them [risk assessments] have disadvantages, and as yet none is clearly the "best one." The risk instruments do produce more accurate predictions than "gut feelings" and general impressions, even those of experienced clinicians, but they produce an unsettling portion of false negatives.[8]

He also suggests that ongoing risk assessment may be useful in identifying the men who pose the most danger and providing them specialized programming:

We have a sub-group of chronically violent men who are unresponsive to treatment. We need to be doing more to identify and contain the most dangerous offenders. In part we can accomplish this by paying more attention to ongoing risk assessments, which includes stronger collaboration with the criminal justice system so we understand their criminal histories and past behavior. A lot of the more dangerous men drop out of our programs. Maybe we need to do more intensive programming at the front end and have specialized groups for high-risk offenders and monitor these men more closely.[9]

Gondolf observes that many offenders and many victims have no contact with law enforcement:

Less than half of the men who killed their intimate partners had contact with the criminal justice system. These offenders managed to escape arrest, which begs the question of whether law enforcement officers (even with pro-arrest policies) are pursuing domestic assault cases aggressively enough. It also implies that many victims who are at risk aren't calling the police or requesting services from battered women's programs.[10]

Given the struggle for funding, programs will probably not be able to offer specialized groups for high-risk offenders any time soon. But even with limited resources, offender programs are in a position to help men beyond simply providing court-mandated counseling. We know that certain social conditions can *inhibit* risk: employment, education, a positive reputation in the community, family ties, support systems, treatment for substance abuse or mental health issues, and systems controls—monitoring, sanctions, and victim options. (Although these conditions decrease risk, their absence does not cause domestic violence.)

Programs might consider conducting an exit interview with each participant before he completes counseling to determine his current status. Does he have a job and a stable place to live? Does he need further counseling? Does he have a support system of family and friends? Is he willing to stay in the program if he is still struggling with his problems? Is there a help line he can call if he is feeling desperate, depressed, or confused?

In addition to asking offender programs to work closely with battered women's programs and the criminal justice system, it would benefit such programs (and the men they are working with) to collaborate with other counseling, faith-based, and service programs in the community.

The documentary that I wrote with Ellen Pence, *With Impunity: Men and Gender Violence,* includes a short clip of a radio talk show being broadcast live from the 2009 Minnesota State Fair. During the show, panelists, including a well-known attorney, joke about when it's okay to kill your wife. People, primarily men, call in to offer examples of when such murders are justified. They are doing so amid lots of laughter and sexist comments. No one ever complained to the management of the radio station or to the state fair that the show was highly inappropriate.

Domestic abuse is not amusing. As counselors in this field, we should be doing more than direct service to end men's violence. While our actions are important, our voices should not be silent.

Veterans and Domestic Abuse

Live to the point of tears.

▶▶ ALBERT CAMUS ◀◀

Hector's Story

When I was working on a project on veterans who were returning home from combat zones with multiple problems, including intimate partner violence, I interviewed Hector Matascastillo, an Army Ranger and veteran. Hector grew up in an abusive home where his father battered his mother and him. He joined the Army when he was young, became a Ranger, and was deployed to combat zones around the world. His experiences exemplify how boys and men learn about manhood from our culture. Like so many men he objectified and used women, believing he was superior to them.

When he returned to Minnesota, he found himself in a standoff with several police officers in a St. Paul suburb after battering his wife. The court believed that Hector needed help, and he was ordered into a counseling program in lieu of jail. His journey has been a long and painful one that continues today. Hector didn't blame his military experiences or his diagnosed post-traumatic stress disorder (PTSD) for his violence or for his sexist beliefs about women.

Hector was born in Guatemala in 1973. His mother's and father's families were on opposing sides of the brutal civil war that was occurring at the time in this small Central American country. Family members were being killed, and loyalty issues were a constant fact of life. Hector's birth created a lot of stress in what were already turbulent times. His parents saw asylum in the United States as an option for some peace and security. In 1974 they immigrated and set down roots in a predominantly Latino neighborhood in Chicago.

> My father told me that there were three reasons why I was alive. One was to work hard; men should always be working and bringing home the resources. The man makes the money and the woman takes care of the house and the kids. The second reason was to protect my mother against everybody. As the oldest male in a Latino family at nine years old, this became my role because my father was an over-the-road truck driver, so I was "in charge." He told me the third reason I was alive was to protect my brother.
>
> I grew up in a fairly Latino community in Chicago where there were a lot of crime and gang activity. The messages I got from Dad were reinforced everywhere in the neighborhood. When he came home from driving the truck, he'd start drinking. I guess he felt he'd earned it. He believed everything in the house should be exactly as he wanted it. The tension began when he started becoming abusive toward my mother, first yelling, then name calling and throwing things, and then the beatings. It seemed like pretty much anything could set him off. That's when it started getting confusing for me to understand what my role was, because Dad had told me that one of my responsibilities was to protect my mother. I'd get in the middle of their fights trying to protect her, and we both ended up getting the hell beat out of us.
>
> People in this part of Chicago rarely called the cops, because they usually wouldn't come into Latino neighborhoods. When they did, they were fairly dismissive. They'd say, "Well, we don't understand your broken English. This is something that *you people* have to handle. This is a family issue, and we can't

get involved." You start feeling trapped. Sometimes they'd tell my father to leave, and he would, but then he'd come back and it would start all over again. It was really scary.

When my father was home there was tension throughout the whole house. His remarks were always edgy. Anything could make him angry. If he wasn't watching TV, he was out in the garage working on the car, and I could hear him cussing. He'd yell, "Hector, get out here and bring me a wrench!" Helping him usually meant that I was going to come back with hurt hands, because I wouldn't give him the right wrench. I can't tell you how many times I got my hands whacked.

After a while he didn't seem to need me, so then I'd go back inside. He'd get upset and start yelling at me for leaving when he needed me. My mom would confront him and sort of plead, "Why don't you just leave him alone?" And then he'd be in my mom's face screaming, "Why don't you stop treating him like a little girl? Why don't you let him be a man?" I felt bad that they were fighting over me, and all I wanted was to not get hit in the hands anymore. Whenever she stood up to him for hurting her children, the violence got worse. It would escalate and get way out of control.

When the fighting would start, I'd push my little brother into the bedroom and turn the cartoons on the television up as loud as I could so he couldn't hear the fighting. I'd be praying, "Please don't let it get any worse." And then you'd hear him throwing her around, and he'd be punching walls and slamming doors. The screaming and crying would get louder, and I realized my brother was really scared. I knew if I didn't go out there soon and intervene he was going to come in and drag me out anyway. So I would build up my courage. As soon as I would go into the living room, I would see my mom being thrown across the room. Then he'd be grabbing her by the hair, punching her, slapping her, kicking her. I would run in the middle of it, and then his rage would be directed at me. He would scream, "So you're a man now?" as he hit me in the face.

Mom would be crying, because now I was being hurt. I would try to fight my own father, but inside I would feel like a little pipsqueak against this big guy. Finally, it would start to de-escalate. Then he'd go on an overnight truck trip and I'd start thinking, "He could be back when I go to school tomorrow. And if he comes back, I'm afraid he's going to kill my mother." Hard to imagine a little boy having to worry about such things, but I did. And, of course, I thought the abuse in the house was my fault, because I didn't do the right thing, or because I didn't hand him the right frickin' wrench.

One time I helped my father make this leather belt. I thought we were making it together for Scouts and this was part of the project. But then he hung it up on the wall and said, "This is the belt I'll be beating you with." And he did. He would hit me with the belt, and if I cried, he'd scream, "Stop crying, you're a man! You're not a girl, stop crying!" Eventually the belt broke and I wasn't crying anymore. He said, "Okay, now that you're not crying and you don't need the belt, I'm going to treat you like a man." At first I didn't know what that meant. I thought maybe there would be some relief. But it turned out what he really meant was that from now on he would hit me with his fists, because men hit with their fists. So I learned not to put my head down, because if I did, that was a sign of inferiority and weakness.

Dad expected me to stand up for myself, including in fights I got into at school. He'd ask, "What do you mean there was a fight at school and you walked away from it?" "What do you mean a kid called your brother names and you didn't protect him? Your brother just came home with a bloody nose." I'd say, "Yeah, Frank picked a fight with a bully." Dad would look at me with disgust and say, "Well, then you go and settle this. Don't come back a loser." So I fought and I fought. That's what I was supposed to do. Dad would sort of feminize Frank because he wasn't a fighter. Frank didn't believe in fighting, or maybe he was just too scared to fight. I felt bad for him, because my dad would call him names in Spanish, implying that he was gay because he wouldn't fight.

The Making of a Warrior

My home life had an incredible influence on the decisions I made as a young man. At seventeen I was very altruistic about my purpose in life. I always wanted to join the military and serve my country. Of course, there were two other big reasons for wanting to enlist. First, I wanted to get out of the house as fast as I could. And second, I knew in the military that I could fight, and I wanted to fight. This may seem counterintuitive, but I guess being around all of that violence had an impact on me. My instinct was to survive—whether from my father's fists or from living in the 'hood.

I thought my ability to withstand suffering would be a perfect fit for the military. And I thought, "I'm not just going to join the military; I'm going to become a Special Operations Ranger"—because the Rangers were direct action. You knew when Rangers showed up in battle because they beat you into submission. They took the will to fight out of you. That's what I wanted to be.

War became the goal. I wanted to go to war, because I wanted to test out all these great skills that I'd learned in training. "Violence of action" was one of the principles we operated under. It meant I'm not going to just put two rounds in your chest. I'm going to unload a full clip in your chest because your buddy might be watching. I want your buddy to vomit and lose his will to continue to struggle. I want him to feel fear. I wanted people to fear me.

We trained and we trained and I was ready, or I thought I was ready, to kill another human being. In my first war zone we engaged the enemy. I killed my first soldier. I remember vomiting, thinking, "This is so unnatural." I got weak and went into shock, because this guy didn't die like I remembered seeing people die in the movies.

I had an NCO who must have recognized the impact killing had on the newer Rangers. He took us into a room and told us we were going to watch a movie. He said, "When you're watching, I want you to think about the enemy." The movie was called *Suburbia,* a punk rock flick about these homeless kids living together in a postwar suburb in California. Part of the story was about some stray dogs in the valley where these kids lived. Men would shoot the dogs that the kids were trying to protect. But as a dog was running and getting shot, it would sort of just roll over its own neck, very unnatural like. It looked like the human being I had just killed. And the NCO said, "Do you see the similarities now? They're just dogs, guys. They're dogs. And as long as you can see them that way, it makes it easier to kill them."

So we started training with that mentality. They're just dogs. It shouldn't affect you. Little by little that concept influenced me and the other guys. Okay, they're just dogs. We're just going to go kill them. It's no big deal.

So killing and fighting were what I was about. When I wasn't in combat, I'd be picking fights in bars in the towns near our installations. If someone messed with me, I'd pop him in the face and take him down. I'd fight other GIs in bars in Savannah or wherever we were stationed. We would actually go looking for fights. I'd tell my buddies, "That guy looks like he's tough. He's the cowboy I'm taking down today."

I served in the military for eighteen years. I had many different job titles, from combat support to combat arms. Infantry was where I spent the majority of my time. I had thirteen different operational deployments, with multiple peacetime operations. I deployed to fifty-seven different countries—the Middle East, Central and South America, the Black Sea region, the Baltics, Bosnia, Kosovo, Albania, and many countries in Africa.

As young warriors it was almost like we got to do what we were trained to do and the enemy was an inconvenience. I would actually get angry when they didn't put up a good fight. I thought they were unworthy of me even killing them. They were wasting my time. I'd think to myself, "Why are they running away? Come back and fight." Even after I put somebody down, I'd still be angry at them. Usually to check if somebody's dead or not, you would kick them between the legs. If anyone was still alive, obviously they would jump after being kicked in the groin. This buddy of mine kicked this downed guy so hard that his foot went through his anal cavity. He pulled his foot out and was really pissed off because he got his boot all dirty. So he started kicking this dead body over and over. We didn't see the enemy as human beings.

I Could Have Killed Her, and I Could Have Been Killed

It was January 24, 2004. I was out of the military and in an undergraduate program at a college in St. Paul. I had a lot on my mind and forgot that I had made arrangements with my wife to go out on one of those last-ditch "let's try to find romance in our relationship before we get divorced" dates. Our marriage had really been going downhill for some time. I called her and told her I had to stay at school late. Of course, she got angry. As usual I got defensive. We were expecting a blizzard that evening, and the weather was getting really bad. I started driving home. The whole way I was arguing with my ex-wife on the phone. She screamed, "Fuck you! Don't come home. I don't want you around here if you're going to be this way!" She hung up on me. I thought, "Well, I don't want to go home, so screw you. I'll just get my coat out of the house and sleep in the truck."

I walked in the door and there she was. She was furious that I came home. The yelling started immediately, and we were both throwing things around the room. She grabbed the remote controls and threw them at me. I put my arms up to block getting hit. The dog came up and put his paws on me, and I started to take it out on him. I threw that poor dog out the door. My wife was pleading for me to stop. When I came back in, I grabbed a knife and said, "You love that fucking dog more than me, and I'm going to take care of this." We struggled and somehow the knife fell out of my hand. I guess something inside told me that I didn't really want to kill the dog, or else I wouldn't have let go of the knife. The whole incident was unreal.

At that point she was really hysterical and demanded that I leave. I grabbed her by the hair and threw her outside in the snow. The next thing I knew, I was facing off with eight police officers with two pistols in my hand. My wife would say, "When the lights went out on Hector, that was the time to be scared, because he was so unpredictable." She had seen the "lights go out" many times in the past, and talking to me or trying to touch me would lead to me putting her in a chokehold. The night of the incident, I kicked her.

So there I was out in my front lawn with my guns in my hands. I'm now in a standoff, but later I realized that I was also was in a dissociative state, which is common with PTSD. I remember seeing one combatant (really, he was a police officer) at about my one o'clock, and he had the drop on me. In my mind I thought I had just cleared a room and lost my Ranger buddy. He was gone. I couldn't see him. There was only this combatant facing off with me. In my world the question was, who's going to die? My pistols are at the low ready.

I was confused. I remember looking over to my left, and I saw my one-year-old son watching me through the front window. I thought, "What the hell is he doing here? I must be losing my mind." And then I heard screaming to my right. At the top window of my split-level home, somebody was yelling. When I looked, it was my wife screaming to the police, "Don't shoot him! Please don't shoot him!" I looked out in front of me, shaking my head back and forth and feeling nauseous and woozy, like I was going to pass out.

I widened my stance and grabbed my pistols a little bit harder. In front of me were cop cars with their lights on. Everybody was yelling at me. "Throw your guns down. Throw your guns down now!" I was thinking, "I don't know how to get rid of my guns. I'm going to die. I'm facing off with eight police officers, and I just got done fighting with my wife and my kid saw all of this. Now my kid is going to watch me get arrested. No. No. I'm going to die here. I'm not going to let this happen." Prior to this, I was a war hero. I've been all over the world and fought for my country. I'm not the terrorist. And now I've become a terrorist. All I could think is, "I'm not going to leave this place alive. I'm not going to let that happen." I yelled out at the street, "Go ahead and shoot me. Go ahead, shoot me."

In the police report it said that I waved the guns at them and was out of my mind. I may have been. Eventually I started putting myself in a compromising position. Surrender. I hit the snow, and they were cuffing my hands and yelling commands. The police retrieved the guns in the street. I don't know if they were kicked down the street or if I threw them. The guy who I believed to be an armed combatant was just a police officer doing his job, responding to the domestic assault call. I was arrested and taken to jail, and then the journey began.

My Violence and Abuse

In the past I was usually abusive to women, but I always blamed my partners for my behavior. With my ex-wife, in addition to the violence, I was really emotionally abusive. I would try and destroy her self-worth. If the house was messy, I'd get in her face and tell her that she was worthless. I'd say, "What the hell are you good for? I could find any other fuckin' woman off the street to come in here and do the things that I expect from a wife." When I was angry, she was scared, and I knew it. I'd just yell and things would automatically ramp up to the next level. My posturing and my yelling were ferocious. I'd be in her face real close, and it was fierce. She would say that the contour of my face would actually change. What was even crueler was how easily I could switch it off and on when I wanted. After raging at her, I'd just be calm. I used to say, "I can make you feel invisible." So then I would. I would withdraw and be completely calm, and the unpredictability of that moment would linger. I wasn't hurting her physically, but she was never sure when it would happen again. I had an enormous amount of power.

I remember having fights with my ex-wife, and I knew I needed to leave the sergeant outside the door. The sergeant shouldn't have any place here in our home. The sergeant's mean. We don't need that ornery bastard in here. I knew I shouldn't be that guy, but on the other hand I knew that behavior was effective at getting what I wanted when I wanted it. The yelling was followed by periods of quiet and calm, and then I would explode again. It became the way I lived, and my ex-wife had to endure it.

Even when the violence stops and when the relationship ends, men who batter can still control their wives. I did. After my arrest and conviction, it was clear that our marriage was over. But even after the divorce, I would use my son as a way of getting back at my ex-wife. Whether it was things I said at a school conference or family court, or when I was on the phone with my son, I know that what I was saying and doing was punishing my ex-wife.

I'd say to her, "I'm doing this because it's best for him. I want him to succeed in school. You're not a good parent. Look at how you're living. Look at the kind of lifestyle you're involving our son in. Who's this guy you're dating? What kind of a person is he? Does he treat you right? I don't want my kid seeing this stuff." I was relentless. It was always about making her second-guess her decisions, attacking her parenting, belittling her, making her question every single thing that she did around him.

Coming to Terms

When I look back at the situation on that snowy night, I realize I could have killed my ex-wife, and I could have been killed by the responding officers. I tell people that when I was on the ground in the snow, it wasn't any different than the way I had been living my entire life. I was living on my belly, and it was then that my journey began, because it was the first time that I was ever picked up off my knees and onto my feet. I learned how to stand up again. I had to be on my knees for a while and learn what it meant to be really down before I could stand up.

When I was arrested, there wasn't a veterans' court. My case was one of the first where people in the criminal justice system started asking questions about the role of military experiences, especially in combat, in criminal acts. Although I was abusive to my ex-wife, I never did anything nearly as violent before my combat experiences. The court started questioning the correlation between PTSD and battering, not as an excuse but as a possible disorder that influences violent behavior.

All I could think of was that I don't want to live my life like this anymore. I was feeling things that I'd never felt before. I didn't want to feel them. The judge, the prosecutor, the probation officer—everybody in the system who knew what happened at my house that night wanted me to get help. The on-call chaplain at the jail came to talk to me because I was suicidal and considered dangerous and potentially homicidal to others. The chaplain realized that they needed to get somebody with a psychological background to talk to me. The person they sent to my jail cell happened to be a Vietnam veteran. He had seen the kind of behavior I exhibited many times before and thought I should be assessed for PTSD.

The judge released me from jail with conditions. He said, "Young man, you need to exorcise your demons. I'm going to give you that opportunity." I was ordered into counseling.

I'm learning that it's going to take years to get over the things that have happened in my life. It's a process. I learned that facing yourself takes courage and that facing the pain inside is hard. This crucible will make you a better person. I learned what it's like to accept what I've done without defending myself or blaming others. And even if redemption was possible, I'd still sit with what I've done. I don't have to rationalize anymore. I did these things to my ex-wife. I am responsible.

My son will most likely suffer because of what I did and what he saw—my violence and my abuse. He will have issues. I know my ex-wife has issues going on in her life. She's told me that she'll never trust men again. I was her first husband. I was her first real relationship, and I blew it with her. Taking responsibility for these things is painful but cleansing.

In my old life, the only woman that could possibly be better than me was my mother. All other women intimidated me, especially women who were confident and strong, women who looked at my tough-guy image and thought I was immature. I saw this as an insult. I'd think or say, "You're just an arrogant bitch." I'd feel this way most intensely if it was a woman I was attracted to. I'd think, "I'm going to bring you back down, because you're far too intimidating for me, because I don't understand where your confidence comes from. I don't understand how you have so much respect for yourself. From everything I learned growing up, women should be dependent on men. You get your confidence from me."

Whenever one of my partners or my ex-wife would do something that made me feel like she was asserting her independence, I'd think, "Wait a minute, what does this mean? I'm going to lose her. She's an object that I have to possess, protect, and control. If I lost her, I wouldn't be a man. I couldn't keep my family together." Maybe she was looking somewhere else, and even if she wasn't, I'd convince myself that she must have been. I thought, "I'm not important to her anymore. I'm insignificant." Whatever it took for me to maintain power over my past partners and my ex-wife I did because I didn't want to feel vulnerable.

On Healing

Healing from the violence and my past is difficult. I have damaged my ex-wife. I can't change that. And my dad can't change what his violence did to me. When my son was born, I was deployed during Enduring Freedom. Because of his birth I got to come back home. My brother Frank had made a room at his house for my wife and the baby. I looked in the room, and there was this tiny little baby. I was playing with him, and I remember my brother saying, "Hey, do you know that Dad is going to come by and see him?" I was stunned. I hadn't seen my father in over ten years. We hadn't even talked.

When Frank told me my dad was coming, I thought, "I'll just leave, and he can play with his grandson." All of a sudden there was a knock at the front door, and my dad was there, earlier than planned. I was in the bedroom with my son, and I realized I couldn't leave because he'd see me. I had no way out. I looked at the window, thinking, "I'll jump out and escape that way." I was panicked. Instinctively I hid in the closet. My father came into the room. He went to my son, who was very quiet. He just kind of stared at my son for a bit and then picked him up.

All this time I was in the closet, and I'm scared to death of this man. I'm scared that he might hear me. I remember thinking that I was going to stop breathing. I didn't move or make a sound. The shame started kicking in. I was trapped. If I walked out of the closet, he would say that I wasn't a man, because I couldn't come out and be in the room with him. I started thinking about everything I had been through with combat and in leadership positions in the military. I faced the fire of war and I've been around the world, and here I am in this closet afraid of this man.

He started talking to my son, telling him, "You know I will do whatever it takes to love you. I couldn't love *your* father. I did everything I could to break him, and I couldn't break him. Please forgive me." He was talking to my son. And here I am in the closet now just wanting to explode. I mean talk about bittersweet. I wanted to run out there and destroy him, rip him apart, and at the same time I wanted to just break down and be held. You know be a little boy again. In many ways I was a just a little boy stuck in a closet afraid of my dad while he was holding his grandson. Talk about humbling.

Helping Men Change

When I work with men who batter, I know how difficult it is to get through the denial, blaming, and minimizing. I engage the men I work with and challenge their perceptions that they are the victims. I go back to a strength that I believe we all have. In our culture there are different ways of viewing masculinity—positive and negative. One value that I think is important is courage. That's not limited to men, but it is valued in male culture. And I don't mean like courage to fight or to do something reckless. I talk about how much courage it takes to become vulnerable. How much courage it takes to turn back into your shame. The courage it takes to take responsibility for your behavior.

When I hear men blaming their partners, the police, or the system, I say, "Let's be courageous and expose ourselves. Let's be honest." The first thing I ask men is, "Is this the way you really want to live your life? Do you need help? Do you have the courage to be vulnerable and look deep inside at what you've done and the people you've hurt?" So I engage them on a strength that we all have. I engage them on their desire to be courageous.

I'm hopeful that men can take a different route, that men and women can have more equal relationships and be violence free. I am hopeful, but I'm scared at the same time. I'm scared how some men may react to a new courage that they haven't seen in other men. When I hear the men in my groups talk about the ways they're now talking to their kids, I'm hopeful. I had a man tell me how he knelt in front of his son and apologized for his behavior. He told me he was scared to death of this four-year-old. His son said, "I've been afraid of you, Daddy." And then he told me that his son hugged him and he had never experienced that kind of feeling before. It was total love and trust, and I can have that by being a better father.

I still worry that sometimes I'm going to become abusive and that I could revert back to the behaviors I'm accustomed to. At the beginning of my relationship with my current wife, we had experiences when I noticed the old me emerging. I'm cautious, and I listen. I'm afraid to go back. I don't like that feeling. I can't imagine going back to that lifestyle; it was energy draining, depressing, and so unhealthy. I don't want to hurt my wife like I hurt my female partners in the past.

I continue to learn every day. I've tried to make amends with my ex-wife, although I know she'll never forgive me, and I don't expect her to. Recently I sent my ex-wife a couple of letters acknowledging my violent and controlling behavior and my effort to change. She responded more favorably than I could ever have imagined. Had she not wanted to communicate, I wouldn't have, but I'm grateful that she responded, and I hope she sees my efforts as genuine.

I have to continually check how I'm responding and how I'm reacting, especially when I'm upset or angry. If I see even a shred of fear in my children's eyes, I need to back away, because my reaction was probably over the top. I never want my kids to be scared of me. The same goes with my wife. When I get angry, I need to step back. My past is about scaring people. My past is about scaring women. I'd go into what they call "military mode"—talking with your hands, screaming, threatening, and making myself unpredictable.

When I feel the old Hector coming out, I go for a run. Sometimes I just sit with it. I need to check out my behavior with my wife and my kids, because I don't want to go backward. I love this new way of living. I love the new feelings that I've been having for the last five or six years. I don't want to go back.

The Casualties of War

The number of American casualties who have returned home from the past two wars have been considerable. The *New England Journal of Medicine* reported that significant numbers of veterans have returned to the United States with PTSD and other mental health problems from their combat experiences in Iraq and Afghanistan. The report concluded that between 5 and 9.4 percent of veterans suffered from PTSD before deployment; after deployment, this went up to 6.2 to 19.9 percent. That's an additional 10,500 cases for every 100,000 United States veterans serving in Iraq.[1]

The Pentagon estimates that as many as 360,000 veterans suffered from traumatic brain injury (TBI), including 45,000 to 90,000 veterans with persistent symptoms requiring specialized care. Colonel Charles Hoge, MD, told a congressional committee in March of 2008 that nearly 30 percent of troops in their third deployment suffered from serious mental health problems.[2]

Serving in the military, especially during war, requires dedication and commitment. Men and women leave their homes, schools, jobs, and families to serve their country, whether or not they support the objectives of the war. Most veterans successfully reintegrate back into civilian life after serving, but there's no way to precisely determine how combat experiences will impact an individual service member. However, statistics suggest that military personnel who do have difficulty adjusting to their combat experiences need help and services.

Military Personnel and Veterans Returning after War

In 2008 the Minnesota House of Representatives passed a bill requiring that the criminal justice system determine whether returning veterans convicted of crimes have combat-related mental health problems, including PTSD, that may have been an influencing factor in their criminal behavior. The idea isn't to excuse criminal behavior but rather to have veterans assessed for PTSD, substance abuse, TBI, and depression related to their combat experiences. If the veteran is found to have a mental health problem, the court can consider treatment as an additional probation condition. If it is deemed appropriate, a domestic violence offender can be made to complete treatment for certain co-occurring conditions (e.g., substance abuse, PTSD) before enrolling in a domestic abuse offender treatment program.[3]

This legislation provided the impetus for the creation of veterans' courts in Minnesota. Specialty courts are relatively new, and often the up-front costs are high. However, the investment is well worth the result. Many drug courts and mental health courts have reduced recidivism by holding offenders accountable. They are closely monitored for their compliance with court-mandated plans requiring behavioral changes and with treatment recommendations. For more information about veterans' courts, visit the Justice for Vets website at www.justiceforvets.org.

Although research continues, the data indicate that veterans with PTSD and TBI are more likely than veterans without these problems to engage in domestic abuse and other criminal behavior. We should expect some readjustment problems for veterans returning to their civilian lives. While such problems are real, however, most veterans, including those who engaged in combat, do not abuse their intimate partners after their wartime experiences. Finding a causal connection between diagnosable mental health problems and domestic abuse is difficult. This is in large part because it's hard to determine whether a service member was a perpetrator before being deployed, or whether his combat experiences contributed to his violent and abusive behavior upon his return. As of this writing most programs at the Department of Veterans Affairs (VA) don't have standardized protocols to screen and assess for domestic abuse, and mental health agencies often fail to identify battering in civilian and military clients. Domestic abuse programs are increasingly expected to provide services to veterans who have not been adequately screened.

Compounding the issue are the gray-area cases. For instance it is clear that Hector's attitudes about women were formed long before he joined the Army, although his military experiences reinforced his sense of superiority and entitlement. He had also been abusive and controlling with women before, during, and after his combat experiences. Following his military service Hector had PTSD episodes associated with his violent behavior, especially his behavior toward his ex-wife. He would be the first to say that his PTSD did not cause his violence. He needed treatment for both his PTSD and his domestic abuse.

Understanding Male Veterans with PTSD and Co-Occurring Conditions

Glenna Tinney, MSW, has extensive experience working in both the civilian and military systems to end violence against women. She was one of the original Navy social workers recruited for active duty and served for twenty-four years working with military families and managing worldwide family violence and sexual assault programs. She rose to the rank of captain before retiring from the military.

Tinney manages a special project for the Battered Women's Justice Project developing a model coordinated-community response to address intimate partner violence (IPV) and co-occurring combat-related conditions such as PTSD. She trains military and civilian victim advocates and other providers on issues affecting military families. In 2013 President Obama awarded her the Champions of Change Award for her work.

During an interview Tinney reflected on the effects of military combat on veterans and their families:

As in the civilian community, there are high rates of intimate partner violence in the military. PTSD is now surfacing as a major issue for veterans returning home from combat zones. As a veteran who has worked in the field for a long time, and as the daughter of a retired Army officer who returned from Korea with PTSD, I understand the challenges for the partners and family members of veterans returning from wars with co-occurring conditions. I also understand the challenges for the criminal and military justice systems obligated to deal with offenders, the mental health practitioners struggling with limited resources to provide the best possible treatment for military personnel and veterans, the military and civilian advocates helping victims, and the offender-intervention programs trying to figure out how best to serve military and veteran offenders.

Our country has been involved in many wars on many different continents. Some combat veterans have returned home from these wars with multiple physical and psychological problems. In the past, veterans with mental health problems had limited options for help, and most of them kept quiet about their war experiences and their feelings.

In all of our wars, some veterans have experienced PTSD, but it was defined and diagnosed differently than it is today. The terms "shell shock" and "battle fatigue" have been used to describe the psychological and behavioral issues service members experience after returning from war. Most service members who have deployed to a war zone have some level of combat stress when returning home. This can result in having sleep disturbances and bad dreams or nightmares; being angry, short-tempered, agitated, irritated, annoyed, jumpy, mistrustful, and easily startled; avoiding people and places; using alcohol and drugs; smoking; and being overcontrolling or overprotective. For most veterans these symptoms disappear within a short time.

However, for some, the symptoms are intense and troubling and don't go away. If they persist, they are probably indications of PTSD. This is a serious but treatable condition that can occur after a person is exposed to death or threatened death, actual or threatened serious injury, or actual or threatened sexual violence. Symptoms include but are not limited to experiencing intrusive, bad memories of a traumatic event; avoiding things that might trigger memories of the traumatic event, such as crowded places or loud noises; shutting down emotionally to prevent feeling pain, fear, or anger; operating on "high alert" at all times; having a very short fuse and/or startling easily; and experiencing sleep problems, irritability, anger, or fear.

Being with someone who has PTSD can be difficult; it can cause problems in daily life and in relationships. Some combat veterans with PTSD may be violent and some may not. When intimate partner violence is also present, the condition may exacerbate the violent behaviors or vice versa.

We haven't fought ground wars like those in Iraq and Afghanistan since the Vietnam War. Because we've moved to an all-volunteer military force, military missions since 9/11 have required that service members deploy multiple times to both Iraq and Afghanistan. Such deployments can exacerbate PTSD. One of the reasons we're seeing a different response from the military (and from society in general) to veterans returning from war with mental health problems is that we're experiencing a sort of collective guilt about the way we treated Vietnam War veterans. As is well documented, returning Vietnam veterans were not provided necessary services, and in many respects they were met with disdain or worse because the war was intensely unpopular. The military, Congress, and state governments are now increasingly paying attention to the needs of veterans, although services are still inadequate.

Being in combat doesn't cause IPV [intimate partner violence], but combat experience can result in PTSD, and its symptoms may be similar to the emotions, responses, and tactics seen in perpetrators. For instance an individual with PTSD who is also a domestic abuse perpetrator may be impulsive or use destructive behaviors, easily become angry or irritable, feel the need to be on guard, have difficulty controlling emotion, or be overwhelmed with feelings of shame and despair. To determine appropriate interventions, it's important to differentiate between stand-alone PTSD symptoms and battering tactics.

Research shows that military personnel and veterans who

have PTSD are more violent with their partners, which is why screening for PTSD is so important. Risk assessments are increasingly being used by health care providers, advocates, treatment programs, and the courts to determine how much danger a victim may be facing.

Whether you're a victim advocate, domestic abuse counselor, or probation officer, the information you have about the pattern and context of abuse may be limited. Police and court reports are helpful, but collateral information from the perpetrator's current or past partner(s) is important to assess for IPV, PTSD, other co-occurring conditions, and risk. Partners can corroborate the context in which the abusive behavior is embedded.

Context includes the previous behavior of the offender, the intent of his violence, and the way this behavior has affected the victim. Examining these factors helps to determine whether an abusive act is a battering behavior (using violence, intimidation, threats, and coercion) or an anomaly, something that is not part of an ongoing pattern of coercive control.

An offender's partner knows whether he was violent or abusive prior to his deployment or if this behavior surfaced after his combat experiences. She can also describe her level of fear living with him. This information is not always easy to obtain. Military personnel and veterans, like other IPV perpetrators, may not be truthful about their past behavior, and victims may be reluctant to divulge information that could jeopardize the service member's career.

I would add, however, that if you screened the general population of nonmilitary IPV offenders, you would find that many of them have trauma histories, PTSD, and co-occurring conditions. For instance it is widely acknowledged in the literature that 70 percent of all male perpetrators grew up observing domestic violence in the home or were themselves abused by a parent or other family member. If trauma alone causes IPV, why don't more women who have experienced similar childhood experiences—being physically or sexually abused—batter their male intimate partners? Women are more likely to internalize their childhood trauma, experiencing hopelessness and depression, blaming themselves, and feeling shame. Men tend to externalize their childhood experiences and, having been socialized as males, often use violence to settle conflict. Perpetrators may claim that the trauma they experienced during combat is a justification or excuse for their violent, aggressive, and controlling behavior in a past or current intimate relationship. In the treatment field, some practitioners also believe that IPV is caused by combat experiences or co-occurring conditions. Although there is a relationship between mental health issues and combat experiences, they are not typically what cause IPV. For instance a veteran could experience dissociative symptoms (breakdown in memory, awareness, identity, or perception), or this could also be a defense mechanism because the perpetrator is struggling with taking responsibility for what he has done.

Although there is a high suicide rate in the military, only half of all suicides have involved veterans who had combat experience. Many military personnel and veterans have had what practitioners are increasingly describing as adverse childhood experiences (ACEs)—trauma histories. This is also true of the general population of IPV perpetrators. ACEs include emotional and physical abuse; neglect, both physical and emotional; family dysfunction, including a mother being abused; household substance abuse; incarceration of a parent; and exposure to other traumatic stressors.

Screening and Assessing Offenders

Domestic abuse programs have limited resources, but a majority of programs have assessment tools that can be enhanced for military personnel and veterans. Most assessment forms provide information about law enforcement involvement in the case, court dispositions and conditions of probation, civil orders for protection and reliefs/conditions, self-reported alcohol and drug use, the offender's personal history with violence as a child, his reported use of violence and abuse in past and current intimate partnerships, a medical and mental health treatment history (including depression, PTSD, TBI, attempted suicide, and mental illness), and risk assessment questions.

The staff of domestic abuse programs should have referral information if they believe that a court-mandated offender may have post-traumatic stress disorder or traumatic brain injury. Many of the current screening tools don't provide the kinds of questions that a domestic abuse program uses to assess battering and risk to an intimate partner. An offender who has been ordered into a program may have co-occurring conditions and hence should be screened for each.

The following websites provide information on PTSD and screening:

The Department of Veterans Affairs National Center for PTSD
www.ptsd.va.gov/professional/assessment/screens/pc-ptsd.asp
www.ptsd.va.gov/professional/provider-type/doctors/screening
-and-referral.asp

National Center for PTSD (lists other PTSD screens)
www.ptsd.va.gov/professional/assessment/screens/index.asp

Counseling Programs That Work with Veterans

In some jurisdictions, mental health agencies or domestic abuse programs have started veterans' groups for offenders, both those who must participate in court-mandated programs and those who participate voluntarily. Some of the veterans have mental health problems and some don't. A number of VA clinics offer anger management classes, but they usually don't explore the battering dynamics that a traditional domestic abuse program does.

Scott Miller, Men's Program Coordinator at the Domestic Abuse Intervention Project in Duluth, Minnesota, says that most communities would like to have separate offender programs for veterans, but it's typically cost prohibitive, since there aren't the numbers to generate a group. Miller's experience with veterans who batter is that they tend to be rather rigid and use their combat experiences to rationalize their aggressive and violent behavior. While generally supporting the concept of veterans' groups, he warns that as in any culturally specific group, participants can get caught up in "group think." This makes it important to have veterans who are violence free facilitating the groups. Again this is not easy for small programs, which are often dependent on meager public funding and participant fees.

That veterans use combat experience as a justification for their violence should not be surprising, since most men who batter rationalize their behavior in one way or another, at least initially. Discussion of combat experience can become problematic in a group, however. Nonveteran counselors are often reluctant to challenge veterans with combat experience, because the counselors believe they can't relate or respond to the reality of combat. Counselors obviously don't want to appear unsympathetic or as if they are minimizing the trauma of a veteran's combat experiences, even though most men who batter have experienced some level of trauma in their lives.

I recently observed an offender group of eight men who were having an in-depth discussion about the elements of a respectful relationship with a woman. The group was facilitated by two experienced counselors who had been doing this work for a long time. One group member, who had returned from the war in Iraq, was constantly bringing up examples of his war experiences—the battle mindset and what he had learned in the military—to make his point about how people respond to conflict. While his assertions seemed genuine, they became a barrier to deeper dialogue. The other men in the group shut down because they hadn't had similar experiences. Even though the counselors tried to be respectful of this man and shift the discussion back to the themes being discussed, the dynamics of the group were negatively affected.

After a while one of the counselors told him that they appreciated his contribution and acknowledged that his military examples had had a profound impact on his life. While noting the emotional significance of his combat experiences, she asked if the group might focus more on the topic for that night—ways participants use isolation to control their partner. The counselors later reported that the second half of the group was much more productive.

This example illustrates the need for counselors to intervene and refocus a group. It also illustrates one of the benefits of having culturally specific groups if a program has the resources. If the counselors had both been veterans, the discussion and the participant's continued explanations for his violence might have been handled very differently.

The decision to start a veterans' group should not be made in a vacuum. Offender programs should work with battered women's programs, the courts, the VA, and other providers to explore potential unintended consequences of starting a veterans' group. For instance will the previous military rank of the veterans' counselors be a problem for some participants? Will perpetrators use PTSD or TBI as an excuse for their battering? Does the idea of a veterans' group send a subtle message to the victims to forgive their abusive partners because of their combat experiences? Are we asking the courts to treat domestic abuse cases differently because an offender was in the military or served in combat?

Counselors who are also veterans are more apt to recognize when a veteran is using his combat experience as a way of deflecting responsibility for his abusive behavior. More research needs to be conducted before veterans' groups are considered a promising practice for offender programs.

Miller acknowledges that many domestic abuse programs around the country receive referrals from the courts to work with veterans who have not been screened and assessed for PTSD and other mental health problems. Ideally domestic abuse programs should screen and assess all domestic abuse perpetrators for co-occurring conditions, not just military personnel and veterans. Unfortunately a lack of resources prevents many programs from providing such comprehensive assessment and treatment. While some programs have the capacity to provide concurrent treatment for PTSD and domestic abuse, others rely on community mental health agencies and chemical dependency programs to treat offenders before they enter a domestic abuse program.

Hector Matascastillo, whose story begins this chapter, started an eighteen-week veterans' group at the Domestic Abuse Program in Minneapolis. (He has since left the Domestic Abuse Program and opened his own practice.) The group receives referrals from the VA, probation officers, and a newly established veterans' court. While it's too new to measure the program's success, anecdotal evidence has been positive. The program makes contact with the participant's partner and has the man complete an abuse/behavior inventory during intake. Staff members examine police and court reports and have ongoing contact with the partner to assess for risk and monitor changes in behavior during the man's participation in the program.

The program uses a cognitive-behavioral treatment model similar to that utilized by other groups affiliated with the Domestic Abuse Project. Like most offender programs, a key feature is asking the participants to take responsibility for their behavior. Hector told me that this assignment is the single greatest predictor of a group member's awareness of his abusive behavior. The group is open ended and typically has twelve members.

Hector describes trauma-informed changes made for the group. In the meeting room, for example, the chairs are placed against the wall so participants aren't distracted by their hypervigilance, which requires them to constantly scan the environment for any perceived threat. He says the participants feel more comfortable in this environment.

Like other cognitive-behavioral treatment approaches, this program has a profeminist analysis. The group helps participants examine the power dynamics in a relationship when a man is using violence, coercion, intimidation, and threats to dominate his partner. Looking at the top-down organization of the military helps participants see the hierarchical structure that they have created in their own intimate relationships. While a top-down structure is necessary in the military to maintain discipline, it is contrary to the kind of egalitarian relationships we promote in our groups.

As a veteran who has both battered and experienced PTSD, Hector can more easily challenge a man who is hiding behind a diagnosis of PTSD to rationalize his behavior. He's been there. He knows about minimizing his abuse and blaming others for what he did. He also has a positive story to tell. Like many of us, Hector believes that each man in his group can change if he is motivated to take those first steps.

A Message to Military Personnel and Veterans

Please share the following information with military personnel and veterans you are working with in counseling or in domestic abuse groups.

If you are a service member or veteran who has battered, or if you're concerned about your escalating abusive behavior with your intimate partner, help is available. You're probably aware that your partner or maybe your children are afraid of you, especially when you get angry. Maybe you were abusive to your intimate partner before you joined the military, or perhaps you've noticed that things have changed when you returned from deployments. As is true for most men, asking for help can be difficult. If you're reading this book, you're obviously concerned about your violence. You may have already lost your relationship, or maybe your current partner is saying she wants you to get help; she may even be threatening to leave unless you change.

Please ask for help. You're worth it.

The following are useful resources for military personnel, veterans, victim advocates, and practitioners in the domestic abuse field:

- Eligible veterans can receive free screening and treatment for PTSD and other combat-related mental health issues, traumatic brain injury (TBI), and substance abuse at VA facilities. However, services related to intimate partner violence were not being provided in every VA facility at the time this book was written.

- Active duty military personnel can receive free mental health services through Department of Defense and TRICARE health-care resources.

- *Returning from the War Zone: A Guide for Military Personnel,* published by the VA National Center for PTSD, contains information on what to expect when returning from combat and how to help military members better transition back to home life. The guide also provides a list of resources. The guide can be found at: www.ptsd.va.gov/public/reintegration/returning _from_the_war_zone_guides.asp.

- *Returning from the War Zone: A Guide for Families of Military Members* is a similar guide for family members. It can be found at: www.ptsd.va.gov/public/reintegration/returning_from _the_war_zone_guides.asp.

- Active duty military and veteran families can contact **Military OneSource at (800) 342-9647,** twenty-four hours a day, seven days a week. Some states have their own hotline programs. Individuals who are attached to a military installation can contact the installation's victim advocate, the Family Advocacy Program (FAP), law enforcement, and/or IPV/domestic violence programs in the local civilian community. Contact information for installation FAPs can be found online using the Installation Locator on the Military OneSource Homepage: www.militaryonesource.mil.

- Additional information for understanding the military response to IPV/domestic violence can be found in the handbook *Understanding the Military Response to Domestic Violence: Tools for Civilian Advocates* at: www.bwjp.org/articles/article-list.aspx?id=30.
- Advocates (military and civilian) will find the e-learning course *Safety at Home, Intimate Partner Violence, Military Personnel and Veterans* useful in providing services to military-related families experiencing intimate partner violence (a link to the program can be found at www.bwjp.org/elearning_course.aspx). Funded by the Avon Foundation, the five-module program was produced by the Battered Women's Justice Project (www.bwjp.org).

You may also contact a local program in your community that provides services for men who batter.

Closing Thoughts

A journey of a thousand miles
must begin with a single step.

►► Lao-tzu ◄◄

Violence gives a man who batters temporary control over his partner. He ends an argument on his terms, vents his anger, and punishes
his intimate partner. But at what cost? Although often getting his
way, he causes incredible suffering in the process.

A man who batters tries to justify his behavior, yet the terror and
disappointment in his partner's eyes are always there as a reminder
that it was he—and no one else—who did something hurtful and
abusive to her. There is no excuse. In their attempt to avoid responsibility, too many men dig in their heels and try not to feel, or try
not to remember. A Buddhist teacher once told me that a man who
batters looks in the mirror, sees that his face is dirty, and wipes the
mirror to get it clean.

Some men do face their problems head on and make commitments to change. You have met some of these men in this book.
I would have stopped doing this work a long time ago if I hadn't
seen some incredible personal transformations. If you have made it
through this book, take the next steps to change—you won't regret
it. Set some goals for your life, and practice what you have learned.
Ask for help. Use the exercises in the workbook to keep you focused
on your goals.

And what of the women who told their stories in this book? I try to imagine how they must have felt as the blows and kicks bruised their bodies. What were they thinking when they saw the rage and hatred in their partners' eyes? How did their husbands and boyfriends who had once professed love and commitment get to such a place? Were these women's spirits broken? Would they ever trust a man again? I hope they have found a path to healing and have found love and support. I also wonder about the children of the men and women in this book. How have they been affected by witnessing the violence? Will we see the boys who were exposed to domestic abuse in our groups in the future, or will the cycle be broken because of our community interventions?

While writing this third edition of *Violent No More,* I somewhat surprisingly became invigorated and hopeful about the future. I finished this book almost exactly on the eleventh anniversary of the deaths of my friends Sheila Wellstone and Senator Paul Wellstone. Both Shelia and Paul were fiercely committed to ending domestic abuse. About two months before they died in a plane crash in northern Minnesota, Sheila told me that she wanted to focus energy on reaching men who were abusing women. She recognized that laws and shelters weren't enough. She knew that men had to change. Since that time there has been a slow but growing acknowledgment that we need to address the culture that produces men who batter.

One final message to men reading this book: Get involved. For too long gender violence has been considered a women's issue. It isn't. Today we can *all* make some serious commitments about how we want to lead our lives. It is up to each of us to change a little piece of the world.

Appendix A:
Creating a Process of Change
for Men Who Batter

The educational process presented in the Duluth curriculum *Creating a Process of Change for Men Who Batter* is based on the work of the late Brazilian educator and author Paulo Freire. Freire's contribution to education came to light with his work on literacy campaigns with the poor. In his groundbreaking book *Pedagogy of the Oppressed,* he emphasized that every human being is capable of looking critically at his or her world despite the level of oppression he or she has experienced.

Through dialogue and critical thinking, students develop an awareness about the world, even if the world is his or her own neighborhood. This awareness leads students to a personal transformation and then to the emergence of what Freire would call a "critical consciousness." Students distinguish what is created by nature from what is created by the culture, and they begin to understand the impact of socialization on the oppressed and the oppressor. They become more reflective about the world around them, raising questions about the inequities in their society and ultimately about how to struggle against oppression.[1]

I met Freire during the 1980s, when Ellen Pence and I were writing the Duluth curriculum. We knew that his educational approach would resonate with battered women who were for the first time hearing and talking about the injustices of oppressive systems—in this case the power their husbands and boyfriends had over them. We didn't know if this approach would work with men who batter.

Over dinner and a couple of glasses of red wine at a restaurant in St. Paul, Freire, Peter Park (one of his academic colleagues), and I discussed men who batter their intimate partners. I asked Freire whether liberation education could work with court-mandated offenders. Always thoughtful, Freire responded by asking whether men who batter would gain empathy from this educational process. And more important he wanted to know whether they would willingly give up their dominance over their intimate partners when they benefit from that dominance. He said he needed time to ponder the questions. He wanted us to report back to him on whether engaging men who believe in their superiority over women could or would change through a dialogical process. Would they gain empathy? Would they give up their power?

Objectives of the Model

The Duluth curriculum is designed to help men stop battering by achieving six objectives:

- to help the participant understand how his abuse stems from beliefs of entitlement that support his control of his partner's actions, thoughts, and feelings
- to increase the participant's understanding of the causes of his violence by examining the cultural and social contexts in which he uses it against his partner
- to increase the participant's willingness to change his actions by examining the negative effects of his behavior on his relationship, his partner, his children, his friends, and himself
- to encourage the participant to become accountable to those he has hurt through his use of violence by helping him to acknowledge his abuse, accept responsibility for its impact on his partner and others, and take specific steps to change

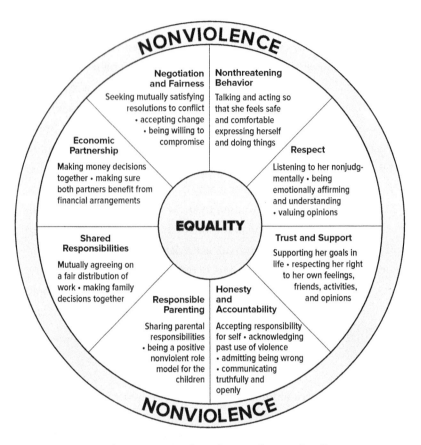

- to increase the participant's understanding and willingness to change by exploring actions, intents, and beliefs that support equality with a woman
- to provide the opportunity for a man to find love, trust, and commitment in relationships with women and children by learning new ways of acting in a relationship

To achieve the above objectives, the curriculum is organized around the themes found on the Equality Wheel and the corresponding Power and Control Wheel. The behaviors and aspects of the relationship shown on the Equality Wheel become the model offered to participants for egalitarian and interdependent relationships with women. The Power and Control Wheel depicts the pri-

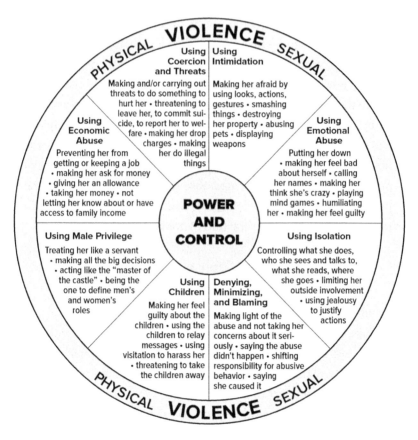

mary tactics and behaviors individual abusers use to establish and maintain control over their partners.

Each theme in the curriculum contains the following three parts:

- Part One explores an aspect from the Equality Wheel.
- Part Two explores the corresponding tactic from the Power and Control Wheel.
- Part Three focuses on becoming nonviolent—for example, more accountable, respectful, trusting, and supportive.

Though each theme has a specific focus, the themes work together to create an integrated whole. Because the group process is dialogical and drawn from examples men raise from their own lives, every session covers several tactics and/or equality themes.

Because of this integration, the curriculum can be adapted to domestic abuse programs regardless of their length. In Duluth the program is thirty weeks. Depending on the length of the program and the needs of the participants, facilitators or counselors can decide which themes to use. When programs are longer than thirty weeks, themes can be repeated. Each time one is repeated, the participants will be in different places in their change process than they were the first time around, so the dialogue will be different. The thinking of men in the groups is challenged through the program's dialogical process, which layer by layer helps them integrate new ways of thinking that lead them in the direction of nonviolence.[2]

Guidelines for Counselors/Facilitators Using the Duluth Curriculum

To effectively use the Duluth curriculum, counselors should:

- have a clear understanding and philosophical analysis about the history and nature of men's violence against women. Otherwise the dialogue will simply become a discussion without challenges to sexist thinking.
- have a significant amount of training and have worked with a skilled and experienced colleague for some time.
- feel comfortable entering into dialogue with group members and facilitating critical thinking. Dialogue requires the group leader to be genuinely curious about the group members' belief systems without colluding and without having a predetermined ending point in the dialogue.
- have the confidence and skill to pose questions and engage group members in understanding the moral and ethical contradictions of their use of violence and their belief in male entitlement.
- help men who batter become more reflective about their lives, and challenge their world view about what it means to be male in our society and why they want a woman in their life.

Dialogue is not an easy process for most counselors. As a former teacher I can attest to the way I was taught to teach in college. Freire refers to traditional education as "banking education," which essentially is a form of indoctrination. With the traditional educational model, the student simply repeats back what the teacher presents. Without an opportunity for dialogue and critical thinking, the student will fail to analyze the material being presented. In a domestic abuse group, a man may hear a lecture, complete an assignment, and listen to a group leader's feedback. But the man will likely repeat back only what the leader hopes he will say. It is questionable whether an altered consciousness will ever emerge through a traditional educational process, because the group member isn't being challenged to investigate and analyze the belief system that guides his world.

There is always a fine line between engaging in dialogue and colluding. Dialogue would completely shut down if the group leader challenged every sexist comment a participant makes. A skilled facilitator can always find ways to reintroduce such comments and put them into a context that is challenging for the whole group.

More information about the curriculum *Creating a Process of Change for Men Who Batter* and the Duluth Model is available at: www.theduluthmodel.org.

Appendix B:
Useful Handouts

The following material may be useful as handouts for counselors and may be reproduced. Please ensure that either the Domestic Abuse Intervention Project (DAIP) or the author is cited on the handouts. The Power and Control Wheel and the Equality Wheel can be found in Appendix A; the rest of the handouts are located in this Appendix, beginning on the following page.

• **Time-Out Rules**
• **Negotiation Guide**
• **Fair Discussion Guide**

Time-Out Rules

1. Take a time-out when you recognize your cues and before you become emotionally or physically abusive.
2. Take a time-out when you feel like you want to become abusive or violent; do not take a time-out to avoid conflict.
3. Tell your partner you are taking a time-out.
4. Tell your partner how long you'll be gone.
5. Do not drink, use drugs, or drive.
6. Call a friend or group member for support.
7. Do calming exercises like walking or jogging, shooting free throws at a basketball court, or meditating.
8. Think positive thoughts. Do not dwell on the problem that caused you to become angry.

9. If you are still agitated, or if you believe you might still become abusive or violent if you go home and you need more time than you agreed to, call or text your partner and let her know.
10. Your partner is not obliged to take a time-out; you take a time-out for yourself.
11. If your partner indicates that she is afraid of you, stay away. Find an alternative place to stay until things have calmed down.
12. When you return, do not insist that you and your partner should solve or resolve the conflict you were having.
13. If you notice your cues again, take another time-out.
14. Whenever you follow the time-out rules, make a note of the positive way you handled the situation and its results.

An Important Note

You may want to practice a time-out when you are *not* angry so that you and your partner understand the process and each other's expectations. Your partner needs to know the rules of the time-out so she knows what to expect.

Negotiation Guide

1. Regardless of how angry or hurt I feel, I will remain nonviolent.
2. If I disagree with my partner's position, I will still be respectful toward her.
3. I will remain seated during the discussion.
4. I will not yell, scream, or use my voice in an intimidating manner.
5. I will not threaten my partner in any way.
6. I will not use put-downs, call my partner names, or be sarcastic or belittling.
7. I will not bring up past incidents to prove a point.
8. I will avoid blaming or shaming statements.
9. I will strive not to get defensive.
10. I will listen to my partner's position and refrain from interrupting.

11. I will commit to work toward a compromise.
12. I will be willing to explore my own issues and take responsibility for mistakes I have made.
13. I will respect my partner's wishes to end the discussion.
14. I will be honest.
15. I will talk about my feelings but will not use them as a way to manipulate my partner.

Fair Discussion Guide

Before you begin: Review these guidelines together, and add any that you both decide are important:

1. Acknowledge that a good discussion requires two people who are ready to talk. Don't force a discussion.
2. Reminder: You know each other's weak spots. Don't use them to hurt your partner.
3. Before you begin a discussion, you must first be committed to a fair process.
4. Define the problem—it may be different for each person. What is negotiable? How does each person perceive and define the problem? Who else will be affected and how?
5. Agree to deal with one issue at a time.
6. Agree on how long you want to discuss the issue—you don't need to resolve everything in one sitting.

Try to:

- Listen. Try to understand what the other person is saying.
- Hear things you disagree with or find painful without reacting defensively.
- Use "I" statements, like "I think" or "I feel."
- Take responsibility for your past actions.
- Be honest.
- Be willing to apologize or state that you are willing to work on an issue.

- Encourage your partner to take equal time to present her position, as well as time to change her mind.
- Work toward a mutually satisfying solution.
- Accept that some things may need to change.

Try not to:
- Interrupt when your partner is talking.
- Raise your voice (for men who have battered, you need to be especially careful with your body language, tone of voice, looks, rolling of eyes, etc.).
- Blame your partner.
- Bring up the past to make your point.
- Walk away from the discussion.
- Make threats.
- Use other people's opinions to make your point.

Before you end the discussion:
- Each person should try to summarize what was stated.
- What was agreed to?
- What have you personally committed to?
- What still needs work?
- Can you agree to short-term and long-term goals?
- What needs to be part of an immediate and then a final solution? If a compromise is needed, list several long-term solutions you both think are fair.
- How did you feel about the discussion process? What improvements would you make in the future?

Notes

Chapter 2: The Roots of Men's Violence Against Women

1. Rebecca Emerson Dobash and Russell P. Dobash, *Violence Against Wives* (New York: The Free Press, 1983).
2. Rebecca Emerson Dobash and Russell P. Dobash, interview in *With Impunity: Men and Gender Violence,* film (Saint Paul, MN: Education for Critical Thinking, 2013).
3. Shannan Catalano et al., "Female Victims of Violence" (U.S. Department of Justice, Office of Justice Programs, Bureau of Justice Statistics, 2009), http://www.bjs.gov/content/pub/pdf/fvv.pdf.
4. Michael Kimmel, interview in *With Impunity: Men and Gender Violence,* film (Saint Paul, MN: Education for Critical Thinking, 2013).
5. bell hooks, *Ain't I a Woman* (Boston: South End Press, 1981).
6. Kate Ratliff and Shigehiro Oishi, "Gender Differences in Implicit Self-Esteem Following a Romantic Partner's Success or Failure," *Journal of Personality and Social Psychology* vol. 105, no. 4 (2013): 688–702.

Chapter 3: How We Learn to Be Violent

1. Rebecca Emerson Dobash and Russell P. Dobash, *Violence Against Wives* (New York: The Free Press, 1983).
2. A. Rosenbaum and K. D. O'Leary, "Children: The Unintended Victims of Marital Violence," *The American Journal of Orthopsychiatry* vol. 51, no. 4 (1981): 692–99.
3. Anne Ganley, in *Treating Men Who Batter: Theory, Practice, and Programs,* ed. P. Lynn Caesar and L. Kevin Hamberger (New York: Springer Publishing Company, 1989).
4. Jackson Katz, interview in *With Impunity: Men and Gender Violence,* film (Saint Paul, MN: Education for Critical Thinking, 2013).
5. Iris Chang, *The Rape of Nanking* (New York: Penguin Books, 1997).

6. James Gilligan, *Violence: Our Deadly Epidemic and Its Causes* (New York: Grosset/Putnam, 1996).

7. Ellen Pence and Michael Paymar, *Education Groups for Men Who Batter* (New York: Springer Publishers, 1993).

8. Cordelia Anderson, interview in *With Impunity: Men and Gender Violence*, film (Saint Paul, MN: Education for Critical Thinking, 2013).

Chapter 4: It's More than Physical Violence

1. S. Spaccarelli, J. D. Coatsworth, and B. S. Bowden, "Exposure to Serious Family Violence among Incarcerated Boys: Its Association with Violent Offending and Potentially Mediating Variables," *Violence and Victims* vol. 10, no. 3 (1995): 163–82.

2. Peter G. Jaffe, David A. Wolfe, and Susan Kaye Wilson, *Children of Battered Women*, Developmental Clinical Psychology and Psychiatry vol. 21 (Thousand Oaks, CA: Sage Publications, 1990).

Chapter 5: Getting Past Denial

1. Ellen Pence, interview in *With Impunity: Men and Gender Violence*, film (Saint Paul, MN: Education for Critical Thinking, 2013).

2. Larry Bennett and Patricia Bland, "Substance Abuse and Intimate Partner Violence" (National Online Resource Center on Violence Against Women, 2008), http://vawnet.org/applied-research-papers/print -document.php?doc_id=1324.

3. Jennifer Katz, et al., "Excuses, Excuses: Accounting for the Effects of Partner Violence on Marital Satisfaction and Stability," *Violence and Victims* vol. 10, no. 4 (1995): 315–26.

Chapter 6: Letting Go of Relationships

1. Jacqueline Campbell, interview with author (2013).

Chapter 7: Making Changes and Staying on Track

1. M'Liss Switzer and Katherine Hale, *Called to Account* (Berkeley, CA: Seal Publishing Co., 1984).

2. Amnesty International and Human Rights Watch, *Truth and Justice: Unfinished Business in South Africa* (2003).

Chapter 9: Healing

1. Marlin Mousseau, "Project Medicine Wheel" (Pine Ridge Indian Reservation, 1989).

2. H. Lien Bragg, *Child Protection in Families Experiencing Domestic Violence* (Children's Bureau, U.S. Department of Health and Human Services, Child Welfare Information Gateway, 2003).

Chapter 10: Prevention: Getting Men and Boys Engaged with Ending Gender Violence

1. Dave Grossman, *On Killing: The Psychological Cost of Learning to Kill in War and Society* (New York: Little, Brown and Co., 1995).
2. James Garbarino, *Lost Boys: Why Our Sons Turn Violent and How We Can Save Them* (New York: The Free Press, 1999).
3. Angela Browne, *When Battered Women Kill* (New York: The Free Press, 1984).
4. Jackson Katz, interview in *With Impunity: Men and Gender Violence*, film (Saint Paul, MN: Education for Critical Thinking, 2013).
5. Advocates for Human Rights, "Morocco: Challenges with Addressing Domestic Violence in Compliance with the Convention Against Torture" (47th Session of the Committee Against Torture, 2012).
6. Larry Cohen, "From Kools to Cancer Sticks: How Quality Prevention Changed Tobacco Norms" (Oakland, CA: Prevention Institute, 2009).
7. Anne Jones, interview in *With Impunity: Men and Gender Violence*, film (Saint Paul, MN: Education for Critical Thinking, 2013).
8. Oliver Williams, interview in *With Impunity: Men and Gender Violence*, film (Saint Paul, MN: Education for Critical Thinking, 2013).
9. Beth Richie, interview in *With Impunity: Men and Gender Violence*, film (Saint Paul, MN: Education for Critical Thinking, 2013).
10. Ann Jones, interview in *With Impunity: Men and Gender Violence*, film (Saint Paul, MN: Education for Critical Thinking, 2013).

Chapter 11: Counselors Working with Men Who Batter

1. Edward W. Gondolf, interview in *A Conversation about Groups for Men Who Batter*, film (Duluth, MN: Domestic Abuse Intervention Programs, 2007).
2. Edward W. Gondolf, "Do Batterer Programs Work? A 15-Month Follow-Up of Multi-Site Evaluation," *Domestic Violence Report* vol. 3 (1998): 64–80.
3. Edward W. Gondolf, interview in *Assessing Domestic Violence Interventions*, film (Duluth, MN: Domestic Abuse Intervention Programs, 2007).
4. Lenore Walker, *The Battered Woman* (New York: The Free Press, 1984).

5. Ellen Pence and Michael Paymar, *Creating a Process of Change for Men Who Batter* (Duluth, MN: Domestic Abuse Intervention Programs, 1986; rev. 1990, 1993, 2003, and 2011).

6. Edward Gondolf, interview in *A Conversation about Groups for Men Who Batter*, film (Duluth, MN: Domestic Abuse Intervention Programs, 2007).

7. Michael Paymar and Graham Barnes, "Countering Confusion About the Duluth Model" (Minneapolis, MN: Battered Women's Justice Project, 2006).

8. Edward Gondolf, *The Future of Batterer Programs: Reassessing Evidence-Based Practice* (Boston: Northeastern University Press, 2012).

9. Ibid.

10. Ellen Pence, interview in *With Impunity: Men and Gender Violence*, film (Saint Paul, MN: Education for Critical Thinking, 2013).

11. David Island and Patrick Letellier, *Men Who Beat the Men Who Love Them* (New York: Harrington Park Press, 1991).

Chapter 12: Risk and Danger in Domestic Abuse Cases

1. Shannan Catalano, et al., "Female Victims of Violence," Bureau of Justice Statistics, Selected Findings (U.S. Department of Justice, 2009), http://www.bjs.gov/content/pub/pdf/fvv.pdf.

2. Carolyn Rebecca Block, "How Can Practitioners Help an Abused Woman Lower Her Risk of Death?" *National Institute of Justice Journal* no. 250 (2003), https://www.ncjrs.gov/pdffiles1/jr000250c.pdf.

3. Barbara Hart, *Assessing Whether Batterers Will Kill* (Harrisburg, PA: Pennsylvania Coalition Against Domestic Violence, 1990).

4. Barbara Hart, Risk Assessment and Safety Planning (adapted by Hart for this book, 2013).

5. J. C. Campbell, et al., "Risk Factors for Femicide in Abusive Relationships: Results from a Multisite Case Control Study," *American Journal of Public Health* vol. 93, no. 7 (2003): 1089–1097. (J. C. Campbell, D. Webster, J. Koziol-McLain, C. R. Block, D. Campbell, M. A. Curry, F. Gary, C. Sachs, P. W. Sharps, S. Wilt, J. Manganello, and X. Xu.)

6. Praxis International, "The Blueprint for Safety" (Saint Paul, MN: Praxis International, 2009).

7. Arkadi Gerney, Chelsea Parsons, and Charles Posner, "America Under the Gun" (Washington, DC: Center for American Progress, 2014), http://www.americanprogress.org/issues/civil-liberties/report/2013/04/02/58382/america-under-the-gun.

8. Edward Gondolf, *The Future of Batterer Programs: Reassessing Evidence-Based Practice* (Boston, MA: Northeastern University Press, 2012).
9. Ibid.
10. Edward W. Gondolf, interview in *Assessing Domestic Violence Interventions,* film (Duluth, MN: Domestic Abuse Intervention Programs, 2007).

Chapter 13: Veterans and Domestic Abuse

1. Charles Hoge, et al., "Combat Duty in Iraq and Afghanistan, Mental Health Problems, and Barriers to Care," *New England Journal of Medicine* 351 (2004): 13–22.
2. Charles Hoge, Testimony to the Congressional Sub-Committee on Health, 2008.
3. Rep. Michael Paymar, Omnibus Public Safety Policy and Finance Bill, Minnesota House of Representatives, 2008.

Appendix A: Creating a Process of Change for Men Who Batter

1. Paulo Freire, *Pedagogy of the Oppressed* (New York: Continuum, 1992).
2. Ellen Pence and Michael Paymar, *Creating a Process of Change for Men Who Batter* (Duluth, MN: Domestic Abuse Intervention Programs, 1986; rev. 1990, 1993, 2003, and 2011).

Resources

The following resources may be useful for men, women, advocates, counselors, and other interveners reading this book. Most states in the United States and provinces in Canada have organizations that provide referral information for victims of domestic and sexual violence and contact information about domestic abuse counseling agencies in their jurisdictions. Included in this list are national organizations that provide training, technical assistance, and resources in specific areas of domestic abuse prevention and intervention.

Resources for Men

National Domestic Violence Hotline
(800) 799-7233   TTY: (800) 787-3224
www.thehotline.org

Counseling Programs for Men Who Batter
Batterer Intervention Service Center of Michigan
www.biscmi.org

United Kingdom, Help Line
www.nationaldomesticviolencehelpline.org.uk

Men's Advice Line, United Kingdom
www.mensadviceline.org.uk

Resources for Women

National Domestic Violence Hotline
(800) 799-SAFE (7233)   TTY: (800) 787-3224
www.thehotline.org

National Coalition Against Domestic Violence
www.ncadv.org

Batterer Intervention Service Center
www.biscmi.org
A full listing of US programs can be found at www.biscmi.org/other
_resources/state_coalitions.html

Child Abuse
The Childhelp National Child Abuse Hotline
(800) 422-4453
www.childhelp.org/pages/hotline-home

Counseling/Mental Health Help and Assistance
Crisis Services/24-Hour Help Hotline—Crisis Call Center
(800) 273-8255
www.crisiscallcenter.org/crisisservices.html

National Suicide Prevention Lifeline
(800) 273-8255
www.suicidepreventionlifeline.org

Technical Assistance
U.S. Department of Justice, Office on Violence Against Women (OVW)
www.justice.gov/ovw

Resources for Advocates
Praxis International, Inc.
A nonprofit research and training organization that works toward the
elimination of violence in the lives of women and children.
www.praxisinternational.org

Danger Assessment Instrument
The Danger Assessment instrument created by Jacquelyn Campbell can be
used by domestic violence advocates and healthcare providers.
www.dangerassessment.org

Veterans and Military Personnel and Their Families
See Chapter 13, the section starting on page 343 called "A Message to Military Personnel and Veterans," for a list of resources related to this topic.

Professionals working with veterans: See Chapter 13, the section on page 339 called "Screening and Assessing Offenders," for websites that provide information on PTSD and screening.

Standards for Batterer Intervention Programs/Domestic Abuse Programs

Batterer Intervention Service Center
www.biscmi.org

RESPECT United Kingdom
http://respect.uk.net/work/work-perpetrators-domestic-violence/accreditation

Other U.S. Organizations
Asian and Pacific Islander Institute on Domestic Violence
www.apiidv.org

Battered Women's Justice Project
www.bwjp.org

Domestic Abuse Intervention Programs
www.theduluthmodel.org

Education for Critical Thinking
http://educationforcriticalthinking.org

Faith Trust Institute
www.faithtrustinstitute.org

Family Violence Prevention Fund
http://nnedv.org/resources/nationalorgs/9-fvpf.html

Futures Without Violence
www.futureswithoutviolence.org

Gender Violence Institute
www.genderviolenceinstitute.org

Institute on Domestic Violence in the African American Community
www.idvaac.org

Institute on Violence, Abuse and Trauma
www.ivatcenters.org

Jewish Women International
www.jewishwomen.org

LGBTQ Relationships and Abuse: National Domestic Violence Hotline
www.thehotline.org/2012/06/lgbtq-relationships-and-abuse

LAMBDA GLBT Community Services
www.lambda.org

Manavi
A women's rights organization committed to ending all forms of violence
and exploitation against South Asian women living in the United States.
www.manavi.org

Mending the Sacred Hoop
http://mshoop.org

Minnesota Center Against Violence and Abuse
www.mincava.umn.edu

National Association of Drug Court Professionals
www.nadcp.org

National Center for Elder Abuse
www.ncea.aoa.gov

National Center on Domestic and Sexual Violence
www.ncdsv.org

National Center on Protection Orders and Full Faith and Credit
www.fullfaithandcredit.org

National Clearinghouse for the Defense of Battered Women
www.ncdbw.org

National Council of Juvenile and Family Court Judges
www.ncjfcj.org

**National Latino Alliance for the Elimination of Domestic Violence
(ALIANZA)**
www.dvalianza.org

National Network to End Domestic Violence
www.nnedv.org

Rape, Abuse & Incest National Network (RAINN)
https://rainn.org

Resource Center on Domestic Violence: Child Protection & Custody
www.ncjfcj.org/content/view/129/250

Prevention/Social Change

See the section "Prevention: What Men Can Do," in Chapter 10, for a list of resources related to this topic.

International Programs
Advocates for Human Rights
http://theadvocatesforhumanrights.org

Amnesty International USA, Women's Human Rights Program
www.amnestyusa.org/our-work/issues/women-s-rights

Women's Aid (United Kingdom)
www.womensaid.org.uk

Books

Adams, David. *Why Do They Kill? Men Who Murder Their Intimate Partners.* Nashville, TN: Vanderbilt University Press, 2007.

Aldarondo, Etiony, and Fernando Mederos. *Programs for Men Who Batter: Intervention and Prevention.* Kingston, NJ: Civic Research Institute, 2002.

Bancroft, Lundy. *When Dad Hurts Mom: Helping Your Children Heal the Wounds of Witnessing Abuse.* New York: Berkley Publishing Group, 2004.

Browne, Angela. *When Battered Women Kill.* New York: The Free Press, 1984.

Campbell, Jacquelyn C. *Assessing Dangerousness: Violence by Batterers and Child Abusers.* New York: Springer Publishing Co., 2007.

Davies, Jill. *Safety Planning With Battered Women: Complex Lives/Difficult Choices.* Thousand Oaks; CA: Sage Publications, 1997.

Dobash, R. Emerson, and Russell P. Dobash. *Violence Against Wives.* New York: The Free Press, 1983.

Edleson, Jeffery L., and Richard M. Tolman. *Intervention for Men Who Batter.* Thousand Oaks, CA: Sage Publications, 1992.

Faludi, Susan. *Backlash: The Undeclared War Against American Women.* New York: Crown Publishers, 1991.

Ferrato, Donna. *Living With the Enemy.* New York: Aperture Books, 1991.

Freire, Paulo. *Pedagogy of the Oppressed.* New York: Continuum, 1992.

Funk, Russ. *Stopping Rape: A Challenge for Men.* Gabriola Island, BC, Canada: New Society Publishers, 1993.

Garbarino, James. *Lost Boys: Why Our Sons Turn Violent and How We Can Save Them.* New York: The Free Press, 1999.

Gilligan, James. *Violence: Our Deadly Epidemic and Its Causes.* New York: Grosset/Putnam, 1996.

Gondolf, Edward. *The Future of Batterers Programs: Reassessing Evidence-Based Practices.* Lebanon, NH: Northeastern University Press, 2012.

Gondolf, Edward. *Men Who Batter: An Integrated Approach for Stopping Wife Abuse.* Learning Publications, 1985.

hooks, bell. *Ain't I a Woman: Black Women and Feminism.* Cambridge, MA: South End Press, 1981.

Jones, Ann. *War Is Not Over When It's Over.* New York: Metropolitan Books, 2010.

Katz, Jackson. *The Macho Paradox.* Naperville, IL: Sourcebooks, Inc., 2006.

Kimmel, Michael. *Guyland: The Perilous World Where Boys Become Men.* New York: HarperCollins, 2008.

Kimmel, Michael. *Manhood in America: A Cultural History.* New York: Oxford University Press, 1998, 2006, 2012.

Kivel, Paul. *Men's Work: How to Stop the Violence That Tears Our Lives Apart.* New York: Hazelden/Ballantine, 1992.

Kristof, Nicholas, and Sheryl WuDunn. *Half the Sky.* New York: Vintage Books, 2009.

Lissette, Andrea, and Richard Kraus. *Free Yourself from an Abusive Relationship: Seven Steps to Taking Back Your Life.* Alameda, CA: Hunter House, 2000.

Martin, Del. *Battered Wives.* Volcano, CA: Volcano Press, 1981.

Paymar, Michael, and Ellen Pence. *Education Groups For Men Who Batter: The Duluth Model.* New York: Springer Publishing Company, 1993.

Pence, Ellen, and Melanie Shepard. *Coordinated Community Response to Domestic Violence: Lessons From Duluth and Beyond.* Thousand Oaks, CA: Sage Publications, 1999.

Pleck, Elizabeth. *Domestic Tyranny.* Champaign, IL: University of Illinois Press, 2004.

Richie, Beth. *Compelled to Crime: The Gender Entrapment of Battered Black Women.* New York: Routledge, 1996.

Schechter, Susan. *Women and Male Violence: The Visions and Struggles of the Battered Women's Movement.* Boston: South End Press, 1982.

Schechter, Susan, and Ann Jones. *When Love Goes Wrong: What to Do When You Can't Do Anything Right—Strategies for Women with Controlling Partners.* New York: HarperCollins, 1992.

Stark, Evan. *Coercive Control: The Entrapment of Women in Personal Life.* New York: Oxford University Press, 2007.

Websdale, Neil. *Understanding Domestic Homicides.* Lebanon, NH: Northeastern University Press, 1999.

Index

CPSIA information can be obtained at www.ICGtesting.com
Printed in the USA
BVOW08s1105060315

390643BV00009B/43/P

9 780897 936651